# Imagining Exile in Heian Japan

# Imagining Exile in Heian Japan

## *Banishment in Law, Literature, and Cult*

JONATHAN STOCKDALE

University of Hawai'i Press
*Honolulu*

Printed in the United States of America

20 19 18 17 16 15 6 5 4 3 2 1



**Library of Congress Cataloging-in-Publication Data**

Stockdale, Jonathan, author.
Imagining exile in Heian Japan : banishment in law, literature, and cult / Jonathan Stockdale.
pages cm
Includes bibliographical references and index.
ISBN 978-0-8248-3983-3 (cloth : alk. paper)
1. Exile (Punishment)—Japan. 2. Exile (Punishment) in literature.
3. Japanese literature—Heian period, 794–1185—History and criticism.
4. Sugawara, Michizane, 845–903—Cult. I. Title.
DS856.3.S76 2015
364.6′8—dc23

2014028760

University of Hawaiʻi Press books are printed on acid-free paper and meet the guidelines for permanence and durability of the Council on Library Resources.

Designed by George Whipple and Lou Robinson

Printed by Sheridan Books, Inc.

# Contents

# Preface

She fell from the sky,
she fell very far,
and Kansas she says
is the name of the star. —*Arlen and Harburg, "Munchkinland"*

In an autobiographical essay written in the form of a tender analysis of the MGM musical *The Wizard of Oz,* Salman Rushdie once remarked, "My own relationship with 'home' has become, let's say, more problematic of late." Drawing parallels between his own experience and Dorothy's, he added that in his post-*fatwā* period, "I've done a good deal of thinking . . . about the advantages of a good pair of ruby slippers."[1] Exiles in fiction, exiles in history, and exiles imagining exile: as the cases of both Dorothy Gale and Salman Rushdie remind us, exile—taken in its broadest sense to indicate the condition of estrangement from one's home or homeland—remains a persistent theme in both the imagined and lived experience of humanity.[2] Given the widespread experience of exile in history—the Babylonian exile, the Trail of Tears, and the Tibetan community in Dharamsala begin to suggest the scope of the topic—it should come as no surprise to find the recurring theme of exile in works of the imagination (Genesis in the Hebrew Bible, Rama's banishment in the *Ramayana,* and the *Divine Comedy* by the exiled poet Dante). The only surprise comes in realizing how much remains to be explored regarding the themes of exile and banishment outside of a few traditionally privileged examples.

In the case of Japan, members of the Heian court would have been immediately familiar with the tale of a maiden who appears from "beyond," an exile from her homeland in the sky, yet finally able to return with the help of a magical item of clothing (Kaguyahime's *hagoromo* feathered robe in this case acting as the equivalent of "a good pair of ruby slippers"). Yet while parallels between Kaguyahime and Dorothy may exist, it is not the goal of this study to provide either a comparative analysis of exile or a metatheory regarding the human imagination. Rather, as one contribution to the cultural history of Japan, my focus is on a three and half–century period at the

Heian court during which execution was customarily abolished in favor of exile. During the same period, Japan's earliest prose tale, its most acclaimed narrative, and one of its most significant religious movements all centered around figures in exile. The goal of my study then is to trace and examine themes and patterns regarding exile that circulated within early and classical Japanese literature, law, myth, and cult.

This project would not have been possible without the training I received at the University of Chicago, where I had the good fortune to study under faculty in both the History of Religions program and in the Department of East Asian Languages and Civilization. For the gift of their critical insight, I am deeply indebted to Gary Ebersole, Frank Reynolds, Bruce Lincoln, Martin Riesebrodt, and Wendy Doniger from the Divinity School, as well as Jim Ketelaar, Norma Field, the late William Sibley, and Hiroshi Noto from the EALC.

Many others enabled this study in diverse ways. In Japan I especially wish to thank Shimazono Susumu of the University of Tokyo, Richard Gardner of Sophia University, Yamada Yūji of Mie University, and Igarashi Akio of Rikkyo University for opening their own doors and many others. Ichizuka Isamu, Fujita Jun'ichi, and Miyakawa Sachihisa provided a welcoming community and helped me stay on target. At the University of Puget Sound, I am fortunate to be part of a rich community of teacher-scholars; I draw support and inspiration from my colleagues in religion, Asian studies, and in diverse locations across campus. Institutionally, a Mellon Junior Sabbatical Fellowship and several faculty research grants provided the time, space, and support for me to undertake revisions, venture further research, and move in new directions of inquiry. Research librarians at the University of Puget Sound, the University of Washington, and Waseda University facilitated each step along the way. I am grateful also for the editorial insight of Patricia Crosby at the University of Hawai'i Press, who assembled a pair of anonymous readers who managed simultaneously to interrogate and affirm an earlier manuscript; the phoenix that emerged from their fire is a much better bird, though I'm sure it is far from flawless. Any errors remaining in fact or judgment are purely my own.

To my parents, as they say, my debt is deeper than the ocean, but it is my own immediate family who have lived the writing of this book from inception to completion: I am truly fortunate to share the journey with beings as lovely as Zoe, Willa, and Theo.

Finally, by way of dedication, I would like to offer this book in memory of two scholars whose critical studies of the Heian period planted the seeds for my own engagement with the topic from the very beginning. Michele Marra and Richard Okada not only wrote the books that inspired my own inquiry into exile in Heian Japan, but both were present when I first offered my research at an Association of Asian Studies meeting; their supportive critique helped me know I had a worthwhile topic on my hands. I regret that their untimely passing means they will not see the finished project—I imagine they would have much to suggest—but it gives some solace to know that their intellectual labors continue to bring new harvest.

# 1

# Introduction

## *The Moon of Exile*

> Akimoto, the middle counselor, once spoke of wishing "to see the moon of exile, though guilty of no crime." It is easy to imagine why he felt so. —*Yoshida Kenkō*

> Every text takes shape as a mosaic of citations. —*Julia Kristeva*

In the earliest work of Heian prose fiction, a radiant princess gazes nightly as the full moon of the eighth month approaches, awaiting the moment when people from the moon will come to escort her back from exile. At the height of that literary tradition, the hero of the *Tale of Genji* reenacts the same gesture, gazing at the full moon of the eighth month from his own place of exile while speaking longingly of the "capital of the moon" (*tsuki no miyako*). And in the wake of that literature, in a work of nostalgia for a past courtly aesthetic, the author Yoshida Kenkō (ca. 1283–1350) quotes approvingly of "wishing to see the moon of exile, though guilty of no crime." Faced with such a string of images, one cannot help but wonder about the role of exile—and its moon—in Heian Japan. What could account for the rich resonance of such a trope within the Heian imagination?

In fact, the act of imagining exile in Japan can be traced back to the earliest extant narrative, the mythic record of the origins of the Yamato court known as the *Kojiki.* In that myth-history, compiled and recorded by 712 CE, the theme of exile helped to chronicle the genealogies of the gods and to align them with those of the ruling house, tracing a divine cosmos and connecting it to the social order of the Yamato court.[1] A few years earlier the court had promulgated the Taihō legal code, naming banishment as one of five penal sanctions, second in severity only to death. As the Yamato court coalesced around the new capital of Nara—and as a previously oral society took on increasingly textual form—exile was somehow part of that process, a centrifugal sanction that accompanied the centripetalizing focus of the early Yamato state.

Following the transfer of the capital to Heian-kyō in 794, the court experienced a period of more than three centuries in which capital punishment was customarily abolished in favor of banishment, making exile the dominant sanction among Heian elites.[2] During the same period, exile emerged widely as a concern within literature and legends, in poetry and diaries, and in the cultic imagination, expressed in oracles and revelations. While on the one hand banishment was simply one sanction available to the state, it was also something more: exile provided a trope through which members of court society imagined the banishment of gods, of heavenly beings from the moon, of legendary and literary characters, and of historical figures, some transformed into spirits.

In this Heian imagination of exile, any divide between history and fiction was thoroughly blurred. Historical exiles served as "informing images" for the heroes of fictional tales,[3] while fictional characters provided patterns and strategies through which historical figures enacted their lives. A storehouse of images, gestures, and quotations regarding exile offered a wealth of signifying possibilities, and in the narratives of exile that appeared throughout the era, the social order was continually revealed, reflected upon, and reimagined.

Such a rich transcript on exile for Heian Japan contrasts sharply, however, with our present lack of a framework for understanding it, and from the outset a number of questions present themselves. Of what service were narratives of exile to members of the Heian court? Was there a poetics of exile, and if so, what was the grammar of its use?[4] Further, how might we understand the relationship between the legal sanction of banishment, on the one hand, and the wider trope of exile within the cultural imagination?

Based on the case studies that follow, I offer here a preliminary suggestion for approaching the study of exile narratives in early and Heian Japan. Clearly, every narrative of exile imagines a certain constellation of power: a privileged "center," and those who are excluded from it. From this we may trace two broad themes, with nearly endless variations. For those in positions of power, the banishment of *others* provided a persuasive trope for asserting their own centrality, as when it was woven into the ruling myths, or into the legal codes of the polity. Yet the trope of exile was also harnessed by those more marginal, in narratives that sought to reimagine the hierarchies of inclusion and exclusion upon which Heian society rested. While narratives of exile in Heian Japan could thus be employed to assert and inscribe various constellations of power, they could also serve to reveal and reimagine the social order and the circulation of power within it, whether sacred or otherwise.

Such an interpretation carries its own risks, however. Foremost is the risk of projecting a modern apparatus of domination and resistance onto the complex desires and situated interests of the Japanese court, an elite social configuration.[5] Moving beyond such binary impulses, how might we account for the "eros" of exile, the numinous quality reflected in narratives of shining princes and radiant princesses in exile? And what of the haunted air surrounding narratives of banished and vengeful spirits? In short, how might we explore the cultural history of Japanese exile in all its dimensions, including not only the role of exile in relation to practices of inclusion and exclusion, but also in relation to "other interests and desires that are neither determined nor captured by the systems in which they develop"?[6] This book is my attempt at such a study.

In the chapters that follow, I examine the imagination of exile in the myth, literature, cult, and law of the Japanese court, starting with the earliest texts and then focusing on the Heian period, before concluding with some implications that arise from the study of exile for our understanding of Japanese religions. Before proceeding to those individual chapters, however, in the remaining introduction I pause to consider several general features relating to exile and the cultural landscape of the Japanese court, including the vocabulary of exile, the very notion of "centers" and "peripheries," the idea of a Heian "imaginary," and the structure of Japanese court society itself.

## THE VOCABULARY OF EXILE

As may be expected, the Japanese court possessed a rich vocabulary relating to exile and banishment, drawn from the diverse spheres of myth, literature, and law.[7] In addition to that specific vocabulary, we must also consider the language of euphemism: cases in which persons were sentenced to exile in everything but name. Further, there are instances in which the structural elements of exile are present though no term is used to name the situation. Part of the work of my study, therefore, is to consider how diverse cases emerging from the Japanese court can be seen to share patterns linked to the imagination of exile.

In the domain of law, the Yamato state possessed a vocabulary for exile taken from the Chinese legal lexicon. With the adaptation of the Chinese legal codes into Japan (a process accomplished no later than 702 CE with the compilation of the *Taihō Ritsuryō*), a continental taxonomy of punishment entered the discourse and practice of the court. In the *ritsuryō* codes, exile (*ruzai*) is listed as one of five categories of penal sanction, organized in descending order of severity as follows:

1. execution
2. banishment
3. penal servitude
4. flogging (heavy stick)
5. whipping (flexible cane)[8]

As I discuss in chapter 5, the substitution of the character for transgression (罪, *zai*) in the *ritsuryō* codes in place of that for punishment (刑, *kei*) from the Chinese codes illustrates just one of the many revisions made to align the legal codes with the worldview of the Yamato court, indicating a process of adaptation rather than simple adoption.[9]

In the realm of early Japanese myth, exile is introduced by the term *kamuyarau,* used in the *Kojiki* to narrate the banishment of the god Susano-o from Takamanohara, the High Heavenly Plain.[10] The archaic language of this pronouncement is recorded in the thirteenth and seventeenth chapters of the *Kojiki* with minor variations to the phrase *kamuyarai yaraiki,* in which Susano-o is the object of the transitive verb.[11] The verb *kamuyarau* has been translated variously as divine banishment or divine expulsion, as in Philippi: "Thus saying, he [Izanagi] *expelled him* [Susano-o] *with a divine expulsion,*"[12] though dictionaries of classical Japanese define the verb specifically as banishment from the realm of the gods.[13]

In addition to legal and mythic terminology, there were also literary expressions and allusions relating to exile in classical Japanese. While the Chinese character *ru* (流) provided the basis for the legal term exile (*ruzai*), the same character (using its Japanese pronunciation) provided the basis for the classical verbs *nagasu* (流す) and *nagaru* (流る), meaning primarily to shed (as with tears) or to flow (as with water). A further connotation of the verbs, however, was banishment. From these general terms for banishment arose more specific compounds, such as *shima-nagashi,* referring to the practice of exile to distant islands. In addition, the semantic range contained in the verbs *nagasu/nagaru* allowed for literary improvisation alluding to exile, as when the banished court scholar Michizane wrote a poem to the retired emperor prior to leaving the capital, requesting his aid:

*Nagareyuku*
*ware wa mikuzu to*
*narihatenu*
*kimi shigarami to*
*narite todomeyo*

Now that I have become debris drifting away,
will not Your Majesty
act as a weir to hold me back?[14]

The verb *nagareyuku* in the poem thus acts on two levels at once, connoting on the one hand a liquid sense of "drifting away," while at the same time evoking the further association with banishment.

Michizane's case brings up a further aspect of the vocabulary of exile: the issue of euphemism. While Michizane is probably the best-known exile of the Heian period—his vengeful spirit engendered one of the most prominent cults of exiled spirits back in the capital—Michizane's banishment was officially proclaimed a "demotion" (*sasen*), from one of the highest offices at court (minister of the right) to a post at the distant provincial headquarters in Kyushu. As I discuss in chapter 4, the fact that Michizane was sent to his post in the manner of a criminal (without a change of horses en route), lived under a form of house arrest once there, and died within a few years amid difficult circumstances helps us to understand that the term *sasen* was in this case little more than a euphemism for the sanction of exile.[15] In his own writing from the Dazaifu regional government, Michizane minced no words regarding his experience as one of banishment.

Beyond the various phrases, allusions, and euphemisms in classical Japanese and Chinese referring to exile and banishment, what of narratives that do not employ any of the available vocabulary but that contain all of the structural elements corresponding to exile? What should we make of the *Tale of the Bamboo Cutter* (*Taketori monogatari*), in which a princess from the moon is "sent" (*owashitsurunari*) to earth because of a past "transgression" (*tsumi*) she committed on the moon and made to stay for a period of time in this "defiled place" (*iyashiki tokoro*) before being brought back to the capital of the moon following the expiration of her term (*tsumi no kagiri*)? While the text itself does not make use of any of the vocabulary for exile discussed previously, I show in chapter 3 that Heian prose narratives such as the *Taketori* cannot properly be understood without examining the crucial ways in which exile structures and gives force to the entire narrative.

## IMAGINING "CENTERS" AND "MARGINS"

Every instance of exile, real or imagined, invokes a certain constellation of power: a privileged center, and those who are excluded from it. Yet the very notion of a "center" with regard to Heian Japan is hardly unproblematic, and scholars in recent years have struggled to get a better handle on this term. There is no denying that the capital of the Japanese court represented an important "center" in various ways—political, economic, ritual, and aesthetic, as well as spatial. Yet the idea of a static center in Heian society can easily obscure the ways in which "centers" and "margins" were continually being constructed, contested, and reconfigured. Studies of the Japanese court have thus shifted over time on whether they focus on the courtly center, on the margins of that court, or on the presence of other simultaneously existing centers and margins. As categories fundamental to our understanding of exile, then, how might we approach the issue of Heian "centers" and "margins"? I begin by noting three important contributions to this issue offered in recent interpretations of the Heian period.

In his work *Uncovering Heian Japan,* Thomas LaMarre focused attention on the importance of the Heian "center" as a means of retrieving the unique features of that period from the projections of the modern scholarly imagination. In that work, LaMarre explored how modern Japanese scholarship has tended to project the contours of a "national imagination" onto the Heian period, too easily finding the fantasies of the modern state existing in the past, including such features as linguistic purity, ethnic homogeneity, and territorial unity. Drawing on the work of Benedict Anderson, LaMarre argued that the early Japanese imagination of community was based on very different principles, among which was a distinct mapping of power across space. As he quotes from Anderson regarding the "dynastic" model characteristic of kingship, "Kingship organizes everything around a high centre. Its legitimacy derives from divinity, not from populations, who, after all, are subjects, not citizens. In the modern conception, state sovereignty is fully, flatly, and evenly operative over each square centimeter of a legally demarcated territory. But in the older imagining, where states were defined by centres, borders were porous and indistinct, and sovereignties faded imperceptibly."[16]

For LaMarre, uncoupling Heian Japan from the modern national imagination enables an appreciation of the period as linguistically diverse, ethnically diffuse, and territorially porous.[17] For my study of exile, LaMarre and Anderson together help to point out an essential difference between the classical model of community and that of the national imagination. In contrast to the modern state, which seeks to overspread its influence homogeneously over every unit of terrain, in the Heian model space was anything but homogeneous: the sense of power and prestige created by court society "faded imperceptibly" as distance from the center increased.

Anderson's classical dynastic model corresponds well to our understanding of the early Japanese state. The emergence of the Yamato courtly center corresponded to a transformation in ancient Japan "from an archaic confederacy of aristocratic clans formed around the leadership of the Yamato clan of the imperial house into a centralized bureaucratic state."[18] The emergence of this state coincided with the first permanent capitals, the reorganization of hereditary status into ranks bestowed by the courtly center, and the adoption of legal codes with which to administer a polity centered around the sovereign. As I discuss in chapter 5, the sanction of banishment should also be seen as one means by which the vision of a centralized order was mapped onto the realm, correlating the sanctions of near, medium, and distant exile to transgressions against the throne of increasing levels of severity.

Moving in a different direction, other scholarship on the Heian period in recent years has taken the very notion of center and periphery itself as "a construct to be contested, redefined, modified, augmented, or elaborated."[19] Seeking to shift our gaze from a dichotomy between the courtly center and its peripheries, a number of scholars have explored the "multiplicity of forces and loci" present in Heian Japan, leading to a variety of centers and margins arising at that time.[20] One example of this type of work can be seen in Bruce Batten's studies of Dazaifu, the popular title for which—"capital of the western periphery"—illustrates the multiplicity of forces existing within a single site, at once an outpost of the court and an important administrative center in its own right.[21] In this light, a simplistic model of "center" and "periphery" framed around the Heian capital and its regional peripheries does not entirely account for the diverse ways in which centers and margins existed and were imagined at the time, nor for the ways in which they continued to arise and decline.

We're thus left with a question: How do we acknowledge the existence of a courtly center exerting a certain kind of power and authority, while acknowledging the existence of other kinds of centers and margins at the same time? A helpful resolution is proposed in the work *Writing Margins,* by Terry Kawashima. In her exploration of the process of marginalization in Heian and Kamakura Japan, Kawashima has written that what is perhaps most valuable is not an exhaustive cataloguing of centers and margins but a greater understanding of the *process* of "marginalization" (and we might add "centralization").[22] At the outset of her work, she asks,

> What is a "margin"? How does one come to conceive of something or someone as "marginal"? In texts from the mid-Heian to the early Kamakura period (tenth through thirteenth centuries) in Japan, certain figures appear, at first glance, to be "marginal," or removed from the "centers" of power. The question is: Why do we see these figures in this way? . . . Who is portraying whom as "marginal"? For what reason?[23]

While Kawashima focuses on the textual construction of marginality, we might pose the same question of centrality as well. By attending both to the process of "centralization" and "marginalization," we can move beyond the reproduction of categories which appear always to have existed in static relation to each other. Again, Kawashima's writing on the construction of marginality helps to clarify this issue:

> Perhaps it is more useful to think that the static categories "center" and "margin" do not exist as such. In other words, these two opposed, abstract, and metaphorical spaces are not themselves the most significant components in marginality. Only the process, marginalization, exists. . . . Marginalization is thus a specific act; no textual instance of marginalization proves the existence of a timeless or universal center and margin. . . . In this paradigm, then, there is no single center surrounded by a single margin; instead, different and fleeting instances of marginalizer/marginalized relationships appear and reappear in a dynamic fashion.[24]

For my study, translating Kawashima's suggestions into practice requires examining how narratives of exile present specific discursive moments of both "centralization" and "marginalization." Such an approach carries with it the premise that existing constellations of power were always subject to negotiation and contestation, and that new "centers" and "margins" could emerge as people continually reimagined and reconfigured their relations with the social order—"fleeting instances" within the Heian imagination behind which lay "seemingly unlimited potential for further change."[25]

## EXILE AND THE SOCIAL IMAGINATION

If every narrative of exile imagines a distinct constellation of power, this also raises the question of how best to understand the "imaginary," or how to understand the relation between "the imagined" and "lived" practice of Heian court life. As suggested by my choice of terms already, in many ways this study finds common ground with the enthusiastic credo that "to study the imagination is to go to the heart of a society."[26] Yet to fully address the relationship between the "imaginary" and Heian social life, it's important to clarify the relationship between strategic social practice and what others have termed "*le imaginaire*."[27]

In my use of the phrase, the "social imaginary" refers to the wealth of images and tropes that combine to form the cultural life out of which, in part, societies are constructed, represented, and reproduced. Along these lines, we may say that the trope of exile occupied a prominent place within the social imagination of the Heian court. That is to say, Heian culture possessed a store of images, gestures, and allusions regarding exile, drawn from legendary, literary, and historical sources, both Chinese and Japanese. As a result, the theme of exile could be invoked through myriad associations, the mere mention of which immediately resonated with members of court society. The beach at Suma, the image of rustic salt makers, the act of gazing in longing at the moon: all were strands within a web of signification created by members of the Japanese court who either experienced, recorded, or imagined banishment from the privileged spheres of court society.

Over time, this storehouse of images grew. As an example, in the *Tale of the Bamboo Cutter,* the phrase "capital of the moon" (*tsuki no miyako*) appeared for the first time with complex resonance, referring as it did to a court more pure, more powerful, and more beautiful than any experienced by members of Heian society. That phrase—having entered the lexicon of the imaginary—then resurfaces in later works, as we glimpsed at the outset of this chapter when the hero of the *Genji* evoked the capital of the moon to frame his own predicament of exile.[28] In this way, a new image joined the storehouse of signs by which people imagined exile, providing yet another trope through which they could narrate their lives or the lives of others, imagined or real.

At the same time, while shared signs circulated within the social imagination, it would be a mistake to suggest that the *meaning* of those signs was shared as well. Instead, when we consider the images and ideas contained within the Heian imagination, it's clear that their meaning was always subject to interpretation and, frequently, contestation. As an example, we might consider the "Picture Contest" ("Eawase") chapter of the *Tale of Genji,* part of a fictional tale but one that weaves references to historical and legendary figures into its own narrative concerning exile. In this chapter, a picture contest is held among the highly literate and aesthetically refined women serving at court, in which two sides are formed—corresponding to two factions within the palace—and over a series of rounds, each side presents paintings that become the object of criticism, debate, and ultimately judgment regarding the relative value of their imagery and subject matter. As with so many activities in court society, at the heart of the contest is an aesthetic struggle for distinction.

In the initial round, the painting presented by the first side concerns the *Tale of the Bamboo Cutter.* Arguing in support of the story (and thus of the painting), the first side praises the purity of the tale's heroine (Princess Kaguya, who had been sent to earth in expiation of a transgression committed on the moon), likening her to a divine being: "Princess Kaguya remains forever unsullied by this world, and she aspires to such noble heights that her story belongs to the age of the gods."[29]

In rebuttal, the opposing team responds by disparaging Princess Kaguya's status because of her humble origins: "Since her tie with earth involved bamboo, one gathered that she was in fact of contemptible birth. She lit up her own house, yes, but her light never shone beside the imperial radiance!"[30]

In this short exchange, two radically different interpretations of Kaguyahime are offered by the two teams, one arguing that her character elevated her above this impure world and the other disparaging her character by focusing on her impoverished beginnings. In a sense, the debate recapitulates the fundamental division narrated within the *Bamboo Cutter* itself, as the first team declares its affinity with the realm of the moon to which Kaguyahime returned, while the second team sides with the realm of court society that tried unsuccessfully in the tale to possess the princess. It's a clash, one could say, between a transcendent imagined order and the actual machinery of Heian court life. As I discuss in chapter 3, the use of a character from a narrative of exile in this section of the *Tale of Genji* is hardly accidental, but rather it provides a trope structuring the entire chapter, as indeed the first team continues to present image after image depicting stories of famous exalted exiles (such as Ariwara no Narihira). The chapter ends in the first team's victory—achieved through images painted by none other than Genji himself, depicting his own exile in Suma.

This episode from the *Tale of Genji* serves as a reminder both of the complexity of signs within the Heian imagination and of how we might view the workings of the imaginary on a theoretical level. Images, signs, and symbols are never fixed, static, and univocal, bearing a single meaning for all members of society. It's not necessary to juxtapose, therefore, some signs whose signification is shared by all members of society against other signs whose particular interpretation reflects ideological concerns—as long as we understand that *all* signs and texts remain unbounded: there can never be a single, closed reading.[31]

Exactly because of this open and unbound quality, every commentary on a text or image may be seen as an attempt to "fix" a particular reading or signification of that text or sign.[32] Indeed, the struggle to establish a particular reading of an image—in competition with other possible readings and out of a particular motivated position—is exactly the process portrayed in the "Picture Contest" chapter of the *Genji.* Our understanding of the Heian imaginary must therefore incorporate this sense of strategic practice, an awareness of the contested life of signs within society.

## THE COURT SOCIETY

A final element regarding exile in early Japan relates to the nature of court society itself, and a single example can help to highlight the importance of this topic. When Prince Sawara was sentenced to exile in 785 and died en route, his *corpse* was sent on and buried on Awaji Island. Later, when his vengeful spirit began to haunt the capital and steps were taken for his pacification, Sawara's grave was transferred back to the home province of Yamato, a shrine was built for his worship in Nara, and he was elevated posthumously to the position of emperor.[33] Such striking symbolic actions hint at the degree to which exile operated under the governing logic of court society, a society structured along axes of inclusion and exclusion. In order to gain a clearer understanding of this particular social formation, we can begin by recalling some of the points made in Norbert Elias' classic work, *The Court Society,* while expanding on them to address the particular case of Heian Japan.

In *The Court Society,* Elias began with the understanding that members of court society were "people whose social existence . . . depends on their prestige, their standing at court and within court society."[34] While arrangement within the social hierarchy of the court was marked by fixed ranks, the possession of those ranks itself was fluid, and one might gain or lose rank in confirmation of one's advancing or declining social prestige.[35]

It goes almost without saying that in such a court society, where all members were drawn into "an especially intense and specialized competition for the power associated with status and prestige,"[36] each individual would be finely attuned to the implications of their words, actions, and appearances toward the overall accumulation of cultural capital. As Elias put it, "In such a society the chance of preceding another, or sitting while he had to stand, or the depth of the bow with which one was greeted, the amiability of the reception by others, and so on, were not mere externals . . . they were literal documentations of social existence, notations of the place one currently occupied in the court hierarchy."[37] The competition for prestige within court society thus provides some of the logic behind "the compulsion to display,"[38] or the constant production, circulation, and consumption of items of prestige, and it also suggests some of the rationale behind the striving for aesthetic mastery that so dominated the life of the Heian court, "the special cultivation of taste in court society."[39] Such cultivation is clearly evident, for example, in the ritual-like performance of aesthetic competitions at the Heian court, as illustrated by the picture contest depicted in the *Tale of Genji* discussed above (and in chapter 3).

According to this view, all of the etiquette, diction, gesture, and performance that comprised daily life in court society functioned not just to calibrate the position of each person within the overall court hierarchy but also to distinguish and sustain the particular social field of court society itself. As a result, one of the foundations of court society lay in its most basic function of *distancing:* "It was only by going to court and living within court society that [members] could preserve the *distance* from everything else on which their spiritual salvation, their prestige as court aristocrats, in short, their social existence and their personal identity depended."[40]

In such a social configuration, the loss of prestige brought about by a sanction such as exile thus constituted a threat to one's social existence, and we might argue that in works of the Heian period the particular dislocation brought about by exile was in no small part due to the collapsing of the "distance" erected between the world of the Heian court and the larger society inhabiting the archipelago. In the poetry of Michizane from the Dazaifu, for example, or in the depiction of Genji's exile on the rustic shores of Suma and Akashi, one is immediately struck by the nearly alien quality of the locals depicted residing there, as if two entirely different worlds had suddenly collided. As the narrator of the *Genji* intones regarding Genji's initial experience in exile, "Everything at Suma was different, *and the very presence of the mountain folk, who were a mystery to him, constituted an affront and an offense*."[41]

While Elias' understanding of the distancing function of court society is crucial, it does not account for the entire structure of the system, for the court was organized not only along an axis of *distance* from those outside the court but also along an axis of *proximity* to the "high centre," embodied symbolically in the figure of the sovereign. This is, after all, what rank at the Japanese court declared: a classification of relative proximity to the throne (which alone, in Japan, was above all rank). The particular sanction of exile thus represented a kind of double inversion, both of the distancing from the world and of the proximity to the emperor that Heian court society normally strived to achieve.

In this light, it makes sense that the literature from exile in Heian Japan frequently lingers over the exiled courtier's relation to the sovereign, so often expressed through the image of the emperor's robes, carried as a treasured keepsake into exile. Time and again, the literature of exile focuses on the fragrance of the imperial robes, clung to by the courtier as the only trace of the imperial presence available to them. As Michizane wrote from the Dazaifu,

> The robe His Majesty bestowed on me, here with me
> now—
> each day I lift it reverently, bow to its lingering
> fragrance.[42]

With such a sign, Heian exiles possessed a particularly resonant trope to express the fracturing of their social order, signifying at once their exclusion from power as well as the fading traces of their former proximity to it.

From this perspective, the threat occasioned by exile has been called a kind of social death,[43] and this helps to explain instances in which people argued for *physical* death in preference to the distancing and dislocation of banishment. In Mikael Adolphson's account of the "warrior monks" of the medieval period, we find the following record regarding the head abbot of Enryakuji, Myōun: "[The retired emperor] Go-Shirakawa . . . struck back by arresting the head abbot, Myōun . . . excluding Myōun from the monk register, deposing him as head abbot, and confiscating both his private and his public estates (attached to the head abbot office) within a couple of days. *A week later, the retired emperor ordered that Myōun be exiled, further angering the Enryakuji monks, who vowed to kill the head abbot rather than let him suffer the humiliation of being exiled.*"[44]

Such a drastic reaction to exile conveys well the severity of the sanction within the logic of Heian court society, yet to the voices of the Enryakuji monks we must also contrast those who spoke longingly of exile, as in the sentiment voiced at the outset of this introduction by the priest Kenkō regarding the moon of exile—a sentiment later quoted by Zeami during his own journey into exile on Sado Island.[45] Considered together, such contrasting views suggest that the signification of exile depends in every case on the specific context in which exile was being deployed and imagined.

These contrasting attitudes toward exile—one abhorring and the other valorizing—demonstrate the need for a nuanced understanding of the diverse social forces that constituted court society. On this point I diverge from Elias' characterization, in which members of court society appear as if caught in a net, powerless to reimagine their particular social formation. As he describes it, "No single person within the figuration was able to initiate a reform of the tradition. Every slightest attempt to reform, to change the precarious structure of tensions, inevitably entailed an upheaval, a reduction or even abolition of the rights of certain individuals and families. To jeopardize such privileges was, to the ruling class of this society, a kind of taboo. . . . So everything remained as it was."[46]

Elias' description of court society conveys a synchronic tone: because the particular social field of the court was unable or unwilling to look beyond its own structures and figurations, true change was only possible as a result of violent revolution. Yet after examining the Japanese cases involved in this study, I suggest that we rethink such a position. While in some sense it may have been impossible for those at the Heian court to think completely outside of or beyond the categories and structures provided by their society, at the same time they did make creative use of the structures and tropes available to them to reveal and, at times, to revise the configurations of power in which they lived. In the works of the Heian imagination to which this study is devoted, the presence of figures of exile envisioned as divinely beautiful, fiercely wrathful, and aesthetically superior reveal that exile provided a deeply resonant trope through which members of Heian society were indeed able to reimagine their world and the circulation of power within it, both sacred and otherwise, and in ways that affected and altered the social order itself, as we will see in the chapters that follow.

Each of the following chapters explores a particular case of exile associated with a particular genre of discourse, highlighting historiographic issues along the way that arise from this study of the Japanese past. Chapter 2—focusing on the banishment of the god Susano-o narrated in the earliest court chronicles—in many ways clears the path for the remaining chapters, premised on the idea that to understand the imagination of exile at the Japanese court, it's crucial to understand the role played by exile in the founding texts of that society. Examining the banishment of Susano-o in myth also helps to raise questions concerning the theories popularized by Orikuchi Shinobu regarding exile, highlighting the need for a new approach to the topic.[47] Subsequent chapters apply that new approach to cases originating in the Heian period: chapter 3 examines the role of exile in Japan's earliest prose narrative, the *Tale of the Bamboo Cutter,* as well as the discussion of that text within Japan's most acclaimed prose narrative, the *Tale of Genji.* In chapter 4, I examine the exile, death, and posthumous return of the statesman Sugawara no Michizane, exploring the widely popular cults of vengeful spirits (*onryō*) that arose alongside the widespread use of exile during the Heian period. Chapter 5 addresses the subject of exile in the legal codes of the Japanese court, paying particular attention to the 347-year period during which execution was customarily abolished in favor of exile. In my conclusion I then tie together the diverse fields of law, literature, and cult to consider the posthumous career of the exiled emperor Sutoku, "the greatest vengeful spirit in the history of Japan,"[48] a discussion that both connects the study to the present and raises implications for our understanding of Japanese religion.

A final note is in order regarding the diverse fields examined in this study. A historian of Japanese religion by training, I began this project out of a desire to trace the shifting paradigms of divinity expressed within Heian narratives of exile. I soon found myself far afield, in disciplines as disparate as Japanese law and literary history. Exploring exile, I found myself tracking what others have called *social energies:* "the social energies that circulate very broadly through a culture, flowing back and forth between margins and center, passing from zones designated as art to zones apparently indifferent or hostile to art, pressing up from below to transform exalted spheres and down from on high to colonize the low."[49] It is with no little trepidation that I delve into fields as diverse as myth, literature, cult, and law. Yet at the same time, I'm convinced there's something to be gained from pursuing a single topic such as exile across disciplinary boundaries, "treating all of the written and visual traces of a particular culture as a mutually intelligible network of signs."[50] A sincere cultural history of exile would seem to call for no less, and it is in this spirit that I offer my study, even while recognizing its inevitable limitations.

# 2

# Origin Myths

## *Susano-o, Orikuchi Shinobu, and the Imagination of Exile in Early Japan*

> Thus saying, [Izanagi] banished [Susano-o] with a divine banishment.
> —*Kojiki*

> In the darkest region of the political field, the condemned man represents the symmetrical, inverted figure of the king. —*Michel Foucault*

The earliest example of a narrative imagining exile in Japan appears in the oldest extant chronicle of the Yamato court, the *Kojiki,* or *Record of Ancient Matters.* In the well-known sequence from that myth-history, the *Kojiki* relates how the god Susano-o was banished not once, but twice: first by decree of the divine progenitor Izanagi and then, following further transgressions on Susano-o's part, by council of the myriad deities. Following this second decree, the *Kojiki* recounts Susano-o's descent from the High Heavenly Plain to the ancient province of Izumo, where his character undergoes a dramatic shift.[1] Rather than continuing to transgress against the constellation of power inaugurated by Izanagi, Susano-o displays his reverent support: upon discovering a sacred sword in Izumo, he offers it up to the sun goddess Amaterasu, who later includes it among the regalia she entrusts to her offspring. Those descendents, according to the *Kojiki,* include the very rulers who ordered the text's compilation, editing, and adoption in the first place, a process finally completed in 712 CE.

The "heavenly transgressions" (*amatsu tsumi*) leading to Susano-o's banishment—including his defecating in the sacred hall used by Amaterasu for tasting the first rice and other acts that caused her to withdraw into the heavenly rock chamber—have inspired some of the more creative exegetical efforts seen in the field of Japanese myth. Writing in the eighteenth century, the nativist scholar Motoori Norinaga (1730–1801) held that Susano-o's acts revealed his true character as an evil deity (*ashiki kami*), in contrast to his kind and benevolent sister, Amaterasu.[2] More recently, Susano-o has been cast as a representative of the warrior class,[3] an archetypal trickster figure,[4] a model of antistructural disorder,[5] and as a cosmic giver and taker of life,[6] among other possibilities. Indeed, if one of the defining features of myth lies in its openness to interpretation,[7] perhaps nowhere is this malleability more on display than in the hands of its scholarly interpreters.[8]

More interesting for an exploration of the theme of exile is the interpretation given by the Japanese ethnologist Orikuchi Shinobu (1887–1953). Beginning in 1920, Orikuchi argued not only that the Susano-o cycle shared in the widespread fascination with exile seen in early Japanese myth, literature, and cult, but also that Susano-o's transgressive grieving expressed the same poignant longing felt by *all* Japanese for a lost spiritual homeland. Nostalgic, essentializing, and ahistorical, Orikuchi's interpretation is scarcely tenable today, yet it does have the value of drawing our attention to the widespread theme of exile seen in narratives of the early Japanese court. And while scholarship since Orikuchi's time has turned toward reconstructing the social, historical, and political conditions surrounding the production of early Japanese myth, largely missing from these efforts has been a sustained, systematic exploration of the topic of exile. As a result, the role of exile in the royal myth-histories—and in the wider court society for which those narratives were produced—remains opaque.

In this chapter, I shed light on narratives of exile concerning the god Susano-o by reconsidering the myth cycle alongside other texts and ritual practices of the early Yamato court. Given the gravitational pull still exerted by his theories, I begin by retracing briefly the conception of exile in early Japan put forth by Orikuchi Shinobu—the most widely known scholar to have identified and theorized the theme—while critiquing his approach as a modern form of mythmaking. I then highlight current scholarly approaches toward the textual projects of the Yamato court that can help illuminate the role of exile in the court's earliest narratives. Finally, placing the court chronicles within the wider frame of early Japanese court ritual, I examine the early state's efforts to establish a kind of public transcript: a sacred script and royal theater authenticating a particular constellation of power centered around the sovereign.

## ORIKUCHI SHINOBU AND THE *KISHU RYŪRITAN* GENRE

If it is true that "any account of early Japan must deal critically with the modern agendas that form the field,"[9] certainly no discussion of exile in early

Japan can afford to overlook the work of Orikuchi Shinobu. While important critiques of his interpretive method have been raised over the years,[10] no one has yet offered a more enduring explanation for the widespread presence of exile as a trope within the narratives of the early Japanese court.[11] Orikuchi's work thus occupies a curious position—still referenced today, even as scholarly currents have largely moved beyond the hermeneutics of nostalgia that led to his conclusions.[12] At the outset of this chapter I therefore begin by retracing briefly Orikuchi's approach toward exile narratives, leading up to his treatment of the banishment of Susano-o as paradigmatic within that genre. In doing so, I'll explain why we must move beyond Orikuchi's framework in order to place exile narratives such as the Susano-o cycle within their more appropriate historical, social, and theoretical contexts.

As part of his quest to uncover the origins of what he felt to be a uniquely Japanese cultural heritage, Orikuchi put forth a number of influential theories, among which one of the most well known is his concept of the *kishu ryūritan* genre. With that phrase, he identified and gave name to an ancient genre of stories (*tan*) that narrated the exile or wandering (*ryūri*) of persons or beings of high birth (*kishu*) to lowly and marginal places. As he described the genre in an early work, "In the narrative poetry handed down from ancient Japan, there are tales that relate the wandering to various lands of frail and delicate people, exalted as of the offspring of divinities. I have come to refer to these together by the name 'tales of exiled and wandering nobles' (*kishu ryūritan*). . . . Such stories are countless; they appeared early on and continued to grow."[13] Building on this concept throughout his work, Orikuchi came to believe he had discovered in the *kishu ryūritan* genre the sentiment animating ancient Japan's mythic and literary traditions, recurring again and again in tales of separation and longing involving exalted figures of exile.[14]

Several features of Orikuchi's theory bear noting here. First, Orikuchi introduced the *kishu ryūritan* concept within his early work, *The Emergence of Japanese Literature* (*Nihon Bungaku no Hassei*).[15] In that study, Orikuchi was concerned to trace the various strands he believed combined to form the Japanese literary tradition, central among which he felt was the lineage of stories concerning "exiled and wandering nobles." As he put it, "Such sacred narratives, which in the beginning came down as the tales of reciters (*kataribe*) from a distant sacred place, came into contact with historical reality and then parted again, gradually growing heavy with sadness as tales of the human world. . . . Threading along in this manner, one after another, a single lineage of *ryūritan* can be found."[16]

Variants on the *kishu ryūritan* theme continued to be generated down through the Heian period, Orikuchi believed, until the genre reached its most complete expression in the *Tale of Genji,* after which changing social conditions led to the decline of new variants.[17] For Orikuchi, the *kishu ryūritan* genre thus provided a crucial link between the earliest utterances associated with the gods and the growth of a native literary tradition, linking archaic myth and orality with the emergence of historical and literary narrative.

Second, Orikuchi held that each of the stories within the genre shared certain structural elements in common, among the most important of which was the presence of transgression. Citing both the *Genji* and the *Tale of the Bamboo Cutter* (*Taketori monogatari*) as examples, he wrote, "The cause of the Shining Genji's banishment (*ryūzan*) to Suma was that a transgression (*okasu koto*) had occurred. . . . And though the transgression was of a different type, the *Taketori's* Kaguyahime too, in the end just before she ascended to heaven, told the old man that she was a heavenly being, but that because of a trivial offense (*isasaka no okashi*) she had committed, she had come to live in the human world."[18]

Incorporating this theme of transgression, Nomura Jun'ichi offers a concise restatement of the *kishu ryūritan* genre: "In this way, Orikuchi Shinobu named a related group of *monogatari* in which an originally noble hero or heroine, usually burdened with having committed a transgression, wanders in a lowly place, and he called them 'tales of exiled and wandering nobles.' "[19]

Third, a crucial feature of the genre for Orikuchi was the emotional appeal he believed such narratives held for their audiences—an appeal rooted in their tragic nature. As he explained in a section of *The Emergence of Japanese Literature* titled "The Tragic Spirit (*higeki seishin*) in Folk Literature," "Even in happy tales, we discover for whatever reason the traces of pure tears flowing."[20] As a result, through all the different manifestations of the *kishu ryūritan* genre, Orikuchi felt that a common tragic storyline imparted an essentially unchanging emotional impact: "There is a sense of wanting to feel sad (*kanashimitai*) about a familiar plot. Even when there are slight changes regarding the insertion of a character or an incident, the broader plot has not been changed. I think we don't even realize how much such things have fostered the spirit of Japanese literature."[21] For Orikuchi, this sentiment—the ability to be moved by poignant stories of separation and longing—itself provided a way of understanding the world. As he put it elsewhere, "to the people of old, the stories leading up to the *Tale of Genji* stimulated their spirits *as a kind of knowledge* (*chishiki*)."[22]

Orikuchi's understanding of the *kishu ryūritan* genre grew over time to include an ever-wider set of narratives that he viewed as variants on a more fundamental theme. From the beginning, however, his approach to the genre revolved around a few basic principles—that a single lineage linked earlier stories about gods with the heroes and heroines of the folk and classical tradition, all of whom, usually due to some transgression, found themselves in exile or wandering far from a distant center. Such stories, according to Orikuchi, helped cradle the Japanese literary tradition from infancy to maturity—from orality to literature—and in doing so, served to move and instruct people's hearts as a native form of knowledge.

## ORIKUCHI AND THE SUSANO-O MYTH

While these features of Orikuchi's genre are generally known to scholars who invoke the *kishu ryūritan* concept, further elements of his theory become visible only upon examining his treatment of particular exile narratives. We can see this by looking more closely at the myth involving Susano-o and observing Orikuchi's method of interpretation. In order to see how Orikuchi employs a kind of wordplay focusing on select details, I begin by quoting the original passage from the *Kojiki* regarding Susano-o's initial banishment. The section opens just after the divine progenitor Izanagi has returned from visiting his dead mate Izanami in the underworld; in the process of purifying himself from the defilement of such a journey, he has generated numerous offspring:

> At this time Izanagi-no-mikoto, rejoicing greatly, said:
>
> "I have borne child after child, and finally in the last bearing I have obtained three noble children."
>
> Then he removed his necklace, shaking the beads on the string so that they jingled, and, giving it to Amaterasu-o-mi-kami, he entrusted her with her mission, saying:
>
> "You shall rule Takama no hara."
>
> The name of this necklace is Mi-kura-tana-no-kami.
>
> Next he said to Tsuku-yomi-no-mikoto, entrusting him with his mission:
>
> "You shall rule the realms of the night."
>
> Next he said to Take-haya-Susano-o-no-mikoto, entrusting him with his mission:
>
> "You shall rule the ocean."
>
> While [the other deities] ruled [their realms] in obedience to the commands entrusted to them, Haya-Susa-no-o-no-mikoto did not rule the land entrusted

to him. [Instead], he wept and howled [even] until his beard eight hands long extended down over his chest.

His weeping was such that it caused the verdant mountains to wither and all the rivers and seas to dry up. At this, the cries of malevolent deities were everywhere abundant like summer flies and all sorts of calamities arose in all things.

Then Izanagi-no-o-mi-kami said to Haya-Susano-o-no-mikoto:

"Why is it you do not rule the land entrusted to you, but [instead] weep and howl?"

Then [Haya-Susano-o-no-mikoto] replied:

"I wish to go the land of my mother (*haha no kuni*), Ne-no-katasu-kuni. That is why I weep."

Then Izanagi-no-o-mi-kami, greatly enraged, said:

"In that case, you may not live in this land!"

Thus [saying], he banished him with a divine banishment (*kamuyarai ni yaraitamaiki*).[23]

Even in this brief passage, we can see how Susano-o's banishment illustrated for Orikuchi key features of the *kishu ryūritan* genre, centering around a hero of divine birth who is forced to wander far from a sacred center due to his transgressive behavior. In his commentary on the episode, however, Orikuchi goes on to discuss the meaning of the myth for the Japanese people and the reason for its enduring impact over time. Focusing on the prolonged mourning Susano-o displayed for his "mother" Izanami and his stated desire to go to the land where she resides, Orikuchi writes, "The mother-land (*haha ga kuni*) that Susano-o cried longingly for, turning green mountains barren, and from which Inahi no mikoto [in the *Kojiki*] came riding along the wave tops, is the spiritual homeland that our ancestors (*ware ware no oyatachi*) longed for. Generations of storytellers have explained that it is called their 'mother's land' because [Susano-o's mother] Izanami and [Inahi no mikoto's mother] Tamayori-hime retired there, *but the truth is that these stories narrate the longing felt by everyone (bannin) for the original land* (*mototsu kuni*)."[24] To Orikuchi, Susano-o's wish to go to "the land of my mother"—*haha ga kuni*—actually revealed the yearning among *all* Japanese for an original, lost "motherland" (a phrase expressed identically in Japanese: *haha ga kuni*). In Orikuchi's creative exegesis, "land of my mother" thus becomes "motherland," which then transforms effortlessly into "the original land" (*mototsu kuni*).

Orikuchi's reference to an "original land" in the passage above refers to a final feature of his theoretical framework, the concept of *tokoyo* (literally, "eternal realm"). While references to a land of the gods known as *tokoyo* appear in the earliest Japanese texts, Orikuchi had his own unique understanding of the term. In his view, *tokoyo* referred to the distantly remembered ancestral homeland—misremembered as the eternal realm of the gods—from which he believed the Japanese people came and now existed as if in a state of exile. To Orikuchi, the beliefs found in Japan regarding an otherworldly *tokoyo* sprang from archaic origins, representing the dimly remembered details told to countless generations of children by their elders about a land from which they had long ago emigrated. Sometime after reaching the Japanese archipelago, Orikuchi believed, the link between these stories and an actual place was forgotten, and what remained was simply a blurred memory of the "otherworld," which endured as a crucial trope in the cultural imagination, inspiring a powerful longing for a forgotten spiritual home. Orikuchi described this process in an early passage from 1920: "About the distant past, when our ancestors came to live in this country, those events are handed down in the tales told by reciters (*kataribe*). Regarding the original land (*mototsu kuni*), archeologists, comparative linguists and ancient historians provide no more than some supporting evidence. Their children and grandchildren may have known faintly about a previous land their parents had never visited, but even this was soon forgotten, and all that remained was a feeling of yearning for the original land, instilled in them by their forefathers. *I believe that this force, which inspired our ancestors one or two thousand years ago, lives on in our hearts even today.*"[25]

As seen in his final sentence, Orikuchi felt that the longing for a spiritual homeland connected the ancient Japanese with his contemporaries in the present; he even described how he, too, had once experienced the force of this longing for the "distant sacred place": "Ten years ago I traveled to Kumano, and as I stood on the very tip of Cape Daiō, sticking out into the ocean and glittering in the midday sun, I couldn't help feeling that our spiritual home (*waga tamashii no furusato*) lay at the end of a distant sea voyage. Even today, I can't pass this off as just the affected sentiment of a hopeless poet.[26] Is it not an *atavism,* an appearance of the *nostalgia* that once stirred the hearts of our ancestors?"[27] Orikuchi's remarks thus speak of more than simply his belief in *tokoyo,* for in that moment at the shore he felt he had encountered the spiritual inheritance of all Japanese people: a poignant feeling of longing born of separation from a sacred homeland.

With Orikuchi's views regarding *tokoyo* in mind, we are now prepared to examine the full context of his *kishu ryūritan* theory. In Orikuchi's broadest understanding, the Japanese literary tradition originated as divine utterances handed down from a "distant sacred place," transmitted initially by oral reciters, which later developed into more complex and varied narratives giving voice to the longing for a lost home, the original "motherland." For Orikuchi, the *kishu ryūritan* genre represented the highest expression of this originary theme of longing, inspiring story upon story that narrated the poignant sorrow of gods, heroes, and heroines who found themselves far from a sacred center.[28] Ultimately, he believed, narratives of estrangement such as Susano-o's captured the hearts of the early Japanese exactly because they replayed an archetypal experience that stood at the beginning of Japanese historical consciousness and that remained dimly present within the hearts of the Japanese all the way down to the modern period.

## THE HERMENEUTICS OF NOSTALGIA

What are we to make of Orikuchi's creative interpretation of the Susano-o myth and of his broader conception of exile narratives? We can begin by acknowledging that Orikuchi at once recognized and misrecognized the exile genre in early Japan. On the one hand, his linking of early myths such as Susano-o with much later literary works such as the *Genji* indeed points to the recurring trope of exile in the narratives of the Japanese court—although in retrospect this does not go much farther than attesting to historical fact. Orikuchi went much further in his attempt to explain the *appeal* of such narratives, however, and this is where his theories quickly become problematic. Without going into an exhaustive discussion of his work, we can simply point to two main faults in Orikuchi's method in order to indicate why we must move beyond the *kishu ryūritan* framework once and for all.[29]

First, Orikuchi's writings betray an ongoing quest to uncover the origins of a purely *Japanese* identity, untainted by "foreign" influence. In the *kishu ryūritan* genre, he believed he had found a uniquely Japanese narrative tradition that predated the absorption of Chinese culture.[30] While Orikuchi acknowledged that "in China there were also numerous people of letters who were exiled," he didn't find in their poetry the same spirit that he perceived in Japanese *waka*.[31] Even *Japanese* poets who wrote in Chinese were constrained in their powers of expression, he felt. Echoing a sentiment expressed many years earlier by the nativist scholar Motoori Norinaga, Orikuchi wrote of such poets, "What a dreadful thing, being confined within the expressions of Chinese verse."[32]

Orikuchi's approach thus reveals the continuing imprint of the National Learning (Kokugaku) movement of the eighteenth and nineteenth centuries, whose leading scholars combined philological rigor and protonationalist zeal to project onto the earliest Japanese texts the image of an idealized community: pure, untainted, and thereby sacred.[33] Such nativist faith in the existence of a pure Japanese spirit—as simple to critique as it is difficult to dispel—plainly overlooks the complex interweaving of what we now see as Chinese, Japanese, and Korean elements in the cultural life of the Yamato court, which extend as far back as textual traces can be found.[34] While Orikuchi sought to disentangle strands of a native tradition from the continental influences that enabled writing to occur in the first place, such claims evaporate the moment we consider, for example, that the Tang Chinese poet (and exile) Bai Juyi (772–846) was among the most acclaimed of the Heian period, or that his Chinese poem, *The Song of Everlasting Sorrow,* frames the opening of the *Tale of Genji,* so cherished by Orikuchi as the apex of the *kishu ryūritan* genre.[35] Such reminders help to underscore the affinities, rather than the differences, that existed between the Yamato and Chinese courts, even—or especially—with regard to exile. More broadly, amid the complex mixture of migration from the Korean peninsula, cultural exchange with the Chinese courts, and the archipelago's own ethnic and linguistic hybridity, the idea of a purely Japanese spirit in antiquity remains fundamentally a nativist fantasy.[36]

In addition to imagining a purely "Japanese" past, a second problem with Orikuchi's approach lies in his appeal to a Japanese spirit that transcends history. As we've seen, Orikuchi located the enduring quality of the *kishu ryūritan* genre in the emotional appeal it held for *all* Japanese—throughout time—due to the longing it stirred for a lost spiritual homeland. His approach thus operates by imposing a modern image of community onto early Japan, seeking to construe ancient narratives as the foundations of a single enduring national identity. Yet as scholars have increasingly pointed out, the original textual community for the court chronicles was entirely different. Locating the texts in the social conditions of their late seventh- and early eighth-century genesis, Jun'ichi Isomae writes, "The constituency of the myths in ancient times was limited to clan members who were integrated according to their political functions into the Yamato court centered on the imperial house. The people [and gods] who appeared in the myths were the ancestors of the clans that constituted the court. . . . Thus, the people who lived in the land of Japan did not look to the myths of the *Kojiki* and *Nihonshoki* for some portrayal of the origins of "the people" (*aohitogusa*) because . . . in antiquity the common people appeared only as objects of the rule of the Yamato court. . . . Because of their political functions, the myths were possessed exclusively by the court."[37]

For modern scholars to claim the myths as a treasury revealing the spiritual heritage of *all* Japanese people thus requires a prior transformation in social relations, textual production, and interpretive practice—not to mention an early modern image of national community. As Isomae points out, this was conceivable only after the political power of the court legitimated by the texts had faded during the medieval period, only after publishing technologies had made the texts widely available (in conjunction with the rise of book lenders), and only after a nativist movement had reinterpreted the texts as the classical site of an enduring national spirit. When all of these elements came together, he writes, "The myths of the *Kojiki* and *Nihonshoki* were freed from their political constraints in the early modern period to become relevant to a wide range of social classes. The constituency of the myths expanded to include all people who lived in the realm . . . [and] because by now the myths did not contain any direct referent [to an existing court society], anyone could take part in them simply by living in Japan."[38] Orikuchi's reading of the Susano-o myth as a poignant expression of the longing felt by all Japanese people, throughout time, is thus an interpretation based on a radical dehistoricizing of the royal myth-histories, a move that fundamentally misrepresents the historical context of the early Japanese court.

More than illuminating the ancient past, Orikuchi's theories shed light most clearly on the historical setting of his own writing. As an influential scholar at Kokugakuin University during the turbulent interwar years, Orikuchi's mythic account of the origins of the Japanese spirit sought to erase any divide between the archaic and modern periods, offering the possibility of a spiritual engagement with the past for the disenchanted modern audiences he was concerned to address. Yet if such expressions of "desire for an origin that could never be reached" remained a hallmark of Japanese scholarship laboring in the wake of the National Learning movement,[39] this also means that scholars today who invoke Orikuchi's *kishu ryūritan* genre do so at the risk of reproducing a distorted image of the Japanese past. Nostalgic, essentializing, and ahistorical, the *kishu ryūritan* theory is genuinely problematic—and a fresh approach to exile narratives in early Japan is long overdue.

## REREADING THE JAPANESE MYTH-HISTORIES

If Orikuchi's interpretation of early Japanese myth in many ways constitutes its own modern mythology, how might we better locate the significance of the royal myths for the court society in which they originally circulated? More specifically, what relations might we trace between myths imagining the exile of a god on the one hand and the social world in which such narratives were produced? And what might this tell us, in turn, about the widespread presence of exile as a trope within early Japanese narrative?

To begin addressing such questions, we can start by examining the nature of "myth" in the myth-histories themselves. In contrast to nativist-influenced views such as Orikuchi's, the work of several generations of scholars clearly shows that the court-sponsored myth-histories were not simply unreflective compilations of early Japanese oral tradition, but resulted instead from concerted efforts by the Yamato court to trace a narrative supporting the claims of the royal house to sovereignty.[40] The preface to the *Kojiki* itself makes this clear, stating that the text resulted from the ruler Tenmu's charge to compile a coherent narrative—"discarding the mistaken and establishing the true"—and we can understand this at one level to indicate a narrative supporting the claims of Tenmu's line to sovereignty.[41] As Kōnoshi Takamitsu has stated more generally regarding the two earliest court chronicles, "The *Kojiki* [712] and the *Nihon shoki* [720] were originally composed as a result of the need of the early *ritsuryō* state to authenticate itself," adding that the texts produced by that state offered "an affirmation of its own world order."[42] That such an authenticating project was fundamentally genealogical is also clear from the outset of the *Kojiki* and *Nihon shoki* narratives, both of which begin by tracing the genealogies of numerous deities and continue by connecting that divine hierarchy to the social order of the Yamato court (through accounts describing the descent from the heavens of the ancestral deities of various court families).

Clarifying the historiographic intent behind the state's textual projects also helps shed light on what has been a stumbling block for many interpreters of Japanese myth: the complex diversity of the mythic record from early Japan. As Kōnoshi points out regarding scholars like Orikuchi, "modern scholarship has regarded the *Kojiki* and the *Nihon shoki,* along with early ritual texts such as *norito* (ritual prayers), as manifestations of a single preexisting mythology," and indeed, "as the cultural foundation of both the folk and the nation."[43] As a result, many scholars have downplayed differences between the two myth-histories as variations or divergences from a presumed "original" narrative.[44] Yet there are good reasons to take such differences seriously: as Jun'ichi Isomae reminds us, "there was never a time when the *Kojiki* and *Nihon shoki* myths constituted a single, unified text: a multitude of variants, as well as the interpretations connected with each of them, coexisted side by side."[45] In this light, rather than a single, unified mythology, the presence of variants within the very earliest texts reveals the existence of diverse sources out of which the myth-histories were composed, each in distinctly motivated ways.[46]

It shouldn't surprise us, then, that the *Kojiki* and *Nihon shoki*—compiled at different moments, in different linguistic modes, and with different sources and audiences in mind—differ from each other on rather fundamental points. Rather than a High Heavenly Plain (Takamanohara), the *Nihon shoki* refers repeatedly to "Heaven."[47] Nor does Izanagi's mate Izanami die in the *Nihon shoki.*[48] Yet the situation is even more complex: not only do the two texts contradict each other, they also contradict themselves, internally. As one example, Orikuchi's exegesis of the Susano-o myth centers around the deity's mourning for his deceased mother, and this mourning is indeed recorded in the *Kojiki* account, yet in the same *Kojiki,* Izanami never gave birth to Susano-o: such a genealogy appears only in the *Nihon shoki.* At moments such as these, there is almost a sense in which meaning hovers in the "mosaic of citations" created between the two texts,[49] as long as we understand this to reflect not so much a single preexisting mythology as the distinctive use in each text of a common archive of mythic variants.[50]

This diverse archive—resulting from differing versions of the royal chronicles (*teiki*) and ancient myths (*kuji*) held by the different clans, as well as regional variants (as can be seen later in the provincial *fudoki)*—is reflected particularly clearly in the *Nihon shoki,* which presents both the official court narrative as well as variants (*issho*) to the main text, resulting in as many as eleven variants for a given passage.[51] At times the juxtapositions within the *Nihon shoki* can be jarring, as when the official narrative establishing Amaterasu as blood ancestor of the royal line is accompanied by three variants in which Susano-o instead is attributed with paternity.[52] Given such diversity within the mythic sources, the privileging of one version as "correct"—the *Kojiki,* for example—or the positing of a single, preexisting mythology, simply doesn't match the available evidence. As a result, as Jun'ichi Isomae has suggested, rather than attempting to locate the "true meaning" or "correct version" of early Japanese myth, we might shift our attention more profitably to those moments in the historical transcript where one group has attempted to "fix" a particular reading of myth—"discarding the mistaken and establishing the true," in the words of the *Kojiki* preface—realizing all the while that such moments come about precisely in light of and in response to the existence of other "variant" readings.[53]

## SUSANO-O MYTHOLOGY IN HISTORICAL PERSPECTIVE

Regarding the production of the earliest court chronicles, Joan Piggott has termed the court's project one of "integrative mythology," referring to the manner in which the earliest chronicles incorporate myths and deities from other regions within narratives supporting the claims of the Yamato sovereign.[54] In doing so, the mythic record reflects the court's expanding presence beyond the Yamato Plain—an expansion Piggott characterizes as occurring not primarily through force but through the assimilation of regional elites into a Yamato-centered "hierarchy of status."[55] In this fashion, she suggests, regional leaders outside the Yamato sphere gradually became self-interested participants in the Yamato polity, receiving titles, privileges, and articles of prestige in return for their submission, loyalty, and tribute to the Yamato center.[56] Likewise, as regional elites were gradually assimilated, so too their clan deities, mythologies, and cultic centers made their way into the Yamato framework as well.[57]

Within the Yamato court chronicles, nowhere is the process of integrative mythology more clearly evident than in the inclusion of the so-called Izumo cycle. Beginning with the exile of Susano-o to Izumo and ending with the famous land-yielding sequence—in which Susano-o's "descendent" Ōkuninushi cedes rule over the land to deities representing Amaterasu—roughly one-third of the "Age of the Gods" portions of the *Kojiki* and *Nihon shoki* are devoted to myth sequences taking place in Izumo and incorporating the chief deity and cultic center of that region. The presence of significant narrative strands involving Izumo within Yamato court texts thus underlies Piggott's conclusion that, in the court chronicles, "a new divine genealogy under Amaterasu's sovereignty incorporated deities from both areas."[58]

Regarding Susano-o, however, an examination of the *Izumo Fudoki*—the compendium of regional data from Izumo ordered by the Yamato court in 713 and presented from Izumo to the throne in 733—suggests once again that the integrative process was something more dynamic than a simple compilation of existing sources. On the one hand, the *Izumo Fudoki* clearly attests to Susano-o's status as a local divinity—mentioning his name ten times, detailing his divine offspring, and narrating the origin of his place of enshrinement at the Susa no yashiro. By comparison, his name appears in no other extant *fudoki*.[59] On the other hand, his status as a local deity in the *Izumo Fudoki* remains notably modest: absent from the text is any mention of the more grandiloquent qualities attributed to Susano-o in the court chronicles—including not only his kinship with Amaterasu and his exile from the Heavenly Plain but also his slaying of the eight-headed serpent in Izumo and his discovery of the Ama no murakumo sword within its body.[60]

By far the greater deity within the *Izumo Fudoki* is Ōnamuchi—known in the Yamato chronicles by the name Ōkuninushi—who is enshrined in the "great palace" of Kitsuki, known later as Izumo Taisha and situated along a major trade route on the Japan Sea coast.[61] By contrast, the relative status of Susano-o's shrine is indicated by its modest setting in the village of Susa and by the mere two rice fields mentioned in the *Fudoki* providing for its economic support.[62] Such disparities between the depiction of Susano-o in the *Izumo Fudoki* and in the Yamato court chronicles thus suggest a process not merely of retelling but of reimagining Izumo content within the royal myth-histories. Rather than an "Izumo cycle" contained within the *Kojiki* and *Nihon shoki,* there exists what more properly should be called a Yamato-centered narrative employing Izumo deities.[63]

Given the richly detailed role played by Susano-o within the royal myths, we might expect a correspondingly rich cultic landscape surrounding the deity *somewhere*—if not in Izumo, then perhaps in the Yamato region. To examine this, we can turn to the *Engishiki*—the mid-Heian record of the ritual and administrative protocols of the *ritsuryō* state—which includes a valuable listing of shrines (the *jinmyōchō*) that were recognized under the *ritsuryō* system and were thus entitled to receive patronage from the state in the form of offerings.[64] Yet of the four shrines appearing on the list whose names suggest the worship of Susano-o, two were located in Izumo, one was in the ancient province of Bingo, and one was in Kii Province—none are found within the Kinai, the home provinces surrounding and including the capital.[65] Here again, the contrast between the strong supporting role played by Susano-o in Yamato myth and the lack of a cultic presence attested him in the capital region is striking.[66]

It remains unclear how such a rich structural figure in Yamato myth could emerge from such modest origins in the Izumo region, or conversely how a deity seemingly lacking a cultic base in the Yamato region could rise to such an important role in the royal pantheon,[67] although the period during which the court chronicles were being composed was certainly a time of "great change" in the cultic as well as social and political spheres.[68] As Matsumae Takeshi frames the situation regarding Susano-o, "There is probably no deity in Japanese mythology whose complexity matches that of Susano-o, nor therefore any who have been the focus of so much scholarly discussion. . . . One could even say that the question of Susano-o is the starting point for research into Japanese myth, the clarification of which might provide an important key to untangling the riddles of Japanese mythology."[69]

At the same time, the question of the exact relation between Izumo myth and the Yamato myth-histories has been called "the hardest problem of all to solve,"[70] and as Kōnoshi Takamitsu has cautioned, as long as we lack a direct window into the process of textual formation, there are reasons to be cautious about peering back any further toward sources for the earliest extant texts: as we saw with Orikuchi Shinobu, all too often such attempts have resulted in the creation of new, modern "mythologies."[71]

## SUSANO-O AND THE IMAGINATION OF EXILE

Questions of mythic origins notwithstanding, one thing about the relation between Izumo and Yamato mythology stands out from the court chronicles themselves: the crucial role played by exile in mapping out a Yamato-based constellation of power. At the most basic level, we see this in how the trope of exile—Susano-o's banishment from the Heavenly Plain—provides the narrative bridge joining the Izumo section to the central Yamato narrative of the court chronicles. Additionally, the theme of exile enables the narratives at once to relate Susano-o with Amaterasu by blood, while also establishing him as the ancestor of the chief Izumo deity Ōkuninushi (Ōnamuchi). Still further, we can say that banishment provides the narrative element relating Izumo deities (such as Ōkuninushi/Ōnamuchi) to those of the Yamato center even while subordinating them through their descent from the exiled god Susano-o. Narrative connection, genealogical relation, and political subordination of Izumo to Yamato: all are accomplished with the exile of Susano-o.

Such readings gain further resonance when we recall that the mythic conflict between Amaterasu and Susano-o was precipitated by tension surrounding the transfer of power from Izanagi to Amaterasu, and that the nature of

Susano-o's transgressions—destroying Amaterasu's heavenly rice fields, desecrating the hall where Amaterasu was to taste the first rice, and interrupting the weaving of heavenly garments—largely signifies efforts to thwart Amaterasu's performance of the Harvest Ritual (Niiname-sai) of the Yamato court whose celebration by Amaterasu would confirm her legitimacy as the sovereign.[72] Through the trope of exile, we can sum up, the court texts vividly imagine and dramatically assert an entire constellation of power, juxtaposing Amaterasu and Susano-o, Yamato and Izumo, center and margin, royalty and loyalty.

Issues of genealogy, sovereignty, and legitimacy continue to reverberate as the Izumo section of the court chronicles draws to a close. Just as the Yamato narratives descend into Izumo beginning with Susano-o's exile, so too the texts pick up the Yamato thread once again as Susano-o's "descendent," the great Izumo deity Ōkuninushi/Ōnamuchi, is called upon to surrender the land to deities sent down from the Heavenly Plain.[73] More specifically, Amaterasu and the deity Takamimusubi send deities down to pacify and subdue the land, which is filled with unruly and troublesome divinities. Their subjugation ultimately requires the submission of the Izumo deity Ōkuninushi—"the great lord of the land"—and the land-yielding myth involving Ōkuninushi thus sets the stage for the divine descent of the sun lineage, clearing the way for Amaterasu's grandson Ninigi to descend and govern the realm.

Interestingly, the initial attempts to subdue the unruly divinities end in failure, as the first deities sent down from the Heavenly Plain (Ame no hohi no mikoto and Ame no wakahiko, according to the *Kojiki*) end up allying with Ōkuninushi instead.[74] Only after the deity Takemikazuchino-o descends and is about to kill Ōkuninushi's son does the great Izumo deity agree to surrender the land to Amaterasu's envoys. The agreement is conditional: in exchange for his submission to the envoys, Ōkuninushi requests and receives recognition for his own status as the deity of the great shrine of Izumo. Quoting the *Kojiki* version,

> Then [Ōkuninushi] replied, saying:
>
> I will yield this Central Land of the Reed Plains in accordance with your commands. Only, if you will worship me, making my dwelling-place like the plentiful heavenly dwelling where rules the heavenly sun-lineage (*amatsu hitsugi*) of the offspring of the heavenly deities, firmly rooting the posts of the palace in the bedrock below . . .
>
> Thus saying, he built a heavenly shrine (*ame no miaraka)* at the beach of Tagishi in the land of Izumo.[75]

Several elements are noteworthy from the land-yielding sequence. At one level, the account operates in the manner of an *engi*—an origin myth for the founding of the great Izumo shrine, the seat of worship for Ōkuninushi.[76] Simultaneously, the myth serves to authenticate claims made by the "sun lineage" for their own sovereignty over the Central Reed Plain and to deny the same for other deities and their possible descendants. Equally striking, however, the episode recapitulates in myth the historical process of incorporation mentioned earlier, illustrating in this case how a regional deity could be integrated into the Yamato hierarchy of status, receiving privileges and prestige in return for submission and loyalty to the Yamato center. As the Izumo section draws to a close in the royal myths, Ōkuninushi withdraws to govern "things unseen" (*kakuretaru koto*),[77] and the main Yamato narrative continues with the descent of Ninigi, bearing among other things the divine sword first discovered in Izumo by Susano-o. Looking back at the Izumo section of the court chronicles—from Susano-o's banishment to Ōkuninushi's surrender—the role of exile in helping simultaneously to connect and subordinate Izumo to Yamato can be charted genealogically, as shown in Figure 1.

## THE DEVELOPMENT OF AN IZUMO PERIPHERY

Given the themes of conquest and resistance animating the narrative of Ōkuninushi's surrender, scholars have long attempted to fathom the degree to which the antagonism expressed in the myth reflects some aspect of the historical record and why Izumo in particular appears on the receiving end of Yamato subjugation in the court chronicles. It was once popularly suggested that Izumo may have been the base of a distinct ruling group that held sway widely over the land, whose eventual conquest came at the hands of the expanding Yamato kingdom.[78] Certainly, all evidence indicates that Izumo constituted a unique and powerful cultural center by the end of the Yayoi period (ca. 400 BCE–ca. 250 CE), as is clear from the unique style of burial mounds found in the region, the great size of these distinct mounds, and the vast numbers of bronze artifacts recovered from local burial sites.[79] Despite evidence of trade networks and cultural exchange between Izumo and other parts of Japan, however, neither widespread Izumo hegemony nor Yamato military conquest is attested.[80]

As a result, scholarship has largely shifted toward exploring the symbolic function played by Izumo in the royal myth-histories. In this light, it's been

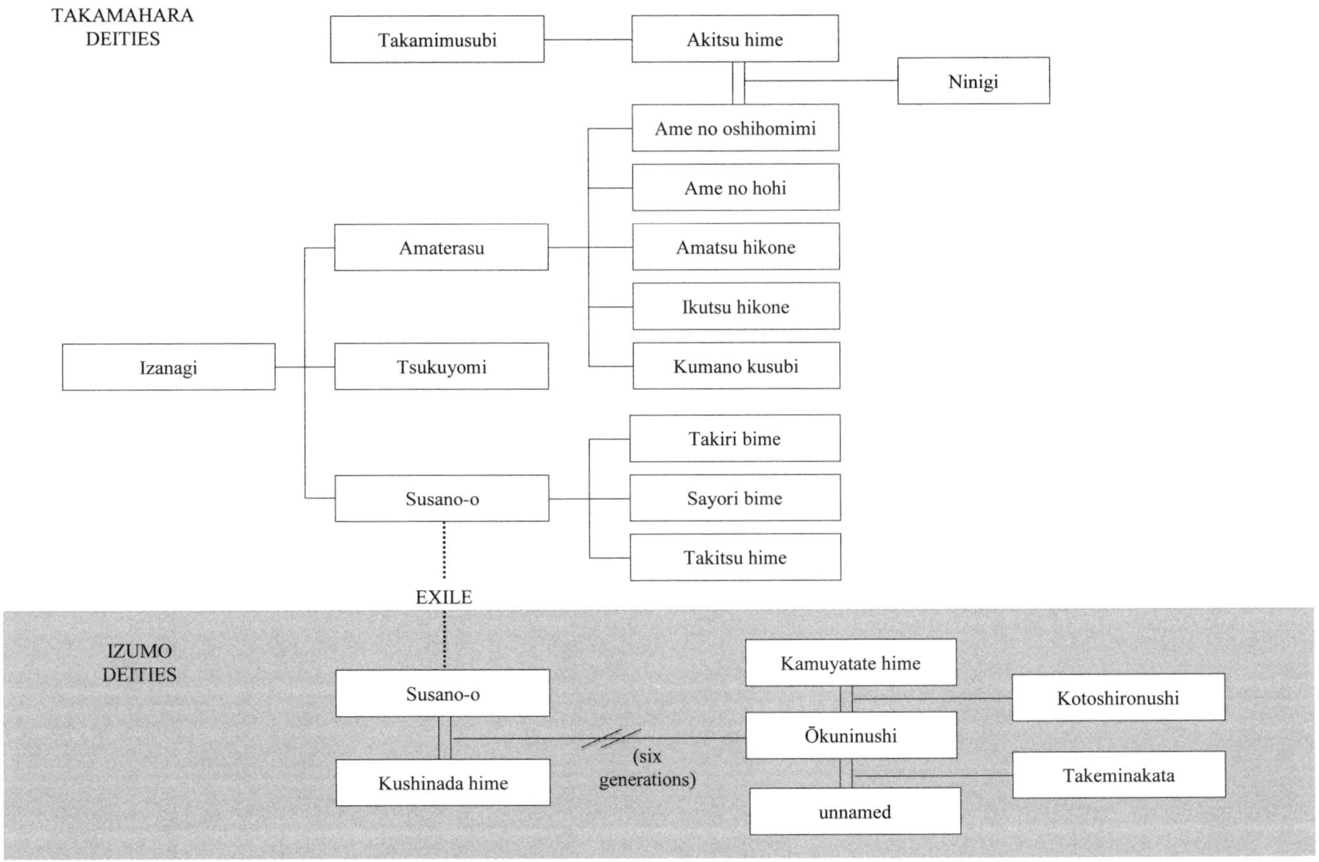


**Figure 1** Genealogies of Exile: The *Kojiki* Perspective

*Note:* In order to avoid mixing genealogies from the *Kojiki* and *Nihon shoki,* this chart pictures the *Kojiki* account. In addition to including several contradictory variants, the main *Nihon shoki* genealogy differs on numerous points: Izanagi and Izanami mutually produce the children Amaterasu, Tsukuyomi, and Susano-o, for example, and Ōkuninushi/Ōnamuchi is considered the immediate offspring of Susano-o through Susano-o's marriage to the Izumo deity Kushinada hime.

suggested that the unique role of Izumo in the court chronicles may evidence Izumo's status as one of the last autonomous regions to be assimilated within the expanding Yamato polity, and that Izumo may thus function in the court texts as paradigmatic of the broader process of Yamato expansion as a whole.[81] Such a function may be reflected, for example, in the way that an Izumo deity—Ōnamuchi—comes to operate in the court texts as the leading representative of all earthly deities: Ōkuninushi. Similarly, the resistance and subjugation of Izumo may have been exaggerated within the court chronicles exactly in order to amplify the actual degree of Yamato authority over territory for which it had in fact only tenuous control. As such examples suggest, while the exact historical background for the myths remains unclear, the singular place held by Izumo in the narrative imagination of the Yamato myth-histories is unmistakable.

Paralleling the mythic assimilation of Izumo deities into a Yamato framework, the archeological record also reflects the gradual absorption of Izumo elites into the Yamato cultural orbit beginning in the Kofun period (ca. 250–592). Distinctive keyhole-shaped tombs, for example—which emerged first in the Yamato region, foreshadowing the rise of a nascent Yamato polity—began appearing in Izumo by the end of the third century.[82] Prestige goods originating in Yamato have been excavated from such tombs in Izumo dating at least to the sixth century, including ceremonial swords inscribed with honorific titles bestowed upon regional elites by the Yamato center.[83] Flowing in the opposite direction, centripetal tribute from the great Izumo Shrine is recorded in Yamato during the same period,[84] suggesting that by the late Kofun era, relations of tribute—in exchange for titles and articles of prestige—were being etched into the larger cultural and political landscape.

## IZUMO MYTH AND YAMATO COURT RITUAL

As we move into the period for which the written records of the Yamato court become historically more reliable, the absorption of Izumo elites into a Yamato-based hierarchy becomes visible in a new dimension: the ritual life of the court. Just as Izumo held a singular position within Yamato myth, the hereditary elite of Izumo also came to hold a privileged position in the ritual life of the Yamato court, in contrast to the role of other similar regional nobility. This can be seen clearly in the prescribed visits to the court of the Izumo no kuni no miyatsuko—the hereditarily appointed regional leader of Izumo—to offer ritual tribute and praise before the figure of the sovereign.[85] While on the one hand the ritual was merely one strand within a much larger tapestry of state ceremony that helped construct and display the sacrality, power, and legitimacy of the royal line, it was also unique in that it is the only known occasion in which a regional *kuni no miyatsuko* came to the court to offer such ritualized praise.[86]

Known by its liturgical name, Izumo no Miyatsuko no Kamuyogoto (Divine Laudatory Words of the Izumo Chieftain), the praise ritual was in fact an elaborate, multiyear affair, set into motion each time the office of Izumo miyatsuko was passed down from one generational leader to the next within the Izumo no Omi family. The process thus began when the incumbent Izumo leader (who was also the chief priest at the great Izumo Shrine) first journeyed to the capital to receive his appointment, along with congratulatory gifts from the state. After his return to Izumo and undergoing a year-long period of purification, the ritual culminated when the new *miyatsuko* journeyed back to the Yamato capital to perform the praise ritual itself.[87] There, before the Yamato sovereign in the courtyard of the Daigokuden—the Great Hall of State within the royal palace—the *miyatsuko* blessed the ruler with words of praise and tribute, including the following:

> Thus do I, inheriting this tradition,
> Perform the worship service,
> And as the morning sun rises in glittering beauty
> Do present, as tokens of homage of the deities
> And as tokens of homage of the Omi,
> The sacred treasures of divine blessing. Thus I humbly speak. . . .
> May you rule as an incarnate deity (*akitsu mikami*)
> The Great Eight-Island Land.[88]

The performance was accompanied by offerings of tribute from Izumo to the sovereign—including jewels, a sword, and a mirror, as well as cloth, a horse, swans, and food offerings—while the Izumo miyatsuko and his followers were further bestowed with gifts and promotions in rank.[89]

As with the Yamato myths involving both Susano-o and Ōkuninushi, the Kamuyogoto liturgy too was infused with themes of genealogy, sovereignty, legitimacy, submission, loyalty, and tribute. Indeed, the ritual acted on one level to assert a connection between the present moment of the participants and the time and space of the royal myth-histories, as can be seen in the motifs that structure the three sections of the liturgy. The first section begins by establishing the credentials of the *kuni no miyatsuko* himself as the chief priest of the great Izumo Shrine, responsible for the worship of both "the blessed offspring of Izanagi" and "the land-creator" Ōnamuchi (Ōkuninushi).[90] In the second section, the liturgy shifts to the time of myth, recalling how the "distant ancestor" of the Izumo leader—the deity Ame no hohi no mikoto—was sent down from the Heavenly Plain to pacify and subdue the land, which Ame no hohi managed to do by causing Ōnamuchi to relinquish control.[91] The final section then narrates the origin of the ritual itself by explaining how the heavenly deities charged Ame no hohi with "blessing the great reign of the sovereign as eternal," a task inherited genealogically by the Izumo miyatsuko in the mythically charged present. As the Izumo leader confirmed during the ritual, "Thus do I, inheriting this tradition, perform the worship service . . . and fearfully and reverently, do humbly speak the congratulatory words of divine blessing."[92]

Echoing the submission of both Susano-o and Ōkuninushi within the Yamato myth-histories, the Izumo chieftain's recitation effectively reiterates the rejection of Izumo autonomy before the "sun lineage" of Amaterasu, offering instead a conspicuous display of loyalty and tribute. For heuristic purposes, we can visually chart homologies between the myth of Susano-o's banishment to Izumo, Ōkuninushi's land-yielding, and the Kamuyogoto praise ritual (see Table 1), drawing attention to the ways both myth and ritual inscribe Izumo within a Yamato-based hierarchy, assimilating and subjecting Izumo elites across distinct moments in mythic and historical time, while confirming the rightful rule of the sun line and, by extension, the Yamato state.

At the same time, such a chart highlights certain elements while obscuring others. Most fundamentally, it presents a vision of power and sacrality centered in Yamato, and we should not forget that texts from Izumo offer a very different perspective. As discussed earlier, none of the passages from the *Izumo Fudoki* connect Susano-o with the royal line, nor do they even mention Amaterasu. Neither does the *Fudoki* ever depict Ōnamuchi (Ōkuninushi) yielding sovereignty over Izumo. Even the text of the Kamuyogoto, performed at the Yamato court, constitutes a deviation from the Yamato-centered myths: whereas the royal myth-histories portray Ame no hohi as a failed envoy of the sun deity who ended up allying with Ōkuninushi, the Kamuyogoto portrays the deity instead as the honored ancestor of the Izumo Omi and the chief deity credited with pacifying Ōnamuchi/Ōkuninushi in Izumo.

**Table 1** Parallel Relationships: Susano-o, Ōkuninushi, and the Izumo Miyatsuko

| | ZONE OF INTERACTION | | |
|---|---|---|---|
| | High Heavenly Plain/ Izumo | Central Reed Plain/ Izumo | Yamato capital/ Izumo |
| Yamato representative | Amaterasu | Envoys of Amaterasu and Takamimusubi | Yamato Sovereign |
| Izumo supplicant | Susano-o | Ōkuninushi | Izumo Miyatsuko |
| Offering, surrender, or tribute from Izumo | sword | rulership over the land | sword, jewels, mirror, and others |

Regarding such discrepancies, it's been suggested that the Kamuyogoto liturgy stakes out a position midway between the Izumo- and Yamato-based texts, mediating between the divergent mythic worldviews of the two regions.[93] In this sense, the ritual performance has been seen as negotiating a kind of settlement, offering a conspicuous display of loyalty and tribute from Izumo in return for greater recognition of genealogical status within the Yamato hierarchy.[94] Matsumae Takeshi summarizes the context for such performances as follows: "For all leading families at this time, the most important concern for establishing one's social standing was to get one's family myths adopted by the court, and to get one's clan genealogies woven into the royal genealogies. There were several ways to bring one's family traditions into the court: by providing one's daughter as a consort to the sovereign, thereby bringing one's natal traditions into the royal family's, or by taking part in the various roles involved in the ceremonies of royal authority—the *Daijōsai, Chinkonsai,* and enthronement ceremonies—by offering performances of one's ancestral rituals and narrating the origin of such rituals as a kind of allegiance myth."[95] Indeed, the Kamuyogoto liturgy offers evidence that Izumo leaders had established one such niche, through which the divine offspring of Ōnamuchi were presented as protector deities for the Yamato sovereign.[96] All of this may help to explain the conspicuous role of the Izumo miyatsuko in the ritual life of the early Yamato court, yet it is also possible to overstate the degree of Izumo prestige or autonomy achieved by the ritual performance of praise. In the end, while the ritual may have provided an opportunity for Izumo elites to press their claims for greater recognition within the Yamato hierarchy, at the same time this opportunity was always framed within a dramatic display of allegiance to Yamato authority, in a liturgy that amounted ultimately, in one scholar's phrase, to "words of submission" (*fukujū no kotoba*).[97]

Interestingly, the earliest known performance of the Kamuyogoto ritual is recorded in a *Shoku Nihongi* entry from 716, which states that an Izumo miyatsuko named Hatayasu conducted the liturgy.[98] The next performance was recorded in 724 by an Izumo miyatsuko named Hiroshima, who was also one of the original editors of the *Izumo Fudoki.* Regarding the 716 performance, scholars are unsure whether the *Shoku Nihongi* entry marks the first occurrence of the ritual ever or simply the first recorded occurrence.[99] It's striking, however, that this first known occurrence takes place a mere four years after the completion of the *Kojiki,* suggesting that both the *Kojiki* and the Izumo Kamuyogoto ritual were aspects of a larger project on the part of the early Yamato court to authenticate its rule. It is also striking that no performance of the Izumo Kamuyogoto ritual appears in the official histories after 833,[100] thus neatly bookending both the rise and the attenuation of the period in which the *ritsuryō* state most conspicuously attempted to assert its rule over the archipelago.

Before concluding, we should take a moment to reflect on the Kamuyogoto ritual in light of the mythic episode with which we began concerning the banishment of Susano-o. In the charged actions performed by the Izumo miyatsuko, the order of things initiated during the age of the gods with Susano-o's banishment was revisited and affirmed. In the royal myths, Susano-o's expulsion from the Heavenly Plain provided the narrative means for tracing the origins of the principle deities of Izumo, at once relating them to the Yamato pantheon while also inscribing their subordination to that center. With the ritual recitation of praise by a sacred representative from Izumo, such asymmetric relations between the two regions were then periodically recalled, reconfirmed, and displayed.

During these reenactments, the Kamuyogoto ritual included an offering of jeweled beads from the Izumo miyatsuko to the Yamato sovereign: white, red, and blue jewels "arranged in orderly strings of noble beads," presented with the words "May you rule as an incarnate deity the Great Eight-Island Land."[101] Such an offering echoes distantly the bestowal of the string of jewels from Izanagi to Amaterasu mentioned in the royal myths describing the original transfer of sovereignty from Izanagi. It is possible, as has been suggested regarding Izanagi's gesture in the myth-histories, that the act of bestowing jewels plays on homonyms contained within the word *tama* (jewel

玉; soul 魂) to signify the transfer of divine charisma from one ruler to the other and hence the legitimation of succession.[102] Yet even if the gesture by the Izumo miyatsuko represented nothing more than the offering of sacred treasure, in such an act as well we glimpse one further convergence between mythic narrative and ritual practice in service of the consecration of power.[103]

## CONCLUSION

We can begin to wrap up by rephrasing a question originally posed by Paul Veyne in an altogether different setting: Did the Japanese believe in their myths?[104] *These* myths? And what about ritual? Before discussing the privileging of "belief" inherent in such questions, we need first to clarify what we might possibly mean by "the Japanese." To reiterate, the audience for the earliest court texts was never any sort of "folk," much less a national community in the sense imagined by the early modern nativist scholars, but rather the nobility who themselves comprised court society, a hierarchy of central and regional elites. Seen in this light, Orikuchi Shinobu's thesis—that the mythic narrative of Susano-o's mourning and exile expressed the yearning felt by *all* Japanese people for a spiritual homeland—is a reading only made possible from the early modern period, following a complete restructuring of the relationship between text, sovereign, and nation. In contrast, the earliest texts must be viewed as part of a historiographic project on the part of the Yamato state, a project that sought to authenticate and consecrate a particular order of power through the medium of mythohistoric narrative.

We need also to consider the question of "belief" more closely. Every study of the earliest texts from Japan is faced with the challenge of balancing the rich trove of symbolic material contained within the myth-histories, on the one hand, with the clearly expressed political intent of the text's compilers. For every study that recovers the rich symbolic logic within the court texts—unveiling the role of double burial, for example, or of silkworm cults within the royal chronicles—there is always the lingering question of how to regard the role of artifice or agency on the part of the myths' "editors."[105] As an earlier scholar of Japanese literature expressed this tension, "Many myths have been suppressed or forcibly altered in order to make them conform to this pattern [of royal domination]. It would be a grave mistake to consider those parts of the *Kojiki* and *Nihon shoki* which deal with the 'Age of the Gods' (*kamiyo, jindai* 神代) as descriptions of *the* mythology of the

Japanese people and it is a very delicate task to define the relative value of the myths collected in these works."[106]

In the delicate task of determining their "relative value," however, perhaps the study of early Japanese myth does not require us to line up on either side of a divide between belief and unbelief. Indeed, perhaps the question of belief itself somehow misses the target.[107] Rather, as James Scott has shown in other contexts, what we witness in myths and rituals such as those produced by the Yamato court may be understood best as the construction of a public transcript, "the self-portrait of dominant elites as they would have themselves seen."[108] In this sense, Yamato myth and ritual should be viewed as a kind of sacred dramaturgy—a script enacted by members of court society to the degree that they were immersed and invested in the Yamato order of things. In considering the conjoining of the court's myth-histories with ritual practice, Scott's points remain suggestive: "The theatrical imperatives that normally prevail in situations of domination produce a public transcript in close conformity with how the dominant group would wish to have things appear . . . and any analysis based exclusively on the public transcript is likely to conclude that subordinate groups endorse the terms of their subordination and are willing, even enthusiastic, partners in that subordination."[109]

If this is the case, such a public transcript should not then be treated as a record of interior belief but rather as a script reflecting the interests of the dominant, who were in a position to produce exactly such "command performances of consent" as we find in the praise ritual of the Izumo miyatsuko.[110] This doesn't negate the possibility of belief in the myths and rituals that helped shape the royal theater of the Yamato state, but it rightly cautions us not to mistake symbolic enactments of power relations—"credible performances"—for outward expressions of interior belief.

If this all seems rather matter of fact, we are ready then to return to the questions we began with. If Orikuchi's exegesis of the Susano-o myth is inadmissible—resting as it does on projections of cultural homogeneity and shared national longing—where does this leave us regarding the widespread presence of exile as a theme throughout Japanese court society? In the departing wake of Orikuchi's *kishu ryūritan* theory, what should we make of the widespread trope of exile seen in the literature, law, oracles, and cultic activity of Nara and Heian Japan?

While rejecting Orikuchi's theoretical approach, I agree that with the banishment of Susano-o as a starting point, we can better understand the particular resonance of the trope of exile within court society. As noted before, every narrative of exile imagines a certain constellation of power: a privileged sphere and those who are relegated to its margins. From this follows two fundamental possibilities, out of which we may trace nearly endless variants. For those in positions of power, the banishment of *others* provides a persuasive narrative trope for asserting and maintaining their own centrality, as when it is woven into the ruling myths of the Yamato court, establishing relations of hierarchy between Amaterasu and Susano-o, and thereby a vision of power with the "sun lineage" of Amaterasu at its center. Yet as we find in other texts that emerged later within Japanese court society, the trope of exile could also be harnessed by those more marginal, in narratives that sought to question and reconsider the structures of inclusion and exclusion upon which Yamato court society rested. Through the politics and poetics of exile, we might say, all members of court society possessed a theme through which to comment upon the social order.[111] To see how this might be the case, in the next chapter we turn to the theme of exile within Japan's earliest prose tale, the *Taketori monogatari,* focusing particularly on the role of its feather-robed heroine, Kaguyahime.

# 3

# The Radiance of Exile

## *The Tale of the Bamboo Cutter* and *The Tale of Genji*

> "Why so silent?" said Her Majesty. "Say something. It's sad when you do not speak."
>
> "I'm gazing into the autumn moon," I replied.
>
> "Ah yes," she remarked. "That's just what you should have said."
>
> —*Sei Shōnagon*

Although neither the precise date nor the author of *The Tale of the Bamboo Cutter* (*Taketori monogatari*) is known,[1] it is considered the oldest extant *monogatari* (prose tale) written in Japanese, dating to around 900 CE. This idea is echoed within Heian sources as well: *The Tale of Genji* itself refers back to the *Bamboo Cutter* as "the ancestor first to appear of the *monogatari*."[2] The story—involving a child found in a bamboo grove by a wood cutter, who grows into a beautiful woman courted by nobles before revealing her identity as an immortal princess from the moon—is thus among the earliest works of prose written in the Heian period employing the newly developed phonetic script, or *kana*. As such, the *Taketori* stands at the cusp of a major transformation in writing practices at the Heian court, a change that engendered a body of literature written largely by, for, or about women and that produced such well-known works as Murasaki Shikibu's *Tale of Genji* and Sei Shōnagon's *Pillow Book,* to name two of the best-known examples.[3]

In addition to attracting the interest of scholars of Japanese literature, the *Taketori* is also a rich source of material for historians of Japanese religion. Written at a time when continental culture enjoyed enormous prestige at the Japanese court, yet while new literary, artistic, and religious forms were developing alongside Chinese and Korean models, the story freely mixes continental themes with references to Japanese court society. While the character of the princess from the moon combines elements of the feather-robed maiden from Asian folklore with the motif of a beautiful Daoist-styled immortal, the plot is filled with historical figures and institutions from the

Japanese court. In the items that the princess requests from her suitors, the story offers a rich mixture of religious symbolism, from the begging bowl of the Buddha to the branch of a tree from a Daoist mountain of immortality. And in the tale's poignant ending, the narrative concludes with a mythic passage in which the worlds of mortals and immortals are clearly separated, with only the smoke rising from Mt. Fuji as a reminder of a time when immortality was possible on earth.

In addition to its interest for the study of Heian Japanese literature and religion, however, the *Taketori* is equally striking for the profound ambivalence displayed throughout the story: a deep antagonism toward Heian sexual politics and toward the constellation of power in court society that arose from Heian marriage practices. In the story's scathing depiction of the failure of court nobles to gain the princess' hand, in its portrayal of an emperor powerless to stop the return of the princess to the moon, and above all in its depiction of the world surrounding the Japanese court as a polluted place (*kitanaki tokoro*) to which celestial immortals come only as a form of punishment, the *Taketori* appears at the dawn of Heian prose fiction as a work of somewhat radical discontent.

While the dissent given voice within the *Taketori* has been explored within postwar Japanese scholarship and taken up more recently by Western scholars,[4] and while the motif of exile in the *Taketori* has also been noted as a kind of literary archetype,[5] the use of exile to convey discontent has remained largely unexplored, and for that reason neither the text's rhetorical stance nor the conditions from which it arose have been adequately explained. To address that oversight, in this chapter I link the *Taketori* to a larger body of stories that employ a "poetics of exile"[6] in order to reimagine the constellation of power in Heian society. In the *Taketori,* we find, the text radically reimagines Heian society by casting the world of the Japanese court as the periphery, in contrast to a higher, more divine, and more powerful center: the capital of the moon.[7]

While the role of the *Taketori* as a narrative of exile remains underexplored today, I also show in the final section of this chapter that the *Taketori* was not so overlooked in the Heian period itself. Rather, in texts such as the *Genji monogatari,* the discontent expressed in the *Taketori* was quite consciously taken up and elaborated upon. In the *Genji,* itself a lament for "a world evermore gone mad,"[8] the divine princess of the *Taketori* is conspicuously placed alongside other celebrated figures of exile and marginalization. The result is an extended discourse on exile, which, in lifting up such fictional and historical figures as Kaguyahime, Ariwara no Narihira, and Genji himself, critiques not only the court society imagined in the text but also the very real world of Heian society in which the text was produced. To explore the rich role of exile in the Heian literary imagination, I begin by focusing on the *Taketori* itself before moving on at the end of the chapter to examine the presence of the *Taketori* within the *Genji monogatari.*

## THE *HAGOROMO* MYTHEME

The theme of a maiden who comes to earth with the aid of a feathered robe (*hagoromo*) and brings riches to her owner, husband, or parents—what Alan Miller has called the bird-formed maiden theme—is a motif the *Taketori* shares with other tales found in early Japanese collections. Its earliest traces in Japan can be found in *fudoki,* the regional records produced in response to royal command beginning in 713 that contain valuable information about place names, early government, and local beliefs in various provinces at the time of the early *ritsuryō* state.[9] Though only the *Izumo Fudoki* survives in its entirety, in fragments of others we find traces of *hagoromo* stories.

One such fragment from the *fudoki* of Tango Province tells the story of a feather-robed maiden who descended to earth to bathe at a spring. While bathing, the maiden's robes were stolen by a human couple, who forced her to stay with them and brew a magical rice wine, which brought the couple wealth. After becoming rich, however, the couple abandoned the maiden. Unable to return to heaven without her feathered robe, she recites a poem:

> *Ama no hara*
> *furisakemireba*
> *kasumi tachi*
> *ieji madoite*
> *yukue shirazumo*[10]
>
> When I gaze upward toward the plain of heaven,
> a mist rises. I lose my way home,
> I know not which way to go.

Eventually the maiden settles in a new village and over time is enshrined as a local deity; the tale is thus included in the *fudoki* as a kind of *engi,* an account of the origin of that village's shrine and of the etymology of its name.[11]

Such textual fragments suggest that while the *hagoromo* mytheme may have been widespread in early Japan, there was no single storyline to which it was attached; instead, the *hagoromo* motif could serve as the backdrop for a variety of narratives. While the *fudoki* fragment shares elements with the later *Taketori*—such as the wealth resulting from the maiden's presence and the feathered robe that is necessary for passage to heaven—there are just as many elements from the *Taketori* not seen in the *fudoki* version: no suitors, no sovereign, no return to heaven (or the moon), and no theme of punishment given as the reason for the maiden's initial descent to earth.

## THE SHINING PRINCESS OF THE SUPPLE BAMBOO

Echoing the *fudoki* fragment, the *Taketori* introduces at the outset a connection between a divine maiden and the magical accumulation of wealth. The story begins in the manner of a folk narrative, opening with an old bamboo cutter who comes upon a small child during his regular outings into the forest, radiating light while concealed within a stalk of bamboo. He takes the child home and with his wife decides to raise her; meanwhile, on repeated trips to gather bamboo, he finds gold within the stalks. With the passing of time—and the accumulation of gold—he becomes a man of wealth.[12]

Part of the bamboo cutter's "cache" lies also in his possession of the child, who in three short months grows into a beautiful young woman, mimicking the quickened growth associated with bamboo. The elderly couple arranges a coming-of-age ceremony for the maiden, and she is given the name Nayotake no Kaguyahime (Shining Princess of the Supple Bamboo), for as the story relates, she continues to emit a kind of divine radiance: "a light filled the house from corner to corner. When the old man felt down or in pain, by looking at the child the pain would stop; anger too would lighten."[13] Numinous radiance is a trait associated with other divine figures of the Japanese court, including of course Amaterasu, the "Heavenly Illuminating Deity" claimed as ancestor by the royal line, but it is also a trait associated with another hero of exile, the shining (*hikaru*) Genji.

As news travels of Kaguyahime following her coming-of-age ceremony, she becomes the object of male desire throughout the land: "All men, whether high class or low, desired somehow to get Kaguyahime, or to glimpse her,"[14] yet she herself remains uninterested, staying concealed within the home of the bamboo cutter. Eventually, frustrated by her lack of response, the number of suitors questing for Kaguyahime dwindles to five men representing the highest ranks of court society. When it becomes clear that their efforts will not cease, the aging bamboo cutter attempts to persuade Kaguyahime, explaining that even though she is a transformed being (*henge,* a term for something nonhuman that takes human form),[15] she still possesses a human form, and a female one at that. For that reason, he states, she must think about the future when the old man will no longer be alive: she must choose a husband.

In response, Kaguyahime explains her deep reticence to marry, stating how sad she would be if, "without knowing the depths of the man's heart, he turned out to be unfaithful."[16] Still, she agrees to test the depth of each man's feelings, assigning to each an item to find and bring to her. The suitors despair when they hear Kaguyahime's requests—the stone begging bowl of the Buddha, the branch of a tree from a mountain of immortality, a robe made of fire-rat fur, a jewel from a dragon's neck, and a swallow's easy-delivery charm—for they are items well known from Buddhist, Daoist, and popular legends and are seemingly beyond human power to obtain. One by one, the suitors fail to accomplish the tasks set out by Kaguyahime, resorting to lying and deceit as they fashion counterfeit versions of the items she requested. One by one, each suitor's deceit is revealed, and having discovered "the depths of the man's heart," Kaguyahime ridicules them broadly and dismisses them. In the story-world of the *Taketori,* Kaguyahime's deep reticence to marry is thus amply justified.

## THE POLITICS OF MARRIAGE IN THE *TAKETORI*

It's striking that while Kaguyahime appears to nurture a deep affection for the old man and woman who raise her, she remains adamantly opposed even to the idea of marriage, later stating that she would sooner accept death for disobedience than serve as a consort in the imperial court. While an initial reticence to enter into relationship is a conventional and understandable trope for women within Heian poetics, the deep reluctance of Kaguyahime, along with the text's mockery of her suitors, invite closer attention. In this light, while on the one hand the *Taketori* draws from the popular strata in which other *hagoromo* stories circulated, at the same time the story reflects upon the culture of the Japanese court at a time when women frequently provided the "capital" through which families competed to elevate their social and political standing. As has often been observed, such politics of marriage during the Heian period facilitated the rise to preeminence of one family in particular—the regent's line of the Northern Fujiwara—who excelled in placing their daughters as imperial consorts, thus managing to insert themselves into the generation and selection of crown princes and hence, future emperors. Given that the *Taketori* was written around the early tenth century, the text evinces a striking attitude of resistance toward marriage even as that institution was being strategically deployed by the regent's line above all others.

The regent's house political system (*sekkan seido*) is worth recalling briefly in order to underscore Heian marriage politics during the time in which the *Taketori* was composed.[17] Specifically, with the Fujiwara rise to power during the mid-Heian period, the authority of the emperor and council of state was steadily eroded by powerful Fujiwara regents who nominally acted as advisors to the emperor but increasingly came to wield actual power. The key to becoming regent was to arrange the marriage of the family's women into the royal line, for the regent was traditionally chosen from among the maternal uncle, maternal grandfather, or father-in-law of the emperor. As *sesshō* (regent for a child emperor) and then *kanpaku* (regent after an emperor had come of age), the regent's line of the Northern Fujiwara gained unparalleled access to power through offices largely outside the system originally imagined in the state's *ritsuryō* law codes.

As I discuss further in chapter 4, the success with which the Fujiwara employed marriage politics to assert control over the royal succession was supplemented by the Fujiwara use of exile to eliminate competing families and rival clan lines. As an example of this tactic, in the Ōtenmon Incident of 866, the Fujiwara regent Yoshifusa was able to eliminate several rivals from among other major families contending for power and influence over the throne. In this incident, when one of the gates to the Heian palace burned down, a witness was produced who implicated the Ōtomo family, and Yoshifusa was able to use this pretense as an excuse to have the leaders of the Ōtomo family and members of the Ki family removed from office and sent into exile.[18]

Regarding the relationship between such politics and Heian literature, literary scholars such a Mitani Eichi have argued that the author of the *Taketori* must have come from among such families, who in former times occupied positions of prestige but who found themselves during the height of Fujiwara power quite literally banished from the center of court society. Only members of such families, Mitani argued, possessed both the sophisticated literary sensibility and the disenchantment with Heian politics that could have combined to produce a work of such striking discontent as the *Taketori*.[19]

In contrast to actual life at the Heian court, however, in the story-world of the *Taketori* the dominance of the Fujiwara is nowhere to be seen, replaced instead by weak, conniving, and unsuccessful suitors, by representatives of the throne who are openly disobeyed, and by a sovereign who is unable either to bring Kaguyahime to his palace or to prevent her return to the moon.[20] An antiromance, the *Taketori* emerges at the time of *sekkan* politics highly critical of marriage and its manipulations, envisioning instead a powerful heroine who cannot be possessed by any man and who would rather choose death, in her own words, than marry and serve at court.

## THE CAPITAL OF THE MOON

If the story of suitors vying for the attention of a beautiful maiden comprises a central component of the *Taketori,* the story of a girl found in bamboo who eventually must return to the moon comprises the other main element, wrapped around and framing the first. As mentioned above, this element shares features in common with other stories in the *hagoromo* tradition, which appear not only in the earlier *fudoki* but also in later Noh dramas and religious performances. The manner in which the *Taketori* employs this motif produces a unique text, however, introducing such characters as the Japanese emperor and his guards, while establishing the superiority—culturally and in terms of sheer power—of the celestial beings with whom Kaguyahime eventually returns.

The story introduces the emperor just after the failure of the last suitor, when we learn that the sovereign has become curious about the maiden who "refused to marry and vainly brought so many men to ruin."[21] Plotting with the bamboo cutter, the emperor promises the potential of court rank if the old man can create an opportunity for him to see Kaguyahime. They agree for the emperor to try and see her while he is out of the palace on a hunting excursion. The plan works to a degree: the emperor surprises Kaguyahime at home, just long enough to catch sight of her numinous beauty. But when he grabs her by the arm and tries to force her to return with him in his carriage, she disappears in a flash of light,[22] and the emperor is left begging her to reappear so that he can retain at least the sight of her. Defeated in his attempt to bring Kaguyahime back to the palace, the emperor departs, feeling "as if he had left his soul behind."[23]

As the tale builds to its conclusion, the emperor learns from the bamboo cutter that Kaguyahime has revealed she is actually an immortal from the moon and that she must return there on the night of the full moon, on the fifteenth day of the eighth month. Hearing this, the emperor orders that she not be allowed to return and commands the royal guards to surround her house on that night in order to stop anyone coming to take her back. Yet here again, the sovereign's power and authority turn out to be nonexistent. On the appointed night, the royal guards—some two thousand strong—take up positions on the roof and gables of the house and wait for the appearance of the people from the moon coming to take Kaguyahime back. When the celestial beings descend, however, the sky is filled with light "as of ten full moons," and the royal guards stand trembling and paralyzed, unable to lift even a finger, let alone notch arrow to bowstring. In a suggestive detail from a tale contemptuous of male desire, when one of the guards does manage to release an arrow, it simply falls harmlessly to the ground.

The mood is almost satirical. When the immortals tell the bamboo cutter that they allowed Kaguyahime to stay with him "for a short while" only because of a minor good deed he performed in a previous existence, he asks pitifully if perhaps they have made a mistake (because he has raised her from infancy) and if they are not perhaps seeking a different Kaguyahime living in some other land. And while the portrayal of the sovereign is not as scathing as that of the suitors—he doesn't lose life or limb, for example—the tone of mockery regarding royal authority stands in the greatest contrast to the image of the divine and powerful sovereign presented in the state's official transcripts of power. Able to catch a glimpse of Kaguyahime only through deceit, the sovereign is ultimately powerless either to bring her to court or to prevent her from returning to the moon.

## THE *TAKETORI* AS EXILE NARRATIVE

How then does the *Taketori* function as a narrative of exile? There are several points worth considering, revolving not only around the structural theme of Kaguyahime's dislocation from the moon and her final return but also around the language used to describe the reason for her presence on earth and her return to the moon.

In the closing section of the *Taketori,* after Kaguyahime has rejected and brought to ruin her five aristocratic suitors and after the sovereign has sought unsuccessfully to bring Kaguyahime back to his palace, we find that she is drawn into an unspeakable sadness: tears fill her eyes nightly as she watches the moon emerge and grow larger. When asked the reason, she finally discloses that she herself is a being from the moon, and that on the night of the full moon of the eighth month she will have to return there. At this point in the narrative, Kaguyahime offers only vague details about why she had been sent to earth or why she must return to the moon, stating that it is the fulfillment of an obligation from the past (*mukashi no chigiri*) that she now must honor.[24] She also reveals that she has a mother and father back on the capital of the moon and that it was intended she stay on earth only a short time. When the appointed night comes and people from the moon descend on clouds to bring Kaguyahime back, we learn additional information about her from their leader, whom the *Taketori* narrator takes to be a king from the moon. When the bamboo cutter begs that Kaguyahime be allowed to stay on earth, the moon-king explains: "Kaguyahime came to live in your poor company for a short time because of a transgression she committed (*tsumi o tsukuritamaekereba*); the term of her punishment is over (*tsumi no kagiri hatenureba*) and so we have come to bring her back."[25]

In the moon-king's explanation, though no word for exile is spoken, we are given a description clearly echoing the trope of banishment within court society: because of a transgression committed, Kaguyahime was sent away from a capital to live in a remote, humble location for a term of punishment. When that term ended, she was brought home. The theme of exile from the moon also provides a context by which the other characters are finally able to "place" Kaguyahime, whose beauty and radiance "unlike anything of this world," together with her utter contempt for royal commands, had alternately enthralled and unsettled everyone around her. In the story's poignant ending, Kaguyahime puts on the feathered robe to return to the moon, and with that gesture she loses all memory of her time on earth and of her earthly parents, while the old man and woman and the sovereign are left behind to mourn her absence ever after.

## *TAKETORI* SCHOLARSHIP AND THE QUESTION OF EXILE

The notion of the *Taketori* as a narrative of exile was explored in the early twentieth century by the Japanese ethnologist Orikuchi Shinobu, whom I discussed in chapter 2. With his influential theory regarding *kishu ryūritan* ("tales of exiled and wandering nobles"), he put forth the idea that the heart of classical Japanese literature lay in its tragic spirit, which was responsible for generating countless tales of young nobles and divinities who were destined to wander the earth, replaying again and again for Japanese audiences the cultural memory of dislocation from a spiritual homeland. In the *kishu ryūritan* genre, Orikuchi included everyone from the exiled god Susano-o in the *Kojiki* and *Nihonshoki* to the hero of the *Genji monogatari,* as well as numerous members of court whose poems of separation and longing appear in poetry collections such as the *Manyōshū* and *Kokinshū.* Fictional characters such as Kaguyahime, Orikuchi believed, both echoed historical figures and in turn influenced them, borrowing details from historical figures to enhance their poignancy, while illuminating later figures as a kind of archetype.[26]

Orikuchi's concept of a *kishu ryūritan* genre has the benefit of pulling together a wide variety of mythic, historical, and fictional characters and tracing the widespread occurrence of the theme of exile. Yet as I suggested in chapter 2, this approach blurs over the distinct characteristics that define each figure and each instance of exile, as well as each retelling of the motif within specific historical contexts. While the imagined figures of Susano-o, Kaguyahime, and Genji share similarities to each other as well as to historical figures such as Ariwara no Narihira, Sugawara no Michizane, and Minamoto no Takaakira, subsuming all of them within a single category without exploring their unique qualities ignores details that may be the most significant element of each case. In short, Orikuchi's ahistorical rendering of exile literature as simply the recurrence of a timeless archetype ignores the very real political and historical conditions that helped create and circulate narratives of exile, both historical and imagined.

Among Western scholars who have spent time on the *Taketori,* less attention has been paid to the theme of exile in favor of other topics such as the competing ideologies of Buddhism and Daoism seen in the text,[27] the originary nature of the language and narrative structure,[28] or its relation as a precursor to the *Tale of Genji.*[29] Okada mentions in passing that the *Taketori* has been called by some a tale of exile but does not delve further into the theme, while Shirane mentions the *Taketori* as one manifestation of the *kishu ryūritan* genre associated with Orikuchi. While both scholars find much of significance in the *Taketori,* the theme of exile remains for the most part unexplored. One scholar, however, has closely examined the passages that I take to describe Kaguyahime's condition of exile, yet he has come to different conclusions regarding their meaning. For that reason, it's worth examining his interpretation in some detail in comparison to my own.

In a chapter devoted to the *Taketori* from his work, *The Aesthetics of Discontent,* Michele Marra contributes to our understanding of the historical and political conditions surrounding the production of the text. Like other scholars, Marra sees the text inhabiting a space extremely critical of the politics of the Fujiwara-controlled court of the mid-Heian period. Like others, he views the probable author of the text as belonging to one of the court families pushed out of positions of power by the rise of the Fujiwara. In the thesis that runs throughout his book, Marra argues that these marginalized families were able to voice their critique by producing great works of culture, positioning themselves as the true practitioners of the aesthetic and cultural ideals of the court, while portraying the Fujiwara by contrast as deceitful conspirators.

In his interpretation of the *Taketori,* Marra focuses in on the Daoist and Buddhist themes and vocabulary that run throughout the text, both in the objects that Kaguyahime requests of her suitors (some of which correspond to Daoist ritual elements designed to gain immortality) and in the Buddhist theme of transience, which is underscored after Kaguyahime returns to the immortal land of the moon, at the moment when the emperor orders her medicine of immortality burned on Mt. Fuji (hence the smoke rising from the mountain), thereby ensuring the transience of all human life. In Marra's reading, these plot elements amount to a layering of conflicting ideological levels—immortality vs. impermanence—and in his conclusion, he states that the "victory" of Buddhism over Daoism in the story—as seen in the finality of impermanence on earth rather than immortality—is one of the "lessons" that the author of the text was trying to convey regarding the Fujiwara, an assertion that Fujiwara rule would one day prove ephemeral.[30]

It is informative to look at Marra's reading of Kaguyahime's term on earth and her eventual return to the moon. Looking closely for elements of the text that relate either to Buddhism or Daoism, he sees the description of Kaguyahime as an exemplary story of karmic retribution such as we find in the tales of the *Nihon Ryōiki.*[31] In his words, "[Kaguyahime] had come to this world 'because of an obligation from the past' (*mukashi no chigiri*), *which can only be explained within the Buddhist logic of karma.* She had been compelled to be born as a human being because of a past crime that she must expiate on earth. . . . After the successful completion of her mission and the maturation of a positive karma, Kaguyahime can—or, rather, must—leave 'this impure world' (*kitanaki tokoro*), an expression echoing the idea of the necessity of abandoning our sinful world in order to be born in Amida's paradise (*onri edo gongu jōdo*)."[32]

While Marra's larger discussion in *The Aesthetics of Discontent* opens up fascinating lines of inquiry regarding the intersection of Heian literature and politics, there are reasons to pause before accepting his conclusions regarding the *Taketori.* Like other scholars who see the Japanese literature of this period as having been governed by a Buddhist episteme,[33] Marra's reading appears to assume an overarching Buddhist worldview, yet in doing so he passes over some of the details that give the story its particular resonance. The story does not explain Kaguyahime's presence as a "mission" to earth—despite the motif of the riches found in the bamboo—but expressly as a punishment for which she is sent to a polluted place. Nowhere does the story mention karma, let alone "the maturation of a positive karma" upon which Kaguyahime may leave, but instead the story speaks of a "term of punishment" after which she will be escorted home. And certainly no mention is made in the *Taketori* of Amida's paradise, although some scholars see in the descent of the moon people a motif structurally similar to that found in Pure Land *raigō* paintings.[34]

In contrast, I would suggest that considering the *Taketori* primarily a "Buddhist tale" (or even a "Daoist" one) imposes modern religious boundaries onto a Heian cultural setting that largely refused to be divided into discrete religious traditions. Rather than a story regarding "the wheel of karma" as Marra describes it[35]—a phrase found nowhere in the text—I suggest that the *Taketori* employs most vividly the trope of exile, a theme that links the story not only to the political and legal realities of the Japanese court but also to the diverse body of exile narratives through which members of the court revealed and reimagined their world at this time.

## THE LEGAL COSMOLOGY OF EXILE

If we compare the situation of Kaguyahime with the structure of banishment (*ruzai*) depicted in the legal codes of the early Japanese state, we find that in virtually every way the two run closely parallel. In both cases, (a) in response to a transgression, (b) a punishment is given, involving (c) removal from a central location (d) to a distant margin (e) for a fixed time required for the expiation of that transgression.[36]

Yet more than simply mimicking the legal codes, the *Taketori* reveals something further: that unique among the available forms of punishment at the Japanese court, exile provided a powerful trope by which members of the court could reimagine such basic categories as "center" and "periphery," thus redefining the structures of inclusion and exclusion upon which Heian society rested. For if the *Taketori* replicates the logic of exile found in the *ritsuryō* legal codes, it does so in a way that neatly inverts the court's own rhetoric of centrality. Whereas exile in the *ritsuryō* codes helped to construct the prestige and centrality of the Japanese court centered around the symbolic figure of the sovereign, in the *Taketori,* Kaguyahime is banished to the world of that court as a form of punishment—a world populated by none other than the emperor and high-ranking members of the aristocracy.

Returning to the ending of the *Taketori,* following the speech in which the moon-king explains Kaguyahime's exile, the celestial immortals twice express their loathing of the polluted world of humans. The second time occurs when a celestial being offers Kaguyahime the medicine of immortality in addition to the robe of feathers, saying "You must feel ill, after eating the foods of this polluted place (*kitanaki tokoro no mono kikoshimeshitareba*)."[37] The motif of eating the food of a polluted place echoes a mytheme from the *Kojiki* narrative, in which Izanagi descends to the underworld—Yomi no Kuni—to find his partner Izanami, only to learn that having already eaten the food of that polluted realm, she can no longer return to the Heavenly Plain. While I don't wish to suggest that the *Taketori* equates the world of the Japanese court with Yomi no Kuni, I would simply point out that in both cases the mytheme of eating the food of a polluted place serves to contrast a purified higher realm with a polluted lower one. And in contrast to a "polluted world" whose inhabitants include an emperor, court nobles, and Kaguyahime's earthly parents, the people of the moon are described as divine, beautiful beyond compare, and radiant, with no knowledge of sickness or death. Through such contrasts—mimicking the legal imagination of exile found in the *ritsuryō* codes while subverting the notions of center and margin to which those codes were attached—the *Taketori* voices a striking note of discontent regarding the Heian order of things.

## THE *TAKETORI* WITHIN THE *GENJI MONOGATARI*

Thus far I have suggested that the trope of exile in the *Taketori* is revealed both in the structure of the narrative—in Kaguyahime's separation from and return to the distant capital of the moon—and in the text's own language, which refers to her time on earth as a period of expiation for a transgression committed earlier. Yet beyond such elements internal to the text, we should also consider whether the *Taketori* was regarded a narrative of exile in its own time, and if so, what role it played within the Heian imagination of exile.[38] Such questions inevitably lead to the *Genji monogatari,* not only the most well known narrative of exile from the Japanese court but also one that incorporates numerous references to other tales of exile, including to Kaguyahime and the *Taketori.*[39]

If the *Taketori* was called by the *Genji* the "ancestor" of all *monogatari,* then the *Genji* must be considered its most celebrated descendent, a complex and monumental work dating to the beginning of the eleventh century that left an enduring mark on Japanese literary and dramatic arts. In addition to what we might call a "genealogical" relation between the two texts, however, the Japanese literary scholar Kojima Naoko has pointed out structural parallels shared by the heroes of each story—Kaguyahime in the *Taketori* and Genji himself. As one example, the two characters are distinguished by a kind of luminosity, for just as Kaguyahime (literally, "radiant princess") consoles the hearts of those around her simply by virtue of her numinous radiance, Genji too is referred to as the *hikaru* or shining Genji, and he too possesses an unearthly beauty that continually moves the hearts of those around him. As Kojima notes, in both tales such radiance is ultimately transgressive, providing a clue to the antistructural positioning of both characters.[40]

Like the *Taketori,* the *Genji* is also concerned to trace the effects of "patriarchal desire"[41] on the lives of its female characters. As Okada has noted, the *Genji* begins "in an ominous, not to say tragic, manner," when Genji's mother, "soon after giving birth to him and without the all-important backing of a politically powerful father, is virtually hounded to death by her court rivals."[42] This opening, Okada suggests, reveals a primary concern of the narrative: "Rather than originating in 'love' or amorous passion as some would have it, the narrator seems to be showing us the tragic underside of a male desire that depends for the prosperity of a family lineage on a feminine presence at the same time that it ignores the consequences of the practice for the women themselves."[43] As with the *Taketori,* Heian sexual and marriage politics are central among the concerns taken up by the *Genji.*

In addition to exploring the negative effects of male desire, the *Genji* also shares with the *Taketori* a deep familiarity with exile. According to one popular account dating at least to the fourteenth century, the *Genji* had its inception when Murasaki Shikibu—an attendant of Empress Jōtōmon-in—was asked to contribute "entertaining stories" to the "literary salon" of Princess Senshi, the great Kamo priestess. According to the apocryphal story, Murasaki Shikibu, "recalling from her childhood the story of the downfall and exile of Minamoto Takaakira, [began] writing the chapter ("Suma") that tells of Genji's exile."[44] Whether or not this story accurately captures the origins of the narrative, it clearly conveys the connections perceived by early audiences between the *Genji* and the politics of exile at the Heian court. An even clearer connection between the *Genji* and the *Taketori* regarding exile is found in the Suma chapter of the *Genji* depicting Genji's own exile. In one of the many moments in which the *Genji* claims its place within the *Taketori* lineage, Genji is shown—on the night of the full moon of the eighth month—expressing his longing to return to the "capital of the moon."[45] The direct allusion to the *Taketori* is at once implicit and overt: not explicitly announced, yet unmistakable to any Heian audience.

While the *Taketori* is referenced several times throughout the *Genji,* the moment in which the *Taketori* is most conspicuously lifted up for discussion occurs in the famous Picture Contest (Eawase) chapter, a chapter depicting a form of aesthetic competition that served to cultivate distinction and redistribute cultural capital within Heian court society. When a picture contest begins to unfold in this chapter of the *Genji,* the *Taketori* appears as the first in a series of examples that are used to valorize paradigmatic figures of exile and marginality, culminating ultimately in the triumphant victory of Genji's forces in the competition, as well as in the court's belated recognition of Genji's nobility during his period of exile.

Although the ninth century at the Heian court saw the rise of poetry competitions (*uta-awase*), no record of a *picture* competition exists for the court prior to the creation of the *Genji* narrative,[46] and indeed the Eawase chapter reads almost like a creation account for such a ritualized contest. The chapter narrates the genesis of one particular picture competition, which begins after two consorts vying for the attention of the young emperor Reizei discover his interest in paintings. As Royall Tyler explains regarding the sexual politics surrounding royal consorts, "a major ambition of many ranking gentlemen in the world of *The Tale of Genji* . . . was to present a daughter to the Emperor or the Heir Apparent,"[47] which means that among those who placed a daughter as royal consort, a struggle frequently ensued over which one's offspring would become the next heir apparent. Tellingly, in the Eawase chapter, the fathers of the two consorts immediately join in the impromptu picture contest, providing each consort with pictures composed by master painters, which in turn become the object of intense scrutiny, discernment, and debate among the female attendants at court. As the competition to attract the young emperor escalates and as the cloistered empress Fujitsubo enters the scene, two teams are chosen from among each consort's retinue, and a more formally organized picture contest ensues.

Thomas LaMarre has described the nature of such contests and their function in the life of court society, which calibrated its hierarchies in no small part on the ability of its members to achieve distinction in aesthetic discernment. Referring to poetry contests but touching on the general nature of various aesthetic competitions at the court, LaMarre notes, "The general structure of an *awase* consisted of a number of rounds in which two teams, left and right, brought forth for comparison objects of a particular kind fixed in advance. . . . Once the topic was established, courtiers selected the leaders and supporting members of the two teams. Then began the selection of poems, the preparation of prayers and offerings at shrines for victory, and the commissions for artisans to design tables and scoreboards. . . . Following the contest, a banquet, with music and dance, accompanied the presentation of gifts in accordance with the excellence of performance. In short, there was an element of potlatch to these large-scale competitions, in which each team strove to outdo the other in lavishness of expenditure *and which resulted in a redistribution of wealth and status*."[48]

The competition depicted in the *Genji* reflects the formalized structure described above while also ranging freely, as characters remark on everything from the aesthetic and technical merits of the paintings to the design of their mounting, the nature of their paper, calligraphy, and line, and the general content of the stories depicted, including the merits and demerits of their main characters.[49]

As the picture contest in the *Genji* moves forward, the supporters of the two consorts spare no expense preparing their paintings for entry in the competition. For the type of pictures used, it's decided that the paintings will be illustrations of famous stories: "famous stories of old" for the Left side (representing the consort Akikonomu, Genji's adopted daughter) and "modern tales" for the Right side, the team representing the Kokiden consort, the daughter of Genji's rival, the counselor Tō no Chūjō.

In the initial round of the contest, the Left side submits for their very first entry picture scrolls illustrating the *Taketori monogatari,* and the debate immediately moves to a consideration of its heroine, Kaguyahime. Not surprisingly, the two sides disagree sharply in their views of Kaguyahime. According to the spokeswoman for the Left—the team sponsored by Genji—Kaguyahime presents a noble and virtuous figure: "*Princess Kaguya remains forever unstained by this world, and she aspires to such noble heights that her story belongs to the age of the gods.*"[50] In rebuttal, the Right side replies that the humble conditions of Kaguyahime's birth—her discovery in a grove of bamboo—disqualify her as a suitable heroine for the refined world of court society, and the debate moves on.

The *Taketori* doesn't appear in isolation; as subsequent rounds move on to new stories for consideration, the Left side continues to present pictures of figures notably associated with the margins of court society. In round two, the Left team presents pictures depicting Ariwara no Narihira (825–880), the hero of the *Ise monogatari.* As is well known, the *Ise* is a collection of poems and experiences relating to Narihira during his time in self-imposed exile, "life in the capital having become difficult."[51] Debating the merits and demerits of Narihira as a subject for painting, the two teams again disagree sharply on his significance for the court. The Left declares Narihira to be an esteemed poet and classical hero of the past: "In rank ignorance of the great Sea of Ise's magnificent depths, must the waves now wash away words thought merely old and dull?" In response, the Right retorts that his condition on the margins of court society contrasts unfavorably to those who serve at the highest levels of the court: "To the noble heart that aspires to soar aloft, high above the clouds, depths of a thousand fathoms appear very far below."[52]

As the contest continues without conclusion, capturing the rapt interest of all involved, Genji himself suggests pausing the competition in order to make arrangements for a full-scale contest in the presence of the young emperor himself. The *Tale* provides a hint of Genji's deeper motivations: "'We may as well decide victory and defeat before His Majesty himself,' [*Genji*] said, pleased by the spirit with which each speaker put her case. *That had in fact been his idea all along, which is why he had kept some exceptional works in reserve; and among these, for reason of his own, he had placed his scrolls of [his own exile in] Suma and Akashi.*"[53]

The picture contest then continues as an even more formalized competition before the young emperor, and as "the contest remained undecided on into the night," the tension in the narrative continues to mount. Finally the time comes for the final round, at which point the paintings done and kept in reserve by Genji of his exile in Suma and Akashi are presented by the Left for discernment and debate. With the unveiling of Genji's art, the Eawase chapter reaches its climax: "This, done at undisturbed leisure by a genius at the art, was beyond anything. Everyone wept, His Highness the first among them. Genji's paintings revealed with perfect immediacy, far more vividly than anything they had imagined during those years when they pitied and grieved for him, all that had passed through his mind, all that he had witnessed, and every detail of those shores that they themselves had never seen. He had added here and there lines in running script, Chinese or Japanese, and although these did not yet make it a true diary, there were such moving poems among them that one wanted very much to see more. No one thought of anything else. Emotion and delight prevailed, now that all interest in the other paintings had shifted to these. The question answered itself: the Left had won."[54]

With the decisive conclusion of the picture competition, a kind of double victory is imagined within the inner circles of power at the Heian court. At one level, in the court of a young sovereign who has yet to produce any offspring, a competition is waged in the form of a picture contest between two factions, embodied in the teams of the Left and the Right. While a victory by one party or another will not ensure any final ascendance to power, it does represent a victory in the larger struggle for preeminence among consorts within the emperor's court. Such a victory affects not only the consort seeking imperial favor but also her potential male offspring, who might become heir apparent, not to mention her supporters, including her father, who might wield power as regent over any progeny. Then there is the larger circle of their allies, which in Genji's case includes a retired emperor and empress. The ripple effect of this "potlatch-like redistribution" of power extends quite widely.

In the *Genji* narrative, after the victory of the Left, the side representing Genji's adopted daughter, Akikonomu, one consort does indeed attain preeminence in the eyes of the emperor. As the narrator of the *Genji* observes in a subsequent chapter, "Genji's support for the Ise Consort [Akikonomu] had succeeded brilliantly, and she enjoyed His Majesty's highest favor. In wit and looks she left nothing to be desired, and he watched over her *as though over a treasure*."[55] A treasure indeed: with a seemingly minor victory in aesthetic competition, an entire network of supporters sees their interests advance at court.

At the same time, the chapter narrates a further triumph: Genji's rehabilitation in the eyes of the court following his return from exile. Having gone into exile following a perceived sexual transgression, Genji is finally called back to the capital only after a series of afflictions begins affecting the emperor and his mother, as if to suggest that their actions in banishing him exceeded the bounds of propriety. As the sponsor of one side in the picture contest, Genji seizes upon a moment of heightened social awareness at the inner court to present before the eyes of the emperor, the retired empress, other princes, and other nobility the poignant depiction of his noble suffering in exile. Just as Genji planned, far from communicating any sense of dishonor regarding his time spent away, his paintings bring about the desired response from his audience—they are moved to tears.

The tears communicate two levels of appreciation at once. On one level, the audience's reaction signifies sympathy for his plight: he has heightened the affinity of those present for Genji and his faction, including the daughter he has presented to the court as imperial consort. Yet beyond mere sympathy, the audience's tearful praise confirms Genji's unsurpassed mastery of the cultural tropes, a mastery that is able to convey to them—through image, poem, and narrative—the experience of exile, a feeling of the shores at Suma and Akashi, and by extension perhaps, sentiments of affinity toward other paradigmatic figures of exile presented earlier in the picture contest.

By the end of the Eawase chapter, the author of the *Genji* has mounted a not-so-subtle critique of the particular constellation of power imagined in the text at the Heian court. Through the selection of images presented by the Left side during the picture competition, a discourse gradually emerges in which figures of exile and estrangement from the court are held up as exemplars of virtue, beginning with Kaguyahime, moving on to include Ariwara no Narihira, and ending with Genji himself. Such a critique operates on multiple levels. In the story-world of the *Tale of Genji,* Genji's triumph in the picture contest provides a gesture of correction, placing him back in the center of court life and establishing before all his mastery of the aesthetic codes. But in the historical world of the Heian court as well, for the society in which the *Genji* was written and circulated, the valorization of noble exiles sends a corrective message to a society well attuned to the powerful afterlife of the exiled minister Michizane and still reeling from the turmoil caused by the exile of figures such as Minamoto no Takaakira, cited by some as a model for Genji himself.[56]

Such critical tones help us to understand the role of both the *Taketori* and the *Genji* within the Heian imagination and help to clarify why themes of exile and banishment recur in the texts of that period. As Haruo Shirane has remarked regarding the *Genji,* "in highly allusive, poetic, aesthetic, and less than apparent ways, the *Genji* dilates on the question of political power."[57] In this sense, the tale is not so much a *reflection* of Heian society as a *critique* of it. Born of a critical spirit engendered by the turmoil of Heian court society—"an age evermore gone mad," according to the *Genji*—tales such as the *Taketori* and the *Genji* actively reimagine the constellation of power in court society. Unlike historical ministers such as Michizane or Takaakira, who either died in exile or were unable to recover their former positions, the noble exile Genji returns to the center of court society and attains a position of unparalleled prestige. And unlike the marriage politics accompanying the Fujiwara ascendance to power, Kaguyahime is able to resist the advances of high-ranking courtiers and emperor alike, finally leaving their polluted world behind to return to a higher, more divine realm. To repeat the admiring remark made by the triumphant side in the *Genji's* picture contest, "Princess Kaguyahime remained forever unstained by this world, aspiring to such noble heights that her story belongs to the age of the gods."[58]

The age of the gods, indeed: yet not of those gods belonging to the imperial sun-lineage, but an entirely different order of divinity. For in the *Taketori* narrative, perfection remains an otherworldly attribute—radiantly numinous as the moon itself—which stands in the greatest contrast to the actual world, the world experienced by members of the Heian court, which the storyworlds of the *Taketori* and the *Genji* both reveal and reimagine.

# 4

# Spirits in Exile

## *Sugawara no Michizane and the Vengeful Spirit Cults*

> Pleasant-seeming things: the master of horses at the spirit-pacification festival . . . *—Sei Shōnagon*

> The fascinating presence of absences whose traces were everywhere . . . *—Michel de Certeau*

It would be difficult to find a historical case of exile that figured more prominently in the Heian imagination than that of the statesman, scholar, and poet Sugawara no Michizane. As is well known, Michizane lost out in a power struggle at court and was "demoted" to the distant Dazaifu in 901, where he died in 903. In the following years, a number of misfortunes struck his opponents at the Heian court, resulting in the deaths of his primary rival, two princes, and several members of the nobility. For many in the capital, the pattern of victims suggested a single cause—Michizane's wrathful spirit. A court history, for example, records the following entry for 923/3/21: "Crown Prince Yasuakira died; age 21. No one could help but weep sadly; the sound of crying was like thunder. People all say it was an act of vengeance by Michizane's spirit."[1]

While fear of Michizane's spirit provided a rationale for the deaths occurring in the capital, it also influenced the conduct of the living. The *Okagami,* for example, mentions extraordinary measures taken during the infancy of Emperor Suzaku, who assumed the throne in 930 at the age of eight: "Through fear of the Kitano god [Michizane], the shutters of that Emperor's residence were kept closed for three years after his birth; he was reared inside a curtain-dais in a room where lights burned day and night."[2] To many, such precautions did not appear unfounded: Suzaku's own father (Emperor Daigo) had taken ill and died a short while after lightning attributed to Michizane struck the imperial palace itself.

These accounts, and others I examine in this chapter, suggest the degree to which Michizane haunted those in the capital in the years following his death. Yet while Michizane's importance during this period is widely acknowledged, the historical study of his deification has not been without reservations. One learned work on Michizane's place in Heian court history concludes, "Michizane was, of course, no god," but rather someone "deserving of admiration, if not necessarily deification."[3] By contrast, my interest in Michizane begins with his exile and death; it is exactly the deification and widespread worship of this most noted Heian exile that attracts my attention and invites closer examination.

Indeed, Michizane's posthumous career places him directly amid one of the most significant religious developments of the Heian period, the emerging cults of vengeful/honored spirits (*onryō/goryō*).[4] As a particularly illustrious member of this group, Michizane's "absent presence" raises a number of important questions regarding exile, power, and divinity in Heian society. How and by whom, for example, was Michizane determined to have returned to the capital as a vengeful spirit? What paradigms of divinity were expressed in the oracles that repeatedly invoked his name? And what connections can be traced between the rise of a cult devoted to an exiled member of the court and the ongoing struggle for power, distinction, and centrality within Heian society? Such questions are crucial not only to our understanding of the role of exile within the Heian imagination but also to our understanding of the diverse ways in which Heian political and religious discourses were entwined with each other in a kind of dialogical fashion.[5]

While in previous chapters I examined the role of exile in myth and in literature, in this chapter I turn to a historical figure, exploring the role of exile in the cultic imagination. Though Michizane was initially sent away by his rivals as a threat to the state, following later oracles and revelations he was posthumously reinstated in the capital, both as a deity and as an official of the highest rank and office. Michizane's case thus offers a particularly vivid illustration of competing visions of power and sacrality in Heian Japan, a struggle in this instance provoked by the sanction of exile. To explore these points, I examine each of the major elements of Michizane's case in roughly chronological order: the wider Heian context of vengeful spirits, the conditions surrounding Michizane's exile, the oracles calling for worship of Michizane as heavenly deity (*tenjin*), and finally, the founding of a sacred site to Michizane in the Heian capital.

## MICHIZANE AND THE EARLY *GORYŌ* CULT

The notion that a member of the Heian court could bring vengeance upon those in the capital after his or her death—especially when that person's untimely demise was the result of political intrigue—was well established by Michizane's time due to the popular *goryō* cults. This religious movement coalesced amid the political turmoil of the Nara period and flourished throughout the Heian era, leaving an enduring mark on Japanese religious practice and thought to this day.[6]

While it was commonly held in early Japan that humans could undergo deification after death and hence could be petitioned as ancestors or deities and thus intervene in people's lives,[7] those known as *goryō* represented a particular class of spirits.[8] When in the late Nara and early Heian periods a series of plagues, deaths, and calamities occurred in the capital region, connections were made between these events and a number of aristocrats who had died after being implicated in various plots against the state. These nobles all died in exile or away from the capital, either through murder, execution, or suicide, and all were thus believed to have perished in a state of turmoil, causing them to become vengeful spirits (*onryō*). The *goryō* cult that then came into existence centered on the pacification and worship of these high-ranking figures, attempting to calm their wrathful natures and transform them from fearsome *onryō* into powerful yet beneficent *goryō*.[9] Perhaps most striking for the study of exile, in every case the pacification of these vengeful spirits required their posthumous enshrinement back in the capital.

The first historical figure to be classified a *goryō* was Prince Sawara, and a look into the circumstances surrounding his death illustrates several features common to the *goryō* cults.[10] Sawara, a brother of Emperor Kammu, was charged in the assassination of Fujiwara no Tanetsugu, which occurred in 785 while the latter was overseeing plans to move the capital from Nara to Nagaoka. Sawara was placed under confinement at a temple near Nagaoka, where he was said to have refused food for ten days (protesting his innocence), following which he was banished to the island of Awaji. He died en route, but his corpse was sent on into exile and buried on Awaji. Soon after, misfortune visited the capital: an empress died, and the crown prince fell ill amid an epidemic. Through divination, these misfortunes were determined to be the work of Sawara. To pacify his vengeful spirit, Sawara's remains were first reburied and sutras recited for his benefit at national temples (*kokubunji*). When misfortune continued, Sawara was elevated posthumously to the position of emperor (known as Emperor Sudō), his grave transferred back to the home province of Yamato, and the Sawara shrine built for his worship in Nara.[11]

In the following years, as the capital was moved to Heian-kyo amid continued strife, Sawara was joined by several more high-ranking figures who died or were executed away from the capital as a result of their alleged participation in plots against the state. Collectively, these spirits were blamed for plagues, famine, flooding, and other conspicuous deaths occurring in and around the capital. In addition to Prince Sawara, the others included the following:[12]

- *Prince Iyo and his mother, Fujiwara Yoshiko:* son of Emperor Kammu, Iyo was arrested in 807 for plotting treason and confined at a temple in Yamato Province, where, along with his mother Fujiwara Yoshiko, he is said to have committed suicide by taking poison. In 819, both were pardoned and posthumously restored to their original rank.
- *Fujiwara Nakanari:* executed in 810 for his role in the Kusuko disturbance (discussed further in chapter 5), in which Nakanari supported retired emperor Heizei's attempt to reclaim the throne and move the capital back to Nara.[13]
- *Tachibana no Hayanari:* one of the "three brushes" renowned for calligraphy during the Heian period and an influential member of court, Hayanari was charged with treason and exiled to Izu but died en route in 842. In 850 he was posthumously pardoned and "restored" to his original office.
- *Bunya no Miyatamaro:* charged with treason, he died in 843 after being exiled to Izu.

As Inoue Mitsuo has pointed out, the six early *goryō* share several features in common: each was a high-ranking member of court who, after losing out in a political struggle, met their death away from the capital, some in nearby locations (such as Yamato) and some in farther, well-known exile locales (such as the island of Awaji or Izu).[14] In every case, pacification led to their eventual enshrinement back in the capital, while some of the *goryō* also had their former ranks and titles restored or even elevated.

A study of the official language of the court histories reveals a further aspect of the *goryō* cult that has not been sufficiently recognized: the *goryō* were popularly regarded as having been unjustly accused of their crimes. The first mention of the term *goryō* in any Japanese text occurs in the *Nihon Sandai Jitsuroku,* the last of the six state-sponsored national histories (compiled by none other than Sugawara no Michizane, among others). In the first entry regarding the *goryō* from 863/5/20, the *Sandai Jitsuroku* explicitly states, "implicated in plots and punished, they cause plagues (*rei*) brought on by spirits of those who die falsely charged (*enkon*)."[15] The term *enkon* is unambiguous in its translation, meaning "spirits of those who die unjustly accused."[16] Thus, in the view officially sanctioned by the state, it was not the case that treasonous politicians died in a deserved state of turmoil, but rather that high-ranking figures lost their lives unjustly. The evidence for this, according to popular reasoning, lay in the plagues and disasters that continued to vex the capital.

In 863, an alarming number of deaths due to famine and plague in the home provinces led to the first court-sponsored spirit-pacification festival (*goryō-e*) held within the precincts of the imperial palace itself, in the imperial garden known as the Shinsen'en. The event is described in the same passage concerning the six *goryō* mentioned above from the *Sandai Jitsuroku,* which also notes that such rites had recently become widespread outside of the capital: "On this day, by proclamation, the four gates to the garden were opened, and people of the capital and local villages were permitted to come and go and watch. The *goryō* [worshipped] were Emperor Sudō, Prince Iyo, Fujiwara Fujin [Yoshiko], the Kansatsushi [Nakanari], Tachibana Hayanari, and Bunya no Miyatamaro. Implicated in plots and punished, they cause plagues (*rei*) brought on by spirits of people who die falsely charged (*enkon*). Recently plagues have arisen with frequency, and the dead are terribly great in number. Everyone believes these calamities to be the work of vengeful spirits (*goryō*)."[17]

The record of the festival suggests that the court's *goryō-e* offered an elite rendition of more popular religious practices,[18] blending ritual elements drawn from both Buddhist and *kami*-cult idioms. The festival included such Buddhist practices as recitations of the *Golden Light* and *Heart* sutras, lectures by learned Buddhist priests, and offerings of incense and flowers. At the same time, these offerings were placed before individual spirit thrones (*reiza*) erected to worship the six *goryō,* and the ceremony included bouts of wrestling, archery competitions, and performances of song and dance, contributing to the festive atmosphere associated with worship in the *kami* cults.[19] Equally striking, elite members of the court rubbed shoulders at the ceremony with commoners from within and outside the capital, who on this day were allowed inside the gates of the Shinsen'en for the first time in history. According to the official record, the number of people attending from all walks of life was so great that "one could hardly breathe."[20]

While *goryō* ceremonies began in this way as *ad hoc* festivals held in times of need to ward off drought, plague, and other calamities, permanent *goryō* shrines soon began to appear in the capital, providing ongoing sites of worship for the *goryō* deities as well as grounds for regularly scheduled *goryō* festivals. An expanded set of eight *goryō* came to be worshipped as a group at two shrines in the Heian capital—the Kami and Shimo Goryō Jinja—while other sites soon emerged as popular centers of *goryō* worship. Famed among these was the Gion shrine-temple complex, known since the Meiji period simply as Yasaka Shrine.[21] The *goryō* festival that developed at Gion by 970 became renowned as the most popular and lavish of its era; commenting on the festival in a diary entry from 1127, Fujiwara Munetada would later muse, "The excesses of this world are beyond measure."[22]

The *goryō* cult in Heian Japan thus illustrates vividly the gradual crystallization of a popular religious movement from periodically held festivals at temporary sites to institutionalization as deities in state-supported shrines. As the Heian capital gradually became "unmoored" from its *ritsuryō* foundations—the western half of the capital declining and the eastern half filling in—the newly established *goryō* sites contributed not only to a new sacred landscape but to a new geography of power as well.[23] As the state grew unable to support the vast number of shrines chartered in the *ritsuryō* legal codes, a smaller set of twenty-two shrines was named to receive state patronage—a process that has been called one of "intensification and consolidation."[24] Among the new *goryō* sites, both Gion and the shrine to Michizane at Kitano (discussed below) made the elite list of twenty-two. As a further mark of the enduring impact of the *goryō* movement, Kuroda Toshio could still write in the latter twentieth century that the Heian *goryō* shrines continued to define the boundaries of the modern *ujiko* districts of Kyoto.[25] To some degree overlooked by modern historians of Japanese religion, the full impact of the Heian *goryō* cults has yet to be fully measured.

Returning to Michizane, by at least 923 his spirit, too, began to be included in an expanded list of eight *goryō* deities,[26] and the Kitano Shrine that would be dedicated to Michizane soon became the site of a major annual *goryō-e*. Before moving on to examine the process of his deification, however, we need to better understand the context of Michizane's exile and of the wider practice of exile within the court that contributed to the emergence of the *goryō* and *tenjin* cults in the first place.

## MICHIZANE AND THE POLITICS OF EXILE

Prior to the first court-sponsored *goryō-e* in 863, the state had already attempted a variety of ritual measures that same year to ward off pestilence and plague—and perhaps to curb growing unrest. Such measures included a great purification rite (*ōharae*), offerings to major deities (*myōjin*) at several shrines, offerings at the Ise Imperial Shrine, and continued sutra copying and recitation efforts.[27] It appears that the state turned to the direct worship of the six *goryō* popularly associated with plagues and famines only as a last measure. In the view of some, this was exactly because conceding the role of the six *goryō* in creating disorder was equivalent to conceding popular criticism of the state's handling of political affairs. Only after customary means of placation proved inadequate did the court attribute the disorder to those "unjustly accused," thereby acknowledging the state's own responsibility in creating the situation.[28] In this light, the 863 *goryō-e* has been interpreted in part as an attempt by powerful leaders of the time—notably Fujiwara Yoshifusa, the grand minister as well as imperial regent—to curb popular unrest linking the *goryō* to plague and famine brought on by political injustices. It seems fair to conclude that on the occasion of the first court-sponsored *goryō-e* in 863, the gates to the imperial palace garden would not have been opened to the masses for the first time in history if the state felt it had any reasonable alternative.

The skill with which the regent's line of the Northern Fujiwara utilized exile in the Heian period to remove potential rivals has already been mentioned in chapter 3, and the performance of the court's *goryō-e* in 863 suggests that this was also recognized by the various classes in the capital at the time. In a sense, the Fujiwara manipulation of marriage politics (discussed in chapter 3) and the strategic use of exile can be seen as two means for achieving the same ends: control over the imperial succession and the offices attending that succession, while preventing rival families from achieving the same. Prominent Heian incidents that were either orchestrated by the Fujiwara or simply used to their advantage include the Kusuko Incident of 810, the Ōtenmon Incident of 866, the case of Michizane in 901, and the Anna Incident of 969. Each of these resulted in the exile of high-ranking members of families in competition with the regent's line of the Fujiwara for positions of power and prestige, as well as the exile at times of competing members within the Fujiwara clan's own branches.

The Ōtenmon Incident, which occurred while Michizane was still a student at the imperial university, provides an instructive study in the Heian politics of exile.[29] Three years after the imperial *goryō-e* discussed above, the Ōtenmon—one of the gates of the imperial palace—burned down suddenly. Ban (Tomo no) Yoshio, a member of the Ōtomo family, accused his rival Minamoto no Makoto of causing the fire. With the backing of Grand Minister Fujiwara no Yoshifusa, Makoto was cleared of the charges, whereupon a witness was produced who claimed it was none other than Yoshio himself who had started the fire. Yoshio, his son, kinsmen, and several members of the Ki family ended up being charged and exiled (as were some of Michizane's own maternal relatives). Yoshifusa for his part succeeded in removing several key rivals from the court, securing the position of regent (*sesshō*) within the Fujiwara line for the remainder of the Heian period. The culture of discontent that arose during this period, as highly educated noble families found their political bases eroded due to the adept maneuvering of Fujiwara leaders, has been well documented.[30]

It is by now a truism to speak of the Fujiwara grip on Heian politics, which coincided with the creation of extra-legal offices such as that of chancellor (*kanpaku*) and regent, positions that came to be occupied customarily by the maternal grandfather of the emperor. By acting as regent during the reign of child emperors (some as young as eight months old) and then in the powerful capacity of chancellor once they came of age, members of the regent's line (*sekkanke*) of the Northern Fujiwara were able at times to achieve an unparalleled grip on power surrounding the throne. Some histories of Japan go so far as to refer to the mid-Heian era as the Fujiwara period, lasting from around 950 to 1086, until being superseded by the age of rule by abdicated sovereigns, or *insei*.[31]

As others have pointed out, it's also possible to overstate the degree of Fujiwara control.[32] It was not a monolithic body, as struggles took place between and within branches of the Fujiwara clan, and in every incident of exile mentioned above, leading members of the Fujiwara never acted alone but achieved their goals with the help of shifting coalitions among the broader aristocracy. That said, the powerful role played by the regent's line of the Northern Fujiwara in Heian politics was unparalleled. During the mid-Heian period, a succession of Fujiwara leaders from Yoshifusa through Michinaga held a near monopoly on the offices of regent and chancellor, where they were then able to act as advisors to emperors, providers of imperial consorts, and selectors of crown princes, inevitably favoring those drawn from the Fujiwara bloodline.[33]

## THE EXILE OF MICHIZANE

While Michizane's case offers another illustration of the Fujiwara use of exile to remove rivals from the imperial succession, Michizane's rise to power actually coincided with a moment of weakness for the regent's line. When Emperor Uda ascended the throne in 887, the powerful Fujiwara no Mototsune was retained as chancellor and grand minister (*daijo daijin*). Yet when the aged Mototsune died without any sons powerful or old enough to succeed him, Uda was able to assert a degree of independence from Fujiwara control. He did this in part by elevating Michizane (age fifty-four) to the position of minister of the right (*udaijin*), while naming Mototsune's eldest son Tokihira (age twenty-eight) to the more prestigious but less powerful role of minister of the left (*sadaijin*). Michizane's rise thus coincided with the beginning of a nearly thirty-eight-year period—in the midst of the "Fujiwara era"—in which there were no Fujiwara regents or chancellors overseeing the emperor and in which a comparatively low ranking scholar such as Michizane was able to rise to one of the highest offices in the land.

As Michizane rose rapidly to power under Emperor Uda, he presented a clear threat to the ability of the Fujiwara regent's line to control the imperial succession. Because Michizane was not only a close advisor to the emperor but also the maternal grandfather of a potential crown prince, he found himself in a volatile position with regard to struggles to control the imperial succession, made more precarious by the fact that he was a nonroyal who had been elevated to an uncommonly high position.[34] When Emperor Uda abdicated in 897 in favor of his son, the thirteen-year-old Daigo, Michizane was left in a particularly vulnerable position. Within three years, most accounts cite Tokihira as the instigator of a classic Fujiwara-styled power maneuver, accusing Michizane in 901 of plotting to replace the crown prince with his own grandson. For what amounted to a charge of plotting against the state, Michizane was exiled to the Dazaifu, although nominally under the sentence of "demotion."[35]

Whether or not Tokihira was the prime instigator, he did not act alone: among his chief allies were Minamoto Hikaru, Fujiwara Sadakuni, and Fujiwara Sugane.[36] Moreover, members of several other court families were also sent into exile at the same time as Michizane. Thus, while the principal actors in the drama were Michizane and Tokihira, it would be more accurate to say that a power struggle had been lost and won among factions at court, of which the two men—who held the highest offices at that time—were simply the most prominent representatives.[37]

## EXILE, DEMOTION, AND THE DAZAIFU

In legal terms, Michizane was never officially given a sentence of banishment (*ruzai*). Although he was expelled from the capital and sent under guard to the distant government outpost on Tsukushi (now Kyushu) on 901/2/1, having been implicated in treason, the term used to designate this action in the chronicles was simply *sasen,* or demotion. The *Nihon Kiryaku* records even more plainly on 901/1/25 that Michizane was *appointed* (*nin*) to the position of provisional governor-general at the Dazaifu government headquarters in Tsukushi, while Minamoto Hikaru was appointed to Michizane's office of minister of the right.[38] Then, in an entry dating ten days later, the chronicle clarifies this appointment as a demotion: "Offerings were made at various shrines. The matter of Minister Sugawara's demotion (*sasen*) was announced."[39]

If, as Jeffrey Mass has pointed out, "the language of the moment and the language of remembrance [are] frequently discordant," is it anachronistic to view Michizane's case as one of exile?[40] Not according to Michizane himself, as expressed in the poetry composed in Chinese during the last years of his life at the Dazaifu. Verses written by Michizane employ a variety of terms referring to his experience of being banished or of being simultaneously demoted and expelled. A poem "written upon hearing the proclamation of the new era name," for example, contains the line: "How lonely—the one who has been banished."[41] Here, the characters 放逐 (*hōchiku*) convey both the meaning "to drive away" (*oidasu*) and "to banish" (*tsuihō*).[42] In another poem from the Dazaifu titled "On Not Leaving the Gate," Michizane writes somewhat more darkly,

> Since I was demoted and exiled and live in a shack
> I crouch and cringe with ten thousand fears of death.[43]

Here, the verb 謫落 (*takuraku*) connotes both demotion and exile simultaneously.[44]

While it may seem contradictory that a person in exile would be given a position of seeming authority—as with Michizane being "appointed" provisional governor-general of the Dazaifu—it's clear this strictly nominal office was sometimes given to Heian officials banished from the capital but without actual responsibility or authority.[45] As Robert Borgen explains, "According to law, punishment for crimes varied according to the offender's status. A man of Michizane's exalted position, when judged guilty of wrongdoing, often was allowed to maintain a vestige of his honor in the form of a nominal official title signifying that he was a noble, not a common, criminal. So it was that, even during Michizane's final years of disgrace and banishment, he was in name the supernumerary governor general of Dazaifu."[46]

Such a rationale is expressed clearly in the edict—recorded in the *Seiji Yōryaku,* a private court chronicle—that sentenced Michizane to exile/demotion on the grounds of plotting against the state: "His words are obedient, but his heart is rebellious. This is known by all in the nation. He is not a person who should serve as a great minister *but deserves punishment under the law.* However, out of special consideration for his position, he shall only be removed from his present office and be appointed supernumerary governor general of Dazaifu."[47]

In fact, on the journey from the capital to the Dazaifu, Michizane was treated in the manner of a criminal, placed under guard and prohibited from receiving fresh horses or rations. Once at the Dazaifu, he lived under a form of house arrest. Finding it difficult to obtain adequate supplies and food, Michizane's last three years appear to have been characterized by deprivation.[48]

Later Heian sources also look back on Michizane's punishment as one of exile. The *Okagami* uses a colloquialism for exile: "In the end—perhaps because fate had ordained it—Michizane was overtaken by misfortune, and they banished him (*nagasaretamau*) to Kyushu."[49] Other interpretive histories such as the *Gukansho* and *Jinnō Shōtōki* mince no words in referring to Michizane's exile and placing the blame for his punishment on particular members of the court. According to the *Gukansho,* the fact that all state documents regarding the affair were later burned proved the illegitimacy of the charges against Michizane: "The diaries of the various houses and the documents of the Council of State that dealt with the incident were all burned by Imperial command, presumably because the Emperor was afraid the incident was due to some terrible misdeed he had committed. Therefore no one really knows what happened. But some brief references to the incident have been found in other places. Moreover, this was such a big affair that details have come down to us by word of mouth. So we probably know the main points."[50]

Ultimately, it's clear that the act of "demotion" was an extension of Heian political-legal procedures, in which punishments were ameliorated based on the social status of those charged—a practice designed to protect the social distinctions on which the court itself rested. In Michizane's case, "demotion" entailed not merely a loss of office but forced removal from the capital, the most severe punishment available for a person of such high standing during an era when capital punishment was abolished. In addition to Michizane, four of his sons were exiled (*sakō*) to various locations. Nine lower-ranking court officials associated with Michizane were also exiled, indicating a clear effort on the part of Michizane's rivals to eradicate his faction in the capital. In every sense but the euphemistic phrasing of the court, Michizane was banished from the capital, while his power base in the capital was systematically and thoroughly dismantled and dispersed.[51]

## THE DAZAIFU AND THE IMAGINATION OF EXILE

Michizane's final years at the Dazaifu connect him to one of the classic sites of exile in Japanese court culture.[52] In its physical distance from the capital, the association of the Dazaifu with marginality was already established by the Nara period, as can be seen in the poems by frontier guards at the Dazaifu included in the *Manyōshū,* the earliest compilation of Japanese poetry. Later, as a number of high-ranking officials were demoted and banished there from the Nara and Heian capitals, themes and events associating the Dazaifu with political alienation continued to layer upon each other well into the Heian period. By Michizane's time, the Dazaifu carried rich connotations of exile from the courtly center.

To cite one influential example predating Michizane, following the Kusuko Incident of 810, in which a plot to overthrow the emperor led to the execution of Fujiwara Nakanari and the suicide of Emperor Heizei's wife Kusuko, Heizei's son (Prince Abo) was exiled to the Dazaifu and appointed provisional governor-general there.[53] Though an imperial prince, he was made a commoner and given the surname Ariwara.[54] His sons Yukihira and Narihira then went on themselves to become leading figures in the production of exile literature. Yukihira's famous poems regarding his own exile in Suma were included in the *Kokinshū,* while the *Ise monogatari,* a classic work combining themes of separation and eros, is commonly attributed to Narihira.[55]

Following Michizane, the practice of banishing powerful ministers to the Dazaifu continued, at times in near repetition of Michizane's own circumstances. Particularly striking are the similarities between Michizane's case and the exile of Minamoto no Takaakira, a figure suggested by some to have been a model for the hero of the *Tale of Genji.* Takaakira, like the fictional Shining Prince, was the son of an emperor (Daigo), yet he was made a commoner and given the name Minamoto (Chinese reading: Genji) in 920. As with Michizane, he served in a number of high positions, finally rising to minister of the left. When his daughter bore a son to an emperor, Takaakira—like Michizane—found himself in the position of being maternal grandfather to a potential crown prince. Because of the power he would hold if his son became emperor, Takaakira became the target of a power struggle probably led by Fujiwara no Saneyori, later known as the Anna Incident of 969.[56] In classic Fujiwara fashion, a treasonous plot was "discovered" whereby Takaakira planned to replace the current crown prince (Morihira) with his own grandson. Like Michizane, Takaakira was then exiled to the Dazaifu, officially having been "appointed" there in the position of provisional governor-general.

As recorded in chronicles and diaries of the period, the response in the capital to Takaakira's sentence suggests the distress that could be evoked by the banishment of a popular minister of the court. According to the *Nihon Kiryaku,* the capital "was thrown into great turmoil" by Takaakira's fall.[57] The *Eiga monogatari* states that Takaakira's banishment was "the most distressing event of the era," one which evoked the other "great Minister, Michizane" in its poignancy.[58] A diary written by a member of court at that time records simply that there were "none whose sleeves are not soaked" over the affair, employing a classic poetic trope to describe the tears that flowed upon Takaakira's departure.[59]

Unlike Michizane, however, Takaakira was able to return to the capital while still alive, though (unlike the fictional Genji) he never reclaimed his former high status. Michizane's death in exile thus placed him in uniquely tragic company, not merely a Heian aristocrat fallen from power and banished to the periphery but one who died a tragic death far from the courtly center. Such circumstances appear to have led some in the capital to regard Michizane after his death as "matter out of place," a disturbing anomaly in the Heian order of things. When tragedy began to strike those responsible for Michizane's fate, he was soon classified within the category of vengeful spirits (*onryō*) believed to be haunting the capital and requiring propitiation.

## MICHIZANE'S RETURN

After Michizane passed away from illness at the Dazaifu in 903, a temple named Anrakuji was erected at his burial site, not initially to appease any perceived wrath but simply to provide prayer and ritual for his spiritual repose, "assisting him toward Buddhist salvation."[60] Meanwhile, Michizane's reputation as a literary figure continued to grow when his last collection of poetry, sent to his friend Ki no Haseo one month before his death, began to circulate in the capital and bring attention to the conditions of his exile.[61] Within a few years, during the period from 909 through 930, a series of deaths occurring in the capital caused popular belief concerning Michizane's vengeful spirit to coalesce into the familiar form of a *goryō* cult.

The first fatality linked to Michizane was that of his main rival, Fujiwara Tokihira, the minister of the left believed to have instigated Michizane's exile. Tokihira died in 909 at the age of thirty-nine; according to one account recorded in the *Fuso Ryakki,* his death was caused by Michizane in the form of a dragon that entered and exited Tokihira's body. While scholars debate the extent to which Tokihira's death was seen at the time as a manifestation of Michizane's wrath,[62] subsequent deaths clearly led to a growing conviction that Michizane's spirit had been responsible in Tokihira's case also. The first of these was the death in 923 of Tokihira's nephew, Crown Prince Yasuakira, at twenty-one years of age. As quoted at the outset of this chapter from the *Nihon Kiryaku,* this death was popularly attributed to Michizane's vengeful spirit.

Within a month after Yasuakira's death, the court took administrative actions aimed at Michizane's pacification. First, the edict concerning his demotion was rescinded, and Michizane was posthumously promoted to the upper second rank and reinstated to his former position of minister of the right. To wipe the slate clean, a new era name (Enchō) was also proclaimed. Yet these measures were deemed inadequate: within two years, Yasuakira's own son (and Tokihira's grandson) died at the young age of five, and in 930 lightning struck the imperial palace itself, killing three nobles and injuring two, including one who had worked to bring about Michizane's banishment.[63] This too was attributed to Michizane, leading to the association between Michizane's spirit and thunder and lightning deities. Three months later, Emperor Daigo—the reigning emperor at the time of Michizane's exile—fell ill and died at the age of forty-six. His successor was the eight-year-old

Suzaku, the child emperor mentioned at the beginning of this chapter who was "reared inside a curtain-dais in a room where lights burned day and night" for fear of Michizane's wrath.

## THE DEIFICATION OF MICHIZANE

Beginning in 941, a series of oracles and revelations occurring around the capital began to articulate the form and manner of worship necessary for Michizane's further pacification, establishing Michizane not just as a *goryō* but also as a unique form of *tenjin,* or heavenly deity. Following these oracles, a new religious site was established for the worship of Michizane as *tenjin,* enshrining his spirit back in the capital while simultaneously rehabilitating the Sugawara clan back into the hierarchy of influential court families. Michizane's cult thus represents a new stage in the *goryō* movement, moving beyond the worship of *goryō* deities collectively to the cult of a single figure at a site uniquely his own.

The oracles and revelations that established Michizane as *tenjin* occurred between 941 and 947, a little more than a decade after Michizane's spirit was believed to have caused the fatal lightning strike on the imperial palace. The revelations were expressed by three figures, each of whom represented a different aspect of the Heian religious landscape: an esoteric Buddhism ascetic, a folk shamaness (*miko*), and the child of a shrine priest. While each person's vision was unique, together they also mapped out some basic similarities: all make an identification between Michizane and various forms of *tenjin,* and all record the desire by Michizane to be worshipped. Surprisingly—or not—the tone of condemnation regarding Michizane's accusers in at least one vision is quite strong.

The earliest vision recorded is that of the Buddhist priest Dōken, dating from 941. Dōken, son of the courtier Kiyoyuki, had spent some twenty-five years in ascetic retreat in mountains near the capital, and his vision is striking for its narration of otherworldly realms. According to his account, one day he entered into a trance-like state, whereupon he envisioned meeting Shakyamuni Buddha in the form of the mountain god, Zao Bosatsu. He next encountered Michizane, who clarified to Dōken that his proper appellation was Nihon Daijō Itokuten. When Dōken responded to Michizane that everyone regarded him as Karai Tenjin, or Heavenly Deity of Fire and Thunder, Michizane explained that thunder beings were merely his messengers.

Michizane went on to say that he continued to seek vengeance upon those who mistreated him, but that if people worship him in accord with Dōken's revelation he would respond to their requests.[64]

Perhaps the most striking element of the revelation comes toward the end of the account. After conversing with Michizane, Dōken was then transported to hell (*jigoku*), where he saw four figures, one of them clothed. The clothed figure, Dōken learns, was none other than the late emperor Daigo, who had occupied the throne at the time of Michizane's exile and as a result was now paying for his transgressions along with several of his ministers. The late emperor also requested that Dōken report his plight so that he too might obtain relief from his suffering.[65]

Several points are worth noting from Dōken's account. First, it provides an important indication that by 941, Michizane was believed not just to be a vengeful spirit but specifically one linked with fire and lightning. Second, while reiterating Michizane's grudge against those responsible for his downfall, it points toward potential benefits for those who worship him. Finally, with the image of Daigo in hell, Dōken's revelation offers a surprisingly strong rebuke toward those who sent Michizane into exile, including an emperor who had died just over a decade before (in 930). In Dōken's vision, the positions of Michizane and his rivals are dramatically inverted: it is Michizane who occupies a position of religious power and authority in the afterlife, while the disgraced emperor Daigo lies in hell, at the opposite otherworldly extreme.

While Dōken's revelation is important as a sign of the emerging *tenjin* cult and as an indication of popular sentiment regarding Michizane and his adversaries, Dōken did not himself become a significant mediator of *tenjin* worship. His vivid description of Daigo in hell, however, later circulated visually through the picture scroll (*emaki*) version of the *Kitano Tenjin Engi* (Records of the Origins of Kitano Shrine), where a Tendai (Buddhist) interest in the six realms of existence (including hell) joined with the growing belief system regarding Michizane as *tenjin*.[66]

A second influential oracle regarding Michizane came from a woman living in the capital known as Tajihi no Ayako, a folk shamaness or *miko*. In a brief oracle dating to 942, Ayako relates that Michizane appeared to her and asked her to create a small shrine for him at Kitano,[67] also telling her that he had already acquired the title *tenjin*. The record accompanying Ayako's oracle states that she then built a small shrine for Michizane as *tenjin*—not at Kitano but near her home—and began worshipping him there at least until 947.

Ayako's account provides further information regarding the developing *tenjin* cult and contains many elements that would remain core parts of *tenjin* worship. It is the first account to locate the worship of Michizane at Kitano, where an important site to Michizane would soon be dedicated. It also refers to Michizane simply as *tenjin,* dropping the reference (seen in Dōken's account) to thunder and lightning but retaining the central part of his title. It mentions for the first time the desire by Michizane to have a shrine and places that request within a *kami*-cult idiom through the use of the term *hokora* for shrine.[68] Finally, the accompanying record indicates that Ayako began worshipping Michizane as *tenjin,* providing the first glimpse into an active *kami* cult developing around Michizane.

While some sources thus credit Ayako with the founding oracle for what would eventually become the Kitano Shrine, a third important oracle appeared in the year the Kitano shrine was actually established, in 947. This oracle was attributed to the seven-year-old son of Miwa no Yoshitane, a shrine priest from the province of Omi, near the capital. According to this oracle, Michizane again requested to be worshipped at Kitano, promising that pine trees would appear there as a sign of his sacred power; he also stated that he would punish disbelievers but reward those who worshipped him. Finally, illustrating the Heian fusion of Buddhist and *kami*-cult idioms, he requested a Lotus Meditation Hall (Hoke Sanmaidō) to be included at the site. According to the records accompanying the text of this oracle, the boy's father Yoshitane then visited Kitano, where he met a Tendai priest, Saichin, who already supervised a temple in the vicinity.[69] After Yoshitane reported his son's oracle to Saichin, numerous pine trees were said to have miraculously sprung up overnight, a manifestation that then led Saichin to support the shrine's creation.[70]

Following these oracles, a shrine was dedicated to Michizane as *tenjin* at Kitano; construction of the worship hall commenced on 947/6/9. In fact, however, the area known as Kitano, in the northern part of the Heian capital, had been the site of offerings from the early Heian period to a heavenly deity associated with thunder known as Raijin.[71] Originally, Raijin was a deity worshipped by farmers as a god who controlled rain and who consequently played a crucial role in agriculture. The term *raijin* itself literally means "thunder deity," and prayers were offered to this deity to bring rain in times of drought, while lightning and thunder were regarded as attributes of the deity. With the growth of the cult of vengeful spirits during the Heian period, the capacity of lightning to do harm and cause destruction came to be further associated with the type of vengeful activities caused by *goryō*.[72] In particular, following the fatal lightning strike on the imperial palace in 930, the work of lightning deities came to be associated with the vengeful spirit of Michizane, so that he was portrayed in some oracles either as identical with thunder deities or as their master. As seen in Dōken's revelation, Karai Tenjin (Heavenly Deity of Fire and Thunder) was one of Michizane's many appellations, and fire and lightning were attributes associated with Michizane as *tenjin*.[73] It's hardly surprising, then, that a shrine to Michizane came to be located at a site traditionally associated with the worship of deities of thunder and lightning in the Heian capital.

## THE FOUNDING OF KITANO SHRINE

Michizane received a specific title when his spirit was officially enshrined at Kitano: Tenman Daijizai Tenjin, or "Heavenly-Filling Great Self-Sufficient Heavenly Deity." Following the dedication of the shrine in 947, actions attributed to his vengeful spirit appear to have calmed for a while. Records from the period immediately following the shrine's founding focus on the human figures who were involved in constructing, overseeing, and expanding the shrine. In 959, only twelve years after its founding, the shrine was expanded with the support of Fujiwara Morosuke, the powerful minister of the right and grandfather of Fujiwara no Michinaga. Coming only one year prior to his own death, Morosuke's involvement may be related to the fact that he was a descendent of Michizane's nemesis, Fujiwara no Tokihira, and perhaps wished to avoid the continued vengeance of Michizane—as well as assist in his own family's prosperity—by supporting Michizane's shrine. Records of the expansion effort specifically note that Morosuke prayed to Michizane's spirit for his family's protection.[74]

As the Kitano Shrine came to assume a position of importance in the capital and following the expansion enabled by Morosuke, records indicate that questions arose regarding the control of the shrine. The evidence for this comes from a successful petition by Michizane's grandson Fumitoki in 976, which asked the court to grant control over the Kitano Shrine to the Sugawara clan, in part because a Sugawara ancestor was enshrined there and in part based on the precedent established at the smaller temple to Michizane located at the Dazaifu, which a Sugawara had earlier been appointed to supervise.[75] Members of the Sugawara family, in turn, chose the priest Saichin to continue overseeing the immediate operations of the Kitano Shrine.[76]

By 976 the Kitano Shrine—which traced its beginnings to oracles from some of the humblest inhabitants of the capital—had come under the control of the Sugawara clan, assisted by members of the Buddhist clergy to supervise the shrine's operations. In this manner the position of the Sugawara family was greatly enhanced. With the establishment of the Kitano Shrine to Michizane in the capital, the Sugawara had gained a sacred site to the clan's most prominent ancestor, which was all the more prestigious due to the growing popularity of the *tenjin* cult in the capital, and in the following years the clan's rehabilitation reached new heights. A passage in Sei Shonagon's *Pillow Book* from the late tenth century, for example, refers to a Sugawara lord simply as the Kitano *no sanmi* (Kitano lord of the third rank), indicating that within a short time the shrine was already popularly associated with the Sugawara family and that the family was once again placing its members in the upper echelons of court society.[77]

As the tenth century drew to a close, the Kitano Shrine and its deity grew even more popular. In 987 the shrine held its own spirit-pacification festival, and by 1004 the shrine received an imperial visit from Emperor Ichijō. Meanwhile, Michizane continued to receive posthumous honors from the state. In 993, perhaps out of concern that an epidemic was being caused by Michizane's spirit, the deceased minister received two final promotions, first to minister of the left (*sadaijin*) and the senior first rank and then to grand minister (*daijō daijin*).[78] In death, Michizane had achieved something unimaginable while alive: the highest rank and office in the entire court bureaucracy and his deified spirit enshrined in the capital at a new center of worship, supported by the Fujiwara clan and emperor alike. His "return" from exile, in a sense, was complete.

## CONCLUSION

During the Heian period, the use of exile as a political strategy was perfected by the regent's line of the Northern Fujiwara above all others, initiating fraught moments of reorganization within the entire court hierarchy. When several high-ranking members of court died in exile or under guard away from the capital, exile became a contributing factor in the emergence of the cult of vengeful/honored spirits, who were believed responsible for a variety of misfortunes befalling the capital area. In every case, the pacification of these spirits involved returning them to the capital, where they were enshrined in sacred sites newly established for their worship. Decrees of banishment were rescinded, titles reconferred, and rank bestowed, in a concerted effort to erase any wrongdoing from the public transcript and to restore the figures to positions of centrality within the Heian imagination.

Of the *goryō,* none played a more prominent role than Michizane, whose astonishing posthumous return from exile saw him elevated to the highest rank and office at court, as well as installed as a heavenly deity at his own sacred site in the capital. Michizane's case thus sheds light on actual historical examples involving the imagination of exile, and in doing so it calls for further examination. While resisting any single line of interpretation, at the most basic level Michizane as *tenjin* illustrates what might be called the dialogical nature of exile in Heian Japan. In other words, in Michizane's case the political sanction of exile was met with a "religious" rejoinder, through which an exiled noble was reinstated in the capital in divine form, continuing the reconfiguration of the political and religious landscape in new and significant ways.

Among scholars, the very success of the *goryō* cults has caused uncertainty about whether to consider the movement an example of popular resistance, on the one hand, or simply hegemony in its subtler forms.[79] The very fact that by 959 the powerful Fujiwara minister Morosuke was himself contributing to the expansion of Kitano Shrine—while praying for Tenjin's protection over his regent's line—could be seen as an indication that the *goryō* cults had been co-opted "to the point that they were given the role of praising the virtues of the establishment and its order."[80] By this logic, a potentially destabilizing discourse concerning vengeful spirits had been co-opted by members of the aristocratic establishment and turned instead into spectacles of "excess beyond measure," as expressed in Fujiwara Munetada's description of the Gion spirit-pacification festival in 1127. In this view, the use of exile as a tactic by Michizane's enemies would be called successful, in the sense that he no longer posed a threat as court minister in the immediate struggle to control the imperial succession.

Such success may be overstated, however, for as expressed in oracles and recorded in court chronicles, Michizane's fate did not end with his exile, and his posthumous spirit was indeed believed to have affected the balance of power. As both *goryō* and *tenjin,* Michizane was seen as delimiting Fujiwara power and authority, not only by eliminating his main rival Tokihira and bringing two related princes to their early deaths, but also by attacking the imperial palace itself and contributing to the demise of Tokihira's protégé, Emperor Daigo. As a result of this "rebalancing," the Sugawara clan benefited greatly from the *tenjin* cult centered at Kitano. In 991 Kitano was included in a list of the nineteen shrines chosen to receive imperial patronage,[81] and its prominence continued to grow: by 1322, at least one author was placing Tenman Tenjin among the five great *kami* of Japan, alongside deities such as Amaterasu.[82] By serving as the "curators" of an extremely valuable resource—the enshrined spirit of the Sugawara ancestor Michizane—the clan was able to reclaim prestige within the court as well as to ensure its continued importance. To this day, notwithstanding enormous changes in the cult over time, *tenjin* shrines continue to play an integral role in the religious landscape of contemporary Japan, while the head priest of the Dazaifu Tenjin Shrine remains a Sugawara and a descendent of Michizane.[83]

Accordingly, in contrast to those who view the *goryō* cults as having been co-opted by the state, others see in the *goryō* and *tenjin* cults a kind of protest movement, "expressing indirectly a critique of power that could not be made openly."[84] As we've seen, for example, the state initially refrained from worshipping the *goryō* directly, preferring instead to reinstate rank and posthumous office and then to give offerings to more traditional divinities. Yet in both the *goryō* and *tenjin* cults, popular sentiment eventually led to state worship of *goryō* deities and the creation of new sacred sites for their worship.[85] It remains striking that the public transcript portrays the *goryō* not as enemies of the state but as figures who died "unjustly accused," acknowledging them as worthy of veneration—and the state as worthy of blame. It's also striking that the state is known to have prohibited a *goryō* celebration at least once, for a gathering that may have been a precursor to the great Gion *goryō-e*.[86] While the full reasoning behind the prohibition isn't known, it hints at the uneasy relations between the state and the populace concerning *goryō* cults, suggesting that the state may not always have been comfortable with the ambience of protest that never lay far from the practice of *goryō* worship.[87] No wonder that when the rebel warrior Taira no Masakado seized three provinces in the Kantō region and declared himself the new emperor, his "certificate of enthronement" was declared by an oracle in 940 to have been issued by none other than the spirit of Michizane.[88]

It would be an oversimplification, however, to reduce the *goryō* and *tenjin* cults merely to protest movements against Fujiwara hegemony. While it's clear that the cult of vengeful spirits was linked to a sense that the deceased had been unjustly punished, it was at the same time a religious movement concerned with placating disorder—the plagues, pestilence, famine, and disasters that repeatedly ravaged the capital. It's helpful to recall that the Heian period was simultaneously an age of extreme aesthetic sensibility for some—where differences in rank could be discerned by the contrast between clothing dyed scarlet or deep purple—and a period in which chronicles repeatedly refer to corpses piling up in the city.[89] Only a century after the establishment of Kitano Shrine, a court history declared darkly, "This year, the final age began."[90] Religious practices such as the spirit-pacification festivals must also be considered against this background, as one means by which people sought to ward off and gain some measure of control over the all-too-prevalent forces of pollution, disorder, and death.[91]

Indeed, beyond its role in symbolically delimiting Fujiwara authority and in addition to its value for the Sugawara, the establishment of a shrine to Michizane contributed a defining feature to the Heian religious imagination, along with the other newly consecrated *goryō* sites. The fact that an exiled minister from the Heian court could return to the capital as one of the most venerated spirits of the time clearly inspired affinity toward a deity whose power exceeded, in some ways, that of any member of the court. To those living in the Heian capital as well as to later medieval historians, the deification and return of Michizane provided a vivid illustration of the process of rectification at work in history—or at least of the kind of retribution possible against those in power whose transgressions of justice upset both the social and natural worlds.

# 5

# Cosmologies of Law

## *Exile in the Legal Imagination*

> The medium faced the retired emperor [Toba], put out her right hand and turned it over, saying, "How about this?" The retired emperor, thinking "this is truly an oracle from the god," slipped off his seat and, joining his hands, said, "that is what I asked. What may it be?" At this the god spoke through the medium, "In autumn of next year you must die (*kanarazu hōgyo naru beshi*). After that the world will become like the turning over of this hand." *—Hōgen monogatari*

> When terms appear or disappear or change their meaning, the movement of history stands revealed. *—Jacques Le Goff*

In the final section of the *Nihon Ryōiki*—an early Heian work devoted to explaining the miraculous workings of the Buddhist dharma—a story is told concerning Emperor Saga, the reigning emperor around the time of the text's compilation (ca. 822).[1] According to the story, Saga was in fact none other than the reincarnation of the esteemed priest Jakusen, who had died some years prior to Saga's birth. As evidence of Saga's karmic merit, the text mentions an example of the emperor's compassionate rule: "Without fail, imperial law executes murderers. This emperor, however, proclaiming an era of 'spreading benevolence' (*kōnin*), sends those who would be executed into exile (*korosu beki hito o ruzai to nashi*); he governs people by sparing their lives. By this, his virtue is clearly known."[2]

In the story, the emperor's compassionate rule reveals his true identity as a reincarnated priest. Yet the passage also yields evidence of another kind, for it provides an important contemporary recognition of a major change in the legal practice of the Heian court begun during Saga's reign: the customary commuting of the death penalty, in favor of exile, for capital crimes. Indeed, historians of Japanese law speak of a period of some 347 years—beginning with Saga's reign and spanning the majority of the Heian era—when the practice of capital punishment was virtually abolished in favor of exile.

Toward the end of the Heian period, however, the practice of execution reappeared dramatically with the Hōgen no Ran of 1156, one of the civil conflicts that fragmented the Heian court and signaled the rise of warrior houses to power. Among several notable incidents resulting from this conflict, the general of the defeated side was sentenced to death—and his son (on the victor's side) was ordered to enforce the beheading. A later chronicle of the conflict describes the event in shocked tones: "*Killing one's father under the mask of 'loyalty' is the gravest perversion of filial piety, the extreme of unrighteousness.*"[3] In discussing the incident, the text further notes that the executions resulting from the Hōgen conflict were the first to take place at court in over twenty-six imperial reigns, dating all the way back to Emperor Saga.

The nearly three and a half centuries stretching from Saga's reign to the Hōgen conflict provide the backdrop for this chapter's investigation into the role of exile in Heian legal discourse and practice. For those attempting to understand Heian cultural history, the cessation of capital punishment and its later reemergence raise a number of important questions about larger movements involving law, religion, and society. For my purposes, foremost among these is the question of the relationship between the rise of banishment as the dominant legal sanction of the period, on the one hand, and the emergence of exile as a widespread trope within the cultural imagination.

Exploring this question raises further issues, however. In what sense can the *ritsuryō* codes themselves be considered imaginative texts? In other words, in what sense can we compare the legal codes with other narratives of exile I examine in this project, each imagining a particular constellation of power enacted in part through the trope of banishment? As with the genres I examine in other chapters—including myth, literature, and oracles—in this chapter I explore the distinct vision of power imagined within the *ritsuryō* codes, the vision of a centralized polity organized around the divine figure of the sovereign. Within the codes, I'll explore how exile helped articulate that vision: by correlating various degrees of transgression against the social order with various degrees of removal from the courtly center, exile once again provided a resonant means by which the imagined community of the *ritsuryō* state was conceived, articulated, and mapped onto the archipelago.

At the same time, the codes did more than merely theorize a constellation of power, and in the second part of the chapter I examine the implementation of the *ritsuryō* codes, focusing specifically on the changes involving execution and exile that occurred following Saga's reign. To investigate the suspension of capital punishment, I consider the various theories put forth by Japanese legal historians to explain the cessation. While the evidence does not allow for a decisive verdict, I suggest that a reexamination of the *Hōgen monogatari*—and the anxiety with which it depicts the return of execution—supports the notion that concern regarding vengeful spirits must be considered an important factor in the earlier suspension of capital punishment. Finally, based on the data presented in the chapter, I suggest that it is scarcely coincidental that just as exile rose to become the paramount sanction in Heian legal custom, it also emerged as a powerful and recurring trope within literature, folklore, and cultic practice.

## THE CENTRALIZING VISION OF THE *RITSURYŌ* CODES

In studies of early Japan, much has been written about a trio of texts considered among Japan's most important early writings. The *Kojiki* (712), *Nihonshoki* (720), and *Manyōshū* (mid-eighth century) were all completed by the Japanese state during the Nara period, and all three serve as valuable resources regarding the rapidly developing political and cultural landscape of early Japan. As imperially sponsored collections, the texts also shed light on the early state's efforts to consolidate and inscribe its authority, legitimacy, and centrality.

Another textual project was completed around the same time, however, and while less has been written about it, the project had arguably an equal or greater impact on the development of the early Japanese state. I refer to the *ritsuryō* codes, an extensive body of law first fully enacted as the Taihō ritsuryō in 702—predating the *Kojiki* by a decade—and superseded by the Yōrō ritsuryō in 757.[4] The implementation of these codes was part of a far-reaching program of change effected in early Japan, providing crucial support for the transformation of the early Japanese polity from "an archaic confederacy of aristocratic clans . . . into a centralized bureaucratic state."[5]

The *ritsuryō* codes—which were adapted from the Tang legal codes used in China—provided a detailed blueprint for the ideal state imagined by the Japanese court. Efforts to implement this vision during the seventh and eighth centuries included, among other developments, "the creation of the administrative apparatus of a central government . . . the imposition of rigid class distinctions . . . the establishment of a province-county system . . . the nationalization and redistribution of farming land . . . and the reorganization of regional warlords and militia forces into a national army."[6] While debate surrounds the actual extent to which the codes were fully implemented (as I discuss below), there can be no doubt that the Nara period (710–784) saw the realization of the codes in far-reaching ways, and that the key *ritsuryō* blueprint of the Yamato state—a centralized court bureaucracy organized hierarchically under the figure of a divine sovereign—continued into the Heian era even as many of its elements were transformed in new and unforeseen ways.

As the name *ritsuryō* suggests, the codes consisted of two parts: the administrative laws (*ryō*) and the penal codes (*ritsu*). A glance at the thirty chapter headings of the *ryō* (which were further divided into 900 articles) reveals a drive to regulate nearly every aspect of life that could be brought under the jurisdiction of the state: from general chapters titled "Offices and Ranks," "Taxation," and "Education," the codes move on to cover such specific topics as "Arable Fields," "Worship of the Gods of Heaven and Earth," "Buddhist Monks and Nuns," and "Funerals and Mourning," among others. The *ritsu* penal code attempted a similar comprehension with regard to possible transgressions and their sanctions, as can be seen in such chapter headings as "Insurrection and Robbery," "Assaults and Accusations," "Deception and Forgery," and "Palace Guards and Internal Security." William Farris has described succinctly the administrative institutions resulting from the early state's drive for comprehensive rule: "Founders of the new Chinese-style state envisioned an emperor controlling all the realm's land and population, and the reigning family needed help to accomplish this basic goal. Tax accountants, military officers, university professors, experts in divination and medicine, scribes and secretaries, imperial servants, local officials, religious overseers, prison wardens—all were necessary to a well-run, centralized government. The Yōrō Code listed over six thousand offices, and by [the year] 750 as many as ten thousand bureaucrats worked for the emperor."[7] In short, the *ritsuryō* codes provided not only the blueprint but also the legal charter by which the state sought to enact its vision of governance.

## TAXONOMIES OF TRANSGRESSION AND PUNISHMENT

While the *ryō* administrative code articulated the state's vision of a centralized social order, the *ritsu* penal code provided an important counterpart, detailing the possible transgressions against that order and their corresponding punishments. Although some chapters of the original text of the *ritsu* are no longer extant, several crucial chapters (including the opening section on general principles) have been reconstructed from later commentaries, providing a clear description of the types of transgressions and punishments envisioned by the code's compilers. Regarding transgressions, the code introduces at the outset a classification of the most severe crimes imaginable called the *hachigyaku,* or the "eight abominations." In addition, the text details five types of punishment referred to simply as the *gokei,* or the "five punishments," that were designed to correspond to all conceivable transgressions. These two important classificatory systems and their underlying principles are worth a closer look.

The *hachigyaku* comprised a list of the eight transgressions against the social order considered most extreme within the worldview of the *ritsuryō* state. In a system of law concerned to organize an obedient society under the figure of the sovereign—and to authenticate imperial rule itself—it's not surprising that the most severe transgressions imagined were those committed against the sovereign. The most "abominable" outrage was that of plotting rebellion against the sovereign, followed next by destruction of imperial palaces or tombs and then by treason against the state.

While in the main text of the articles defining the eight abominations the crimes are given rather general names (the literal translation of "plotting rebellion against the sovereign," for example, is simply "plotting rebellion"), the accompanying commentary provided within the code further clarifies their meaning. Thus "plotting rebellion" is defined as "planning to endanger the state" (*kokka o ayōgusemu to hakareru*), while the annotated remarks provided by the modern editors add that "endangering the state" in this case refers to the crime of preparing to kill the sovereign (*kunshu ni taisuru satsujin yobi zai*),[8] and that in both the Chinese and Japanese codes, "the state" (*kokka*) in this instance functions as an honorific reference to the emperor.[9] The act of "plotting" is defined in turn either as a group of two or more people involved in a conspiracy or simply one person with concrete plans to commit a crime.[10] In either case, the punishment for plotting rebellion against the emperor is already the most severe possible—death by beheading—and since that punishment is mandated already for the act of *plotting* rebellion, the codes need not specify any further punishments for those who actually carry out such a plot.[11]

The complete list of the eight abominations reads as follows:

1. plotting rebellion against the emperor
2. damage to imperial palaces or tombs

3. treason against the state
4. violence against or murder of one's kin
5. murder of one's wife or more than three members of a family
6. theft or damage of imperial or religious property
7. unfilial acts toward one's parents or senior kin
8. murder of one's superior or teacher[12]

As can be seen by the list, the three most severe transgressions involve crimes against the imperial line (including the graves and palaces of the imperial ancestors) and insurrection against the state/emperor, while the remaining "abominations" refer to crimes that particularly transgress the Confucian-influenced vision of a sacred social order.

Following the list of the most severe transgressions, the code spells out a taxonomy of available punishment. The five punishments listed in the *ritsu* code follow closely those prescribed in the Chinese codes on which the Japanese *ritsuryō* were based.[13] Arranged from least to most severe, the punishments read as follows:

| | |
|---|---|
| 1. whipping (light stick) (*chizai*) | 5 grades: 10 through 50 blows |
| 2. flogging (heavy stick) (*jōzai*) | 5 grades: 60 through 100 blows |
| 3. penal servitude (*zuzai*) | 5 grades: 1-, 1.5-, 2-, 2.5-, and 3-year sentences |
| 4. exile (*ruzai*) | 3 grades: near, medium, and far |
| 5. execution (*shizai*) | 2 grades: strangulation and beheading |

As indicated by the list, while there were five basic categories of punishment, each category was further divided into several grades, resulting in some twenty different levels of punishment that could be correlated to the specific severity of different transgressions. In the case of capital punishment, for example, both beheading and strangulation are mentioned, but beheading was considered the more severe of the two and was thus handed down for the most severe transgressions.[14] The five categories consequently made available a detailed system of punishment for the legal authorities, who then had to consider for every transgression a complex set of factors (including the relative social status of both offender and victim); these factors could either increase or decrease the severity of the punishment given. A crime normally punishable by death through strangulation, for example, might find that punishment increased in severity to death through beheading or mitigated to far exile, depending on the context surrounding the incident.[15]

With regard to exile, the Japanese codes borrowed the Chinese concept of banishment from the capital to near, medium, and distant locations. One difference was that while the Tang codes prescribed exact measurements for the amount of distance considered near, medium, and far (2,000, 2,500, and 3,000 *li,* equivalent to 1,000, 1,250, and 1,500 kilometers), the Japanese code leaves the exact distance unspecified. In actual practice, the state chose locations that had customarily been used for exile prior to the completion of the *ritsuryō* codes; an edict by Emperor Shōmu recorded in the *Shoku Nihongi* from 724 attempted to codify the corresponding provinces as follows: near exile: Echizen, Aki; medium exile: Suō, Iyo; distant exile: Izu, Awa, Hitachi, Sado, Oki, Tosa. An examination of the ancient provinces shows that these corresponded roughly to near, medium, and far distances from the ancient capital, though not with the exact measurements mandated in the Chinese codes.[16]

Regarding the correlation of punishments with transgressions, capital punishment is mandated for the four most severe *hachigyaku:* for rebellion against the emperor, destruction of imperial palaces or tombs, insurrection against the state, and violence against or murder of one's kin.[17] Execution is also mandated in some cases of the fifth abomination as, for example, in the murder of three persons from the same family, but for this transgression exile also appears as a punishment, as for the crime of plotting the murder of certain members of one's own family. The punishment of exile begins appearing more consistently with the sixth abomination, in response to such crimes as stealing articles from shrines or causing damage to great shrines (*taisha*). Exile was also considered when a more serious transgression occurred with mitigating considerations. We should clearly note, however, that the text of the penal codes explicitly mandated execution for a variety of transgressions and that the early court's own histories indicate that capital punishment was indeed regularly carried out.[18]

Over time, however, the actual implementation of the codes came to differ in significant ways from the system envisioned within them, as with the cessation of execution beginning in the early ninth century. As a result, when execution was customarily abolished for a majority of the Heian period, exile rose to become the paramount sanction practiced by the Heian state, a position disproportionate to that imagined by the original drafters of the Japanese penal codes.

## THE RITSURYŌ CODES: A METAPHYSICS AND MICROPHYSICS OF POWER

In addition to a formal reading of the *ritsuryō* codes themselves, we should also consider the social and cultural contexts surrounding the development and promulgation of those codes. As scholars of law have repeatedly shown, legal codes frequently rest on larger cultural assumptions not explicitly articulated in the codes themselves. In order then to explore more fully the role of exile in the legal imagination, in this section I draw upon two theorists whose work can help illuminate the worldview and concerns of the early Japanese codes. I begin with the legal anthropologist Rebecca R. French, focusing on her concept of legal cosmologies, before turning to Michel Foucault's studies concerning the cessation of execution. After this discussion of the imagination of exile within the *ritsuryō* codes, I move on in the following section to examine how the codes were actually practiced historically.

In her studies of Tibetan secular law, Rebecca French offers a particularly vivid reminder of the way legal codes can both be grounded in and help to perpetuate religiously influenced worldviews. Her work on the Tibetan "legal cosmology" is especially helpful because by showing how legal codes—no less than myths—can be enmeshed in metaphysical discourses, she underscores the principle that the anthropology of law must begin by tracing the worldviews, assumptions, rituals, and practices that frequently lie behind a culture's understanding and practice of law.[19]

In *The Golden Yoke,* her work on the Tibetan "secular" legal code, French defined her concept of legal cosmology generally as "a system of thought and practice about how the world operates."[20] Elsewhere, she's elaborated that this "system of thought and practice" provides a kind of "cultural backdrop" consisting of a host of beliefs and principles never explicitly articulated in the law codes themselves: "myths, relations of power, concepts of time, space and personal identity, the legal rituals, history, religious principles, reasoning patterns, procedures, available roles, symbols—a backdrop which I call *Legal Cosmology.*"[21]

Although the subject of French's study is the secular legal code used in Tibet prior to 1959 (as opposed to the religious code, based on the *Vinaya,* which traditionally governed the Tibetan Buddhist monastic order), her work is concerned to show that even in the *secular* legal system, a deeply embedded Buddhist worldview pervaded the legal vision: "Non-Western ideas of reality and illusion, karma, the cyclical nature of rebirth, nonduality, and multiple concepts of time and causation directly affect Tibetan understandings of the nature of law."[22] As she explains with regard to Tibet, this "cosmology" can be seen in such areas as the kinds of statements legal actors made about the world and about the law or in the principles to which actors made recourse in their argumentation. The result, she writes, is that in the actual practice of legal argumentation and adjudication, Tibetan legal specialists could make arguments based on the future lives of the deceased, or Tibetan judges could make decisions that took into account the possible rebirths of the guilty party, among other examples.

While French's work concerns the Tibetan legal system, her findings can help illuminate our study of the *ritsuryō* codes used in early Japan. As with the Tibetan example, multiple systems of law existed in Nara and Heian Japan. For the Buddhist ecclesiastical order in Japan, as in Tibet, there was a partially self-governing code, again linked to the *Vinaya,* the authority for which ultimately rested on its claim to represent the teaching of the historical Buddha.[23] The larger political realm, however, was governed by the state's *ritsuryō* code, which might cautiously be called a "secular" code in contrast to the Buddhist ecclesiastical laws.

As in Tibet, Japan's *ritsuryō* code also reflected a "legal cosmology," resting on metaphysical assumptions about the nature of the universe and the place of humanity within it. In contrast to the Tibetan case, however, the "system of thought and practice" that lay behind the Japanese codes reflected less a Buddhist worldview and more the Chinese cultural origins of Japan's codes. These origins combined a Confucian-inspired vision of the social order, a legalist inclination toward the precise codification of law, and yin-yang and five phases cosmological theories, all of which influenced the development of the Chinese codes during the Sui and Tang dynasties.[24]

As a result, a fundamental concern in the codes of both China and Japan centers around the proper maintenance of social order, premised on vertical relations of hierarchy and subordination, which themselves are presented as reflections of a larger cosmic principle in which "heaven overspreads, and earth upbears."[25] This order is further reproduced in the archetypal Confucian relationships: those between ruler and subject, husband and wife, father and son, elder and younger brother, and between friends.[26] In this system, the correct functioning of each set of relations was portrayed as crucial not just to the proper ordering of society but to the harmonious functioning of the cosmos as well, including the proper course of the seasons and spheres.

Indeed, the metaphysical vision of a hierarchic social order was a principal reason behind the appeal of the Chinese codes to the nascent Japanese state. As Ryūichi Abe has written, "The emperor's authority derived from his being the Son of Heaven who, relying on Heaven's mandate, rules the world with his virtue, the virtue of the father, for all of humanity. It was, therefore, the master metaphor of familial coherence of the Confucian discourse that justified the traditional authority of the Japanese emperor."[27]

Many areas could be chosen to illustrate the metaphysical and social principles informing the Chinese codes—as, for example, with the regulations concerning mourning relations that helped to enforce "in a striking and obvious fashion" the notion of filial responsibility.[28] In the area of punishment as well, the codes sought to align common practice with cosmological "truth." Reflecting the influence of yin-yang and five phases theory, the codes stipulated that capital punishment—associated with yin—could be carried out only during the yin seasons of fall and winter.[29] Examples such as this underscore the fact that the *ritsuryō* codes, no less than the Tibetan legal codes, were grounded in a legal cosmology—a set of assumptions, beliefs, and practices about the cosmic order and about the implications of this cosmic order for human relations. As one Chinese text put the matter succinctly, "the sages made the five punishments in imitation of the five elements."[30]

One danger of invoking a legal cosmology implicit within the early Japanese codes is the error of assuming that the codes merely reflected the existing worldview of the early Japanese court. In fact, the *ritsuryō* codes themselves were adopted as a tool to effect far-reaching changes in early Japan: to enable a major redistribution of power and to charter a new kind of polity in the form of a centralized bureaucratic state. We need to understand better, therefore, how the codes sought to inscribe a particular metaphysics of power across the archipelago by means of this particular vision of law. To help us understand this process of transformation, we can draw upon the work of Michel Foucault, whose own studies of the cessation of execution provide valuable insights not only into the microphysics of power more generally but also by extension into the role of exile in the early Japanese legal imagination.

In his classic work *Discipline and Punish,* Foucault articulated several points—not merely about punishment and law but about power, knowledge, and classificatory systems more generally—that can help illuminate our study of early Japanese law. Among Foucault's fundamental assertions was the idea that penal systems, far from being the sole or even primary sector of society devoted to repressive or disciplinary measures, are no more than one element in a vast network of institutions that serve to implement a "micro-physics of power," one that focuses particularly on the bodies of society's members. Though the exact nature and source of *power* in Foucault's work remains vaguely defined at best, two aspects of his analysis are particularly suggestive for the study of law in early Japan: the notion of "penality" as merely one element within the larger field of the operation of power, and the related concept of "positive" as well as repressive dimensions of punishment and power.

It's helpful to recall that Foucault's study of law and punishment reflected a larger concern on his part to trace the disciplinary foundations of contemporary society. As with this chapter concerning exile in the Heian period, Foucault took as his subject the disappearance of public execution in early modern France. While others had read into the cessation of public executions a narrative of progress, Foucault argued instead that the older system of punishment had merely given way to equally disturbing modes of discipline. In place of older techniques, he believed a modern system of "penality" had taken hold not just of the bodies of the incarcerated but of their "souls," giving rise to ever-deeper levels of subjugation, in part through that system's connection to disciplines of knowledge and understanding.[31] Explaining what may have seemed a counterintuitive approach to the disappearance of execution and torture, Foucault argued, "We must first rid ourselves of the illusion that penality is above all (if not exclusively) a means of reducing crime. . . . We must analyse rather the 'concrete systems of punishment' . . . we must situate them in their field of operation, in which the punishment of crime is not the sole element."[32] Elsewhere, clarifying his approach in a series of methodological dicta, he stated that we should "analyse punitive methods . . . as techniques possessing their own specificity in the more general field of other ways of exercising power. *Regard punishment as a political tactic.*"[33]

Notwithstanding the distance in time and culture between early modern France and Heian Japan, Foucault's approach is suggestive for our study of early Japanese law. With regard to the early legal codes, we may first underscore the point that the *ritsuryō* codes should be viewed not so much as reflecting a particular stage in the "evolution" of Japanese systems of law and punishment but more specifically as part of a distinct project to consolidate and wield power on the part of the early Japanese state. Punishment in the *ritsuryō* codes should therefore be analyzed not simply as a means of reducing "crime," but in the context of the particular vision of power desired by the state.[34] Because the codes envisioned nothing less than a new order of power, superimposed upon an older network of social relations, we may then ask in what ways specific sanctions such as exile served to assert and inscribe this particular order. In this light, we can see that by correlating various degrees of transgression against the social order with various degrees of removal from the courtly center, exile provided a powerful means by which the centralizing vision of the *ritsuryō* state was conceived, articulated, and mapped onto the archipelago.

*Discipline and Punish* also contains some of Foucault's most suggestive writing about what he termed the "positive effects" of power. In Foucault's understanding, penal technologies should be understood as not merely repressive but as part of a larger system that produces "positive" effects. In another one of his theoretical dicta, he advised, "Do not concentrate the study of the punitive mechanism on their 'repressive' effects alone, on their 'punishment' aspects alone, *but situate them in a whole series of their possible positive effects*."[35] And elsewhere, he wrote that "We must show that punitive measures are not simply 'negative' mechanisms that make it possible to repress, to prevent, to exclude, to eliminate; *but that they are linked to a whole series of positive and useful effects which it is their task to support*."[36] In Foucault's somewhat novel understanding, power had a dual nature that was both positive and negative. In discussing the body as the site of the inscription of this field of power, he wrote, "The body becomes a useful force only if it is both a *productive* body and a *subjected* body."[37] This double-sided view of the circulation of power is especially illuminating for the study of law within Japanese court society.

Considering just one aspect of the social order of *ritsuryō* Japan—the state's construction of a governing "center" and its peripheries—we may note that court society functioned as a vertically stratified hierarchy organized around a courtly center, most significantly represented in the figure of the sovereign. The higher one's rank in court society, the closer proximity one was allowed to the emperor, whose "sacrality" was thus established (as Durkheim might say) by being that which was "set apart." As is often remarked, at the higher levels of court society were those deemed "above the clouds" (*kumo no uebito*), nobility who were allowed entrance to the Courtier's Hall (Tenjō no ma) of the Seiryōden, the emperor's residence within the imperial palace where official business of state was carried out.[38] In a positive sense, then, we may say that the hierarchic and concentric structure of Heian society made it possible to invest subjects with power along a vertical axis of proximity to the throne.

Yet the "positive" effects of this vertical structure of power were always linked to the negative potential for their possible withdrawal. This constituted the repressive dimension of power: the center toward which subjects aspired was the same center from which they could be excluded. Exclusion from the center, as conveyed in the penal codes by the sanction of exile, thus represented dislocation from the sources of meaning and power that the court hierarchy ordinarily worked to construct and maintain.

The negative, repressive dimensions of power in Japanese court society were thus inextricably linked to positive dimensions, both of which circulated like twin currents through the social body. Or, as Foucault stated in slightly different terms, we may say that the "kingly" body and the body of the "condemned" represented two aspects of a single, "nervous" system: "At the opposite pole [from the body of the king] one might imagine placing the body of the condemned man; he, too, has his legal status; he gives rise to his own ceremonial and he calls forth a whole theoretical discourse, not in order to ground the 'surplus power' possessed by the person of the sovereign, but in order to code the 'lack of power' with which those subjected to punishment are marked. *In the darkest region of the political field the condemned man represents the symmetrical, inverted figure of the king.*"[39]

Understanding these twin currents helps to explain why the poetics of exile in Heian Japan frequently lingers over the exiled courtier's relation to the emperor, so often expressed through the trope of the emperor's robes, brought as a treasured keepsake into exile. Time and again, the poetry of exile focuses on the lingering fragrance of the imperial robes, clung to by the courtier as the only trace of the imperial body available to them in exile. Such a sign provided a particularly resonant trope for the fracturing of the social order experienced by members of the court in exile, signifying at once their exclusion from power as well as the fading traces of their former proximity to it.[40]

As we move on to examine the historical implementation of the *ritsuryō* codes in the next section, several points taken from the study of law and punishment can help orient our discussion. First, recalling Rebecca French's notion of legal cosmologies, we may say that every concrete system of power imagined within law proceeds from and implies a *metaphysics,* a system of thought and practice about how the world operates; the work of the codes consists of aligning this vision of reality with the practice of everyday life. From this perspective, the vision of sovereignty asserted within the early Japanese codes was no less transcendent than that envisioned within royal myth-histories such as the *Kojiki* and *Nihon shoki* themselves.

Second, following Foucault, we may say that every system of law attempts to employ specific techniques—a *microphysics of power*—to cast individual bodies within a larger network of power relations. The technology of punishment in any system of law should then be examined in connection with this particular vision of power, within a system that manifests both repressive and productive dimensions. From the perspective of such a system, exile from the Japanese court illustrates particularly well Foucault's assertion that "the condemned man represents the symmetrical, inverted figure of the king."

## THE *RITSURYŌ* CODES: ENACTMENT, ADAPTATION, AND AMENDMENT

Up to this point we've explored the vision of power imagined within the *ritsuryō* codes. An entirely different discussion involves the actual implementation of the codes, including the radical changes in legal practice that occurred during the Heian period. In order to explore these issues with regard to the practice of execution and exile, it's helpful first to distinguish several different stages in the implementation of the codes. To do so, in this section I divide the question of implementation into three categories: the general question regarding the degree to which the codes were implemented, the process of adaptation from the Chinese legal models, and the issue of amendments to the codes following their promulgation in Japan.

Among earlier scholars of Japanese history in the West, an influential and skeptical view regarding the codes was expressed by George Sansom, who held that the codes attempted from the start an ill-fated marriage of Chinese bureaucratic forms and Japanese social conditions. In Sansom's view, "We may say that political history from the time of the Taihō reform (701) is essentially a record of the gradual breakdown of the elaborate, logical, symmetrical system of government that had been borrowed from China by ardent admirers without adequate experience of the problems of civil administration. . . . In fact it is scarcely correct to say that it broke down, seeing that hardly any of the provisions of the codes which dealt with land ownership and land revenue had been fully observed since they were promulgated. In a general way this can be accounted for by saying that the Chinese system was unsuited to Japan, that it was premature to impose upon an unregulated and expanding society a complicated procedure which could not possibly work where communications were poor and where there were not enough competent and reliable local officials to enforce the law impartially."[41]

Since Sansom's time, however, a good deal of work has been done on the nature of the early Japanese state and on the function of the early law codes. One of the more important advancements was the recovery by archeologists of troves of *mokkan,* wooden tablets used for record keeping during the *ritsuryō* period, which provide a previously unavailable archive of document artifacts from that period.[42]

Scholarship that utilizes findings from the *mokkan* discoveries has led to a more generous assessment of the importance of the early law codes and the degree to which the codes were actually put into practice. Arguing against the opinion expressed by Sansom, Joan Piggott, in her study of the development of kingship in Japan, asserts that the codes in Japan were no less than the "regalia of a Chinese-style state,"[43] and that their successful implementation can be observed in the fact that "local elites from east to west competed for official appointments, obeyed commands to construct provincial and district headquarters, carried out registration, collected tribute and oversaw its dispatch to the capital, constructed Buddhist temples and roads, and opened new public rice fields in response to proclamations by the heavenly Sovereign."[44] The most successful period of the codes, Piggott thus argues, "witnessed the full penetration by integrative *ritsuryō* networks to the frontiers of the insular realm. As a result the *tennō's* government grew substantially more powerful."[45]

While Piggott argues for recognition of the "penetration of integrative *ritsuryō* networks" across the archipelago, at the same time her work seeks to improve our conception of the centripetalizing function of the early Japanese state. In Piggott's view, the term "centralized administration" is something of a misnomer, for Japanese rulers never imagined a state that could be governed by means of power simply imposed outwardly from the center. Instead, Piggott attributes the success of the *ritsuryō* system to its integration of elites both at the courtly center and at the periphery within a complex hierarchical network,[46] a network not merely imposed by the court onto the realm, but that instead was the result of a process of "negotiated settlement"[47] between capital and regional elites.

In this view, to a certain degree the *ritsuryō* codes served to routinize preexisting power relations, defining new titles and offices for central and regional elites that preserved their status while rationalizing their authority in the idiom of a new hierarchical bureaucracy. "Lacking the means to displace local chieftains," Piggott writes, "central authorities relied on them as intermediaries."[48] Regional elites in the countryside remained substantially in control of their local sphere, but in the new system such control was legitimized by their position within a hierarchy of power articulated in the *ryō* (civil and administrative) portion of the codes. As a result, in Piggott's terms, the state was not exactly *centralized:* "Alliance and symbiosis among contemporary elites throughout the realm formed the basis on which the *ritsuryō* process vertically integrated—centered, rather than centralized—the *tennō's* realm."[49] While the codes envisioned a society *centered* under the figure of the sovereign residing in the imperial capital, the actual power wielded by that center was a matter of negotiation, rather than imposition.

In addition to the question of how successfully the *ritsuryō* codes were implemented, a further debate among scholars of Japanese law concerns the degree to which the Japanese codes replicated the Chinese codes from which they were borrowed, or whether they reflect significant transformations of the Chinese models. This debate is primarily a question of emphasis, however—it is clear that the Japanese compilers made conscious changes to the codes in an effort to adapt the Chinese framework to the Japanese cultural and political context.[50]

Adaptations made to the Chinese codes related to diverse areas of Japanese social and political practice. As Ross Bender notes, a clear example of the adaptive process is the founding of the Jingikan, or Council of Divinities, "charged with oversight of native (Shintō) institutions and clergy . . . [which] had no parallel in the Chinese bureaucratic structure."[51] Similarly, in the area of marriage customs, the Tang codes dictated a system of exogamy, where marriage between members of the same clan sharing the same surname was not allowed. By contrast, in the Japanese case—where endogamy was an accepted practice—the codes were drafted in some cases to *prevent* marriage outside the clan. Certain women of imperial descent, for example, were effectively "forbidden to marry outside the imperial clan."[52]

In the area of punishments, scholars of Japanese law have frequently stated that while the compilers of the Japanese codes made adaptations to the Chinese administrative codes, the penal codes were imported almost without change—yet this is not entirely accurate.[53] As mentioned earlier, the Chinese codes classify the most severe transgressions imaginable into ten abominations, while in the Japanese case these have been reduced by two, omitting prohibitions regarding incest, for example, which in Japan were not subject to the same taboos.

While the compilers of the Japanese *ritsuryō* codes clearly made changes to the Chinese models, it's important to distinguish this initial process of adaptation from a third topic: the process of amendment that commenced after the Japanese codes were already enacted. Almost as soon as the earliest complete *ritsuryō* code was enacted in Japan (as mentioned above, this occurred no later than the Taihō ritsuryō of 702), officials in the court bureaucracy began issuing revisions and regulations to the codes in a continuing attempt to make the laws practical within the social, political, and cultural context of early Japan. It should also be noted that this process of amendment itself followed Chinese legal custom, in which amendments were issued in two categories known as *kyaku* and *shiki*. *Kyaku* referred to "revisions" that actually altered or adjusted a law, while *shiki* referred to "procedures," the detailed provisions for carrying out certain laws whose regulations had raised questions of interpretation. Both *kyaku* and *shiki* were legally binding and were issued either in the form of edicts by the sovereign or as directives from the Council of State.[54]

As an example, within five years of the enactment of the Taihō code the first *kyaku* were issued, revising the code's articles concerning taxation and the structure of the bureaucracy.[55] In 762, the Nara court for the first time ordered the compilation of the various *shiki* issued up to that point into a collection, although if it was produced, such a collection is no longer extant. In 820, the Heian court produced the Kōnin kyakushiki, the compilation of all *kyaku* revisions and *shiki* procedures up to that point.[56] Further collections of *kyaku* and *shiki* continued to be compiled during the first half of the Heian period, culminating in the famous Engi period collection of *shiki* compiled in 927. While the final *ritsuryō* code (the Yōrō ritsuryō) had been enacted by the Nara court in 757, the compilation of legal revisions and procedures continued until 927, after which there were no further attempts to codify law during the Heian period.[57]

For some scholars, the fact that so many revisions and procedures came to be issued during the Nara and Heian periods has been taken as a sign that the state continually battled to make the legal codes suitable for the political and social conditions in early Japan and to make them acceptable to the various groups upon whom the state depended for the successful administration of government. Some see this as a battle that the state ultimately lost, as the vision of a *ritsuryō* state centered around the figure of a divine sovereign eventually transformed by the end of the Heian period into what some see as a kind of tripartite system of governance shared between the imperial court, the *bakufu* warrior government, and independent religious institutions.[58]

In my view, it's important to keep in mind the far-reaching changes brought about by the implementation of the codes, while acknowledging at the same time the tension that always existed between the vision of power imagined within the *ritsuryō* codes and the ability of the state to enact that vision. Even as scholars such as Piggott see the Nara period as the height of the implementation of the codes, an era when a sovereign could garner support from throughout the land for monumental building projects like the Great Buddha at Tōdaiji, others point out that the state was ultimately unable to finish construction on the Chinese-inspired capital in Nara, and even following the move to Heian-kyō, work on that capital was abandoned half finished by 819.[59] By the early ninth century the imperial treasury was nearly exhausted, and the labor necessary to erect the architecture of state was increasingly difficult to obtain.[60] Similarly, by the mid-ninth century, many of the official positions originally detailed in the *ritsuryō* codes were unoccupied, another sign that the realm was growing increasingly "unmoored" from its *ritsuryō* foundations.[61]

## FROM EXECUTION TO EXILE IN THE HEIAN PERIOD

Keeping in mind the debates surrounding the adaptation and enactment of the *ritsuryō* codes, we may now focus more specifically on changes regarding the practice of execution and exile. As mentioned at the outset of the chapter, it is commonly noted that the practice of capital punishment in Heian Japan ceased under Emperor Saga's rule, making the killing of Fujiwara Nakanari during the first full year of Saga's reign (810) the last execution of a member of court for nearly 350 years. Because Nakanari's death occurred as a result of an attempted coup of Emperor Saga—a conflict known as the Kusuko Incident—this event bears further examination as we move on to discuss reasons for the cessation of execution.

The Kusuko Incident (Kusuko no hen) occurred in connection with the abdication of Emperor Heizei in 809, following a period of illness. Heizei's younger brother then ascended the throne as Emperor Saga, but when Saga himself fell ill in 810, a plot developed for Heizei to reclaim the throne. Chief among those held responsible for the plan were Heizei's consort Fujiwara no Kusuko and her brother Nakanari, members of the ceremonial branch (Shikike) of the Fujiwara clan. Together with Heizei, they actually attempted to move the capital back to Nara and to reenthrone Heizei in the old seat of government, from where he once again began issuing decrees. For a brief moment in 810, there existed two "emperors" in two separate "capitals," each pressing their claims to the throne.

Saga responded to the attempted coup by arresting Nakanari and ordering the banishment of Kusuko.[62] In response, Heizei and Kusuko tried to flee to eastern Japan in an attempt to raise support, but they were soon captured by Saga's forces. Heizei was allowed to continue residing in Nara as a retired emperor but was forced to take the tonsure. Kusuko is said to have committed suicide, though some believe she was forced to drink poison.[63] Kusuko's brother and accomplice Fujiwara no Nakanari was executed for treason.[64] Interestingly, Nakanari was shot to death with arrows rather than being dispatched by either of the methods prescribed for the execution of those guilty of treason according to the *ritsuryō* codes.

Japanese scholars are nearly unanimous in stating that following the killing of Nakanari, execution ceased to be practiced for the next 347 years, throughout the majority of the Heian period. According to no less an authority than Inoue Mitsusada, chief editor of the modern edition of the *ritsuryō* codes, "If one examines examples of the performance of executions under the *ritsuryō* legal system, it is said that from the first year of the Kōnin period [810] when Fujiwara Nakanari was sentenced to death during the Kusuko Rebellion, until the Hōgen Rebellion three hundred and forty-seven years later, none occurred."[65] Similarly, in a major reference work on the Heian period, Takashio Hiroshi writes, "From the first year of the Kōnin period when Fujiwara Nakanari was punished with death, until the first year of the Hōgen period [1156] when Minamoto Tameyoshi and others were beheaded, for three hundred and forty-seven years, the performance [of capital punishment] did not happen."[66] Takashio goes on to state that in terms of legal procedure, *sentences* of execution were still handed down during the Heian period, but they were always accompanied by a decree of partial amnesty, lowering the sentence one grade to distant exile.[67]

The execution of Nakanari for treason was fully within the provisions of the *ritsuryō* code. The question thus remains why his was the last instance of execution for the next 347 years, in spite of a number of later cases that were also considered transgressions against the state and that would normally mandate capital punishment. There are no documents from Saga's reign explaining the decision to cease executions, however, and as a result, Japanese scholars have offered a variety of theories to explain the change, though no consensus on the issue has ever been reached. Each of the principle theories is worth examining in turn.

Ishio Yoshihisa is representative of those Japanese scholars who believe that significant elements of archaic Japanese religious custom continued to be influential even after the early state moved to adopt Chinese-based legal procedures. According to Ishio, in the archaic paradigm that predated the adoption of Chinese-styled laws, punishment was regarded as a form of expiation (*harae*) for transgressions committed (*tsumi*), an expiation that required both offerings and disciplinary measures.[68] In Ishio's view, the switch from execution to exile can be explained in part because exile was in a sense equivalent to capital punishment, in that both were regarded as divine punishments for transgressions against the cosmic order: "In Japan, exile was like execution: both were punishments based on the principle of 'divine sanction' (*kami no seisai*)."[69] Thus, he argues, the shift from the sanction of execution to distant exile during Saga's realm must be understood within the context of a fluid boundary between the two punishments, especially because banishment resulted not infrequently in the death of the offender.

In other words, according to Ishio, there *wasn't* any great change effected during Saga's reign—simply the substitution of one punishment for another, both having more or less the same intended effect. One problem with this theory, however, is that it still does not explain why the court would avoid one punishment in favor of another: If the two were truly regarded fluidly, it would seem not to matter which sanction was enacted, and we could expect to see both punishments used without preference for one over another. More glaringly, Ishio's interpretation does not explain why the court would continue to hand down sentences of capital punishment, only then to immediately commute the sentence one degree to distant exile.

Another explanation commonly offered for the cessation of capital punishment involves the influence of Buddhism upon Japanese court culture, and specifically the ameliorating effect of the Buddhist precept against taking life on the state's practice of execution. This explanation is mentioned—though not necessarily supported with evidence—by Ishio Yoshihisa, Inoue Mitsusada, and in some reference texts that examine the topic of capital punishment and exile.[70] The explanation is rejected, however, by another scholar of Japanese law, Ishii Ryōsuke, who argues that the notion of Buddhism as a causal agent for the cessation of execution is logically insufficient: If Japan was not alone in adopting Buddhism, he asks, why wouldn't other countries influenced by both Buddhism and Chinese law have followed the same path of rejecting capital punishment?[71]

Ishii's rejection is itself problematic, however: Japan's history contains numerous examples in which the culture synthesized elements of Buddhism in unique ways. Yet the theory of Buddhism's ameliorating influence on execution in Japan does leave important questions unexplained. Most importantly, why did the Heian court begin to avoid capital punishment at this particular time? Certainly, the influence of Buddhism in Japan had been at work for more than two centuries prior to Saga's reign, and execution was frequently practiced during that period. Further, if there is any evidence for a "gentling" trend in Heian culture, the quote cited at the outset of this chapter regarding Emperor Saga would seem to credit this to an embrace of Confucian rather than Buddhist paradigms. As the *Nihon Ryōiki* mentions in the context of the cessation, Saga proclaimed his era one of "spreading *benevolence,*" citing a fundamental Confucian value regarding the essential quality of an ideal sovereign.

The solution offered by Ishii Ryōsuke in place of Buddhist influence is no more tenable, however, as he falls back on a discourse regarding the uniqueness of the Japanese spirit. While rejecting Buddhism as the determining factor on the change in legal practice, he asserts instead that it was none other than the Japanese national spirit that resulted in the avoidance of execution: "The fact that capital punishment did not occur over a period of nearly three hundred and fifty years is probably due to the gentleness of our national character."[72] Again, we might ask why this perceived "gentleness" did not assert itself either before or after the cessation of execution. And, while it might be conceivable that certain factors coalesced during this period to produce a *culture* less prone to corporeal violence, Ishii's assertion based on an essential Japanese *character* does not begin to address the specific historic elements that might have coalesced at this time to change Heian legal practice.

Yet another explanation for the cessation of execution in the Heian period has been offered by Rikō Mitsuo, a scholar of early Japanese law who has written specifically on the topic of exile within the *ritsuryō* system. According to Rikō, the abolition of capital punishment did not occur, as some have claimed, out of any Buddhist sense of compassion or moral reverence for life. Instead, Rikō asserts, the cessation of executions resulted in large measure out of the fear of wrathful spirits of the dead (*onryō*), the religious movement that became increasingly influential during the Nara and Heian periods. Therefore, Rikō states, the change that occurred from Saga's reign onward should not properly be referred to as an *abolition* or even a *suspension* of capital punishment but simply its *avoidance* whenever possible among the nobility.[73]

One strength of Rikō's theory is that the period during which executions ceased correlates directly with the era in which the cult of vengeful spirits gained wide popularity. As discussed in chapter 4, the *goryō* cults involved the pacification and worship of the spirits of particular nobles who had suffered untimely deaths as a result of political intrigue and who were believed to possess the power to haunt those responsible for their downfall, as well as the more general population around the capital, by means of plagues and other disasters. The first member of court usually classified among the *goryō* deities was Prince Sawara (posthumously named Emperor Sudō), who died in 785 during the reign of Saga's father, Emperor Kammu. Further vengeful spirits arose under the rule of Saga's brother and predecessor, Emperor Heizei, when a prince and his mother committed suicide for their participation in a plot against the throne.[74] And the first state-sponsored spirit-pacification festival, or *goryō-e*—which some take as a belated recognition by the state of the popularity of *goryō* worship—was sponsored in 863, a mere twenty years after Saga's death. Thus, Rikō's theory has the advantage of explaining the suspension of capital punishment in light of a contemporaneous historical development—the emerging *goryō* cult—with which it overlapped.

Rikō maintains, in fact, that executions *did* occasionally take place in Heian Japan, though extremely rarely, and he cites three examples listed in the court chronicle the *Nihon Kiryaku* in which executions are recorded. Rikō points out that the three examples (in 985, 992, and 1024) were each carried out upon criminals who were not members of the court aristocracy, at the hands of low-level military or extra-legal police officers (*kebiishi*) acting under their own power, outside of the legal process requiring imperial consent.[75] Pursuing Rikō's lead, for example, the *Nihon Kiryaku* records that on 992/11/30 in the province of Awa, sixteen pirates were executed and their heads put on display (*kyō*).[76] The examples are significant, Rikō argues, not simply because they indicate the existence of the practice of execution but because in each case the *Nihon Kiryaku* mentions a reward given to the enforcing officer by the court for carrying out the execution. For Rikō, this detail suggests that the court did not abolish capital punishment out of a moral stance that precluded the taking of life, but rather due to the desire to avoid as much as possible any direct involvement in executions that might produce vengeful spirits. In Rikō's view, such aversion was not necessarily shared by military and police officials, especially in connection with the execution of lower-ranking members of society, and the rewards given to them indicate the court's tacit approval.[77]

As a result of Rikō's research, scholars must modify their views of the history of exile and execution in the Heian period. At the very least, the often-quoted figure of 347 years in which the death penalty was not practiced—a figure sometimes cited as the earliest period in world history for a state to abolish execution—requires reexamination.[78] Contrary to the overwhelming majority of scholarship on Heian Japanese legal practice, and notwithstanding cultural developments that led to the nearly complete cessation of execution, there appear to have been rare instances in the mid- and late Heian period when the state tacitly condoned the use of capital punishment.

## EXECUTION AND VENGEFUL SPIRITS IN THE *HŌGEN MONOGATARI*

As discussed above, no consensus exists on the exact reason either for the initial cessation of capital punishment under emperor Saga or for its long duration throughout the majority of the Heian period. This is partly due to the lack of documents on the topic from the court of Emperor Saga. Yet in the absence of records from the beginning of execution's avoidance, we may also look for evidence around the end of its suspension, taking note of the reaction by members of court society to the return of the practice. Such an examination leads us to the Hōgen no Ran, the conflict that vividly reintroduced execution to the capital after a period of some 347 years.

The Hōgen Disorder was a succession dispute that broke out following the death of retired emperor Toba in 1156 and that signaled in important ways the shifting balance of power between the imperial court and military houses toward the end of the Heian period. The dramatic changes set in motion by the conflict are hinted at in the passage quoted at the outset of this chapter from the *Hōgen monogatari,* a later retelling of the conflict and its aftermath. The opening of the narrative recounts Toba's last years, including his ominous encounter with an oracle in 1155 during a religious pilgrimage to Kumano, in which the oracle foretold his imminent death: "In autumn of next year you must die. After that the world will become like the turning over of this hand."[79]

Toba died the following year, and with the powerful retired emperor gone from the scene, a succession dispute erupted as Toba's elder son—retired emperor Sutoku—challenged the earlier accession to the throne of his younger brother, Go-Shirakawa.[80] Just as the dispute split the imperial house into two factions, it also proved uniquely divisive among the leading aristocratic and military families in the capital. Thus while Sutoku's military forces were led by Minamoto Tameyoshi (accompanied by his son Tametomo), Go-Shirakawa's forces were led by Tameyoshi's other son, Yoshitomo. And while Taira no Tadamasa joined Sutoku's forces, his nephew Kiyomori served Go-Shirakawa. As for the leading aristocratic family, Sutoku had the support of the head of the Fujiwara regent's line, Fujiwara Yorinaga (along with his father Tadazane), while Go-Shirakawa had the support of the regent himself, Yorinaga's brother Tadamichi.

The actual battle that constituted the Hōgen conflict lasted only a day, as Sutoku's forces in the capital were quickly overcome. While the highest-ranking leaders on both sides largely escaped injury, the notable exception was Fujiwara Yorinaga on Sutoku's side, who died after being shot with an arrow. Sutoku, captured while seeking asylum following the battle, was sentenced to exile and sent to Sanuki Province (now Kagawa Prefecture, on Shikoku) by order of his victorious younger brother, Emperor Go-Shirakawa. According to the retelling of the episode in the *Hōgen monogatari,* Sutoku, on his way into exile, passed through Suma—the exile location of such noted figures as Ariwara no Yukihira and the fictional Genji—where he is said to have added his own lament to the exile tradition: "What they call living, but separated from life—this must be it!"[81] He would die in exile in Sanuki eight years later, in 1164.

Rivaling the exile of an emperor as one of the most dramatic outcomes of the conflict were the executions carried out upon Sutoku's defeated forces, including his leading general, Minamoto Tameyoshi. Upon Sutoku's defeat and surrender, Tameyoshi sought clemency from the opposing military commander—his own son, Minamoto Yoshitomo. Yoshitomo, however, had been given an imperial command to execute Tameyoshi. Although the *Hōgen monogatari* states that Yoshitomo hesitated, protesting that he must either disobey an imperial command or commit one of the "five abominable crimes" of killing one's parent, the *monogatari* account may or may not be correct; in the end he fulfilled the command, enforcing his father's beheading.

Regarding the account of the conflict narrated in the *Hōgen monogatari,* it's difficult to assess the degree to which the sentiments and words attributed to historical figures in the tale align with historical reality. On the one hand, the *monogatari* offers a retrospective ordering of events, narrated at some distance from the conflict it describes. In addition, the tale represents a victor's history or, more accurately, a tale that sympathizes with the defeated side in the Hōgen, written with the knowledge that the Taira victors in the conflict (such as Kiyomori) would be vanquished at the hands of the Minamoto three decades later. Further, there are passages in the *monogatari* reflecting popular beliefs that only began circulating decades following the conflict. As one example, Yamada Yūji has shown that the episode depicting Sutoku writing a blood oath of revenge—on sutras copied by his own hand in exile—is based on a legend that isn't attested in the capital until 1183, nearly two decades after Sutoku's actual death.[82]

On the other hand, it's reasonable to assume that many of the sentiments expressed in the tale would have aligned with the feelings of those in the capital who supported Sutoku and his allies during the conflict and in defeat. In this regard, it's striking that the *Hōgen* narrative lingers not only over the execution of Tameyoshi but also over its historic significance, commenting on two things in particular. The first concerns the length of time that had passed since the sanction of execution was last carried out at court: "To propose and carry out death sentences which had been suspended ever since they executed Nakanari in the first year of Kōnin (810)—in exact terms, for twenty-six imperial reigns and three hundred forty-seven years—was excessively harsh."[83]

The second concerns how the execution of Tameyoshi by his son was perceived to violate a fundamental relationship within the Confucian moral order, an order that also underpinned the legal codes of the Japanese state. In the words of the *Hōgen* narrative, even in ages when execution had been allowed, there had never been one such as this: "Was not the matter of having Yoshitomo kill his own father a thing unheard of in previous ages? . . . Killing one's father under the mask of 'loyalty' is the greatest perversion of filial piety, it is the extreme of unrighteousness (*fukō no daigyaku, fugi no shigoku*). . . . But perhaps it was because [Yoshitomo] violated righteousness that . . . in the end, before very long, he brought ruin on himself."[84]

In addition to Tameyoshi's beheading, there were further repercussions for the defeated: approximately seventy other members of Sutoku's forces were also executed, including Yoshitomo's younger brothers; Tameyoshi's wife drowned herself, and Taira no Tadamasa was executed by his nephew, Kiyomori. Adding to the alarming acts on the part of the victors, the body of the minister of the left (Yorinaga) was exhumed in order to verify his death, then left exposed along the roadside. Returning to the *monogatari* for a litany of the events resulting from the conflict, an early version of the *Hōgen* text intones, "It was in the Hōgen Disorder there was a child who cut off his father's head, there was a nephew who cut off his uncle's head, there was a younger brother who exiled his older brother, there was a woman who drowned herself in grief. These things are unnatural events in the annals of Japan."[85]

In the historical account narrated by the *Hōgen monogatari,* while in the first third of the text the world is thrown into disorder by Sutoku's rebellion and while in the middle section this disorder leads to even greater transgressions by the victors, in the final third of the text a semblance of order is restored—at the hands of Sutoku's vengeful spirit. As the text moves toward its conclusion, one by one the victors in the Hōgen conflict begin to encounter retributions attributed to Sutoku's wrathful spirit (*onryō*). Significantly, that retribution extends far beyond those immediately responsible for Sutoku's exile: all of the leading figures associated with "unrighteousness" on Go-Shirakawa's side suffer Sutoku's vengeance. Thus Yoshitomo, who had his father beheaded, meets an early death in the provinces. The corpse of Shinzei—the counselor who had advocated Tameyoshi's beheading despite the reluctance of other ministers and who was later killed—is dug up and displayed along the highway. And finally, Taira no Kiyomori (who had beheaded his own uncle) and Emperor Go-Shirakawa each suffer their own setbacks and personal tragedies in the following years. Within the *monogatari,* such actions are ascribed to the vengeful spirit of the deceased emperor in exile: "People said that this was no ordinary thing, it was the curse of Sutoku-in."[86]

The shocked tones that accompany the return of execution to the capital in the pages of the *Hōgen monogatari*—and the fact that the ruin of those responsible was attributed to the work of a vengeful spirit—suggest an anxiety connecting execution and vengeful spirits that may offer a clue to the earlier suspension of execution during Emperor Saga's reign. While it would be possible to attribute Sutoku's vengeance simply to his own defeat and death in exile, it's striking that his retribution was believed directed against all those who—from the perspective of the losing side in the Hōgen Disorder—were responsible for acts of "extreme unrighteousness."

Not only in the account provided by the *Hōgen monogatari* but in the historical life of the capital as well, it's clear that a *goryō* cult to Sutoku began emerging in the years following his death in exile in 1164. As with the case of Michizane, this appears to have resulted from efforts led both by Sutoku's supporters—whose reentry into court society was greatly assisted by Sutoku's rehabilitation—and by those principally responsible for his demise: in this case, the now retired emperor Go-Shirakawa. The first traces of an emerging *goryō* cult to Sutoku can be seen in the year 1177, following a year in which several of Go-Shirakawa's close family members died and just after Go-Shirakawa's plot to depose Taira no Kiyomori had been exposed, leading to Go-Shirakawa's own house arrest. In the eighth month of 1177, the retired emperor responded in ways familiar from the pacification of other vengeful spirits. He first ordered that Sutoku no longer be referred to as the Sanuki-in (roughly, "the retired emperor in exile") but as he is still known today: Sutoku ("reverent virtue"). Additionally, he ordered that a series of eight lectures on the *Lotus Sutra* be offered to Sutoku at Jōshōji, a temple in the capital personally established by Sutoku in 1139. And finally, he ordered that Fujiwara Yorinaga—Sutoku's ally who had been mortally wounded in the Hōgen conflict—be restored posthumously to his former rank and office.[87]

Perhaps spurred by new rumors of the existence of an oath of vengeance written by Sutoku using his own blood, in 1183 Go-Shirakawa further ordered a new shrine constructed for the pacification of both Sutoku and Yorinaga at the site of Sutoku's residence during the Hōgen rebellion (the Shirakawa Palace); the shrine was completed by the third month of 1184. Later that same year, Go-Shirakawa added another shrine to Sutoku at Sutoku's temple, Jōshōji. Finally in 1191, after Go-Shirakawa himself fell ill, only a year before his own death, he further ordered the construction of an image hall (*miedō*) for memorial rites to Sutoku at the site of his tomb in exile in Sanuki. Immediately following Go-Shirakawa's death, actions attributed to Sutoku's vengeful spirit appear to have quieted down. Not only within the textual horizon of the *Hōgen monogatari* but also for those in the capital concerned with such things, a semblance of order appears to have been momentarily restored.[88]

## CONCLUSION

As discussed in chapter 1, one lens by which to view the social configuration of the early Japanese court is through the "classical dynastic model" of community described by Benedict Anderson, in which "kingship organizes everything around a high centre . . . and sovereignties faded imperceptibly [at the margins]."[89] Certainly the legal codes adopted by the *ritsuryō* state imagined such a community—a hierarchical realm centered around the figure of a heavenly sovereign—and during the *ritsuryō* era the state exerted great effort to transform the archipelago in line with this vision.

As Anderson noted, a crucial feature of the classical dynastic model was its treatment of space. In contrast to the modern state, which seeks to overspread its influence homogeneously over every unit of terrain,[90] in the older model envisioned at the Japanese court the sense of power and prestige created by court society dissipated as distance from the center increased. As shown in this chapter, the sanction of exile within the *ritsuryō* codes helped to construct this classical vision of community. By correlating various degrees of transgression against the state with various degrees of removal from the courtly center, exile provided a unique means by which the social order was constructed (along an axis of inclusion and exclusion), mapped onto the realm, and imbued with power and powerlessness.

While both execution and exile are attested during the early period of the *ritsuryō* state, execution was customarily abolished (with a few rare exceptions) for the majority of the Heian era, over a period of some 347 years. In other words, during the lifetimes of most members of the Heian court, the actual practice of execution did not exist, and exile was the paramount legal sanction in the land. This development calls for some explanation. Some scholars have pointed to changes in *ritsuryō* practice as a sign of the state's inability to implement or enforce its own laws, calling into question the degree to which the codes were put into practice in the first place. By contrast, drawing from Rebecca French and the findings of Japanese legal historians such as Rikō Mitsuo, I suggest that the practice of the *ritsuryō* codes required adaptation in order to reflect the shifting legal cosmology of Heian Japan. More specifically, a period steeped in concern for the vengeful spirits of the dead appears to have rendered the practice of execution fraught with undesirable consequences.

A reading of the *Hōgen monogatari* supports this idea. As the primary text chronicling the end to Japan's 347-year suspension of capital punishment, the *Hōgen* provides valuable clues concerning the anxiety that appears to have attended the reintroduction of execution within the capital. Though written at some remove from the events it describes and while clearly reflecting a partisan perspective, the shock recorded in the narrative over the execution of Tameyoshi and others appears to reflect accurately the sentiments held by some in the capital in the aftermath of the conflict. Only when the retribution unleashed by the wrathful spirit of an exiled emperor targeted those responsible for such "unnatural events" was it perceived that a measure of balance had been restored. Within the textual horizon of the *Hōgen* as well as in the historical record of the court, a certain logic connecting the unrighteousness of execution and the retribution of vengeful spirits resonates powerfully.

If the social trauma accompanying execution in some way prompted an expectation for retribution by vengeful spirits—if this was indeed a way of looking at the world—then we have a potential clue to the reasoning behind the earlier cessation of execution in the Heian period. In other words, the widespread popularity of the cult of vengeful spirits in the early ninth century—immediately contemporary with the virtual cessation of capital punishment—appears not merely coincidental, but related. While other factors no doubt also played a role, I suggest that a growing belief in *onryō* influenced changes in the practice of "penality" during the reign of Emperor Saga, leading to the customary cessation of capital punishment. Yet amid the series of civil conflicts that ushered in the end of the Heian period—and with them, the rise of the military houses employed to wage them—the practice of execution once again returned to the court. In this regard, the severed heads displayed in the capital following the Hōgen Disorder provided a clear sign that customary forms of courtly justice begun under Emperor Saga were being abandoned. And with the introduction of idioms of punishment now associated with and administered by warriors, a new chapter in the history of Japanese law was underway.

6

# Conclusion

## *On the Margins of Japanese Religion*

> Why [do I wish to write this history]? Simply because I am interested in the past? No, if one means by that writing a history of the past in terms of the present. Yes, if one means writing the history of the present.
> —*Michel Foucault*

> Historians, like the fishes of the sea, regurgitate fragments.
> —*Caroline Walker Bynum*

If the preceding chapters have treated myth, literature, cult, and law as separate fields of inquiry—a move that reflects contemporary disciplinary boundaries more than the historical nature of things—it is time now to bring those inquiries together within a single frame. And if the preceding chapters have explored moments that seem irrevocably "past," it is time now to connect those moments to the present. To accomplish both aims, we can focus upon a single historical figure, that of the emperor who died in exile at the end of the Heian period, the "greatest vengeful spirit in the history of Japan,"[1] retired emperor Sutoku. Let us consider the following sequence of developments.

In the year 1168, four years after the death in exile of retired emperor Sutoku, the poet/priest Saigyō crossed the inland sea to reach the island of Shikoku. His purpose was to visit sites associated with two figures: the exiled emperor Sutoku, and Kūkai, the founder of the Shingon sect of Japanese Buddhism.[2] Saigyō's choices were hardly arbitrary: he was tracing a path to two figures with whom he felt a deep personal connection. Before becoming a renunciant, for example, Saigyō had served in the elite corps of the North-Facing Warriors (Hokumen no bushi) guarding the cloistered palaces of both retired emperor Sutoku and his father, Toba; he took the tonsure only after receiving Toba's permission to leave his service.[3] Upon ordination as a Shingon priest, Saigyō then spent lengthy periods "deep in the mountains" on Mt. Koya, the temple complex founded three centuries earlier by Kūkai.[4]

Reaching the shores of Shikoku at Matsuyama, where Sutoku first dwelled in exile, Saigyō reported finding no trace of the emperor's former residence. Instead, he composed the first of two well-known poems on Sutoku from this journey:

*Matsuyama no*
*nami ni nagarete*
*koshi fune no*
*yagate munashiku*
*narinikeru kana*

The ship that came,
washed on Matsuyama's waves,
in no time faded
into nothingness![5]

Written to no one in particular, Saigyō's poem offers a brief meditation on impermanence, brought about through reflection on Sutoku's dramatic fall from power. At the same time, the poem plays on the semantics of exile, making use of a term for the washing of the waves (*nami ni nagarete*) that poetically signified banishment. Kūkai's religious name—ocean (*kai*) of emptiness (*kū*)—may also have been on Saigyō's mind.

There are complex undercurrents beneath Saigyō's visit to the distant periphery of the Heian court, offering poetry at sites associated with a banished emperor. Saigyō's pilgrimage has been seen as a final act of service to his former lord, but more specifically we should understand this service as an act of pacification toward the spirit of an emperor who was soon believed to have died in a state of turmoil. Such intent is expressed in the second poem from Saigyō's pilgrimage that became widely known and was later included in the *Hōgen monogatari*. Saigyō's headnote states that it was composed beside Sutoku's gravesite in exile, located at a mountain temple known as Shiramine, where Saigyō also performed memorial services (*mihaka no haberi*):

*Yoshiya kimi*
*mukashi no tama no*
*yuka totemo*
*kakaran nochi wa*
*nanika wa sen*

Long ago you may have dwelt, my lord,
in jewel floored palaces,
but what good is that to you now?[6]

Once again, Saigyō's poem conveys a Buddhist didactic element, written to console the emperor's spirit through a brief meditation on nonattachment. As I discuss below, later narratives would embellish Saigyō's poetic offerings to Sutoku still further, adding such details as Saigyō reciting sutras to aid the emperor in the afterlife or even conversing with Sutoku's lingering malevolent spirit.

While it cannot be known whether Saigyō's pilgrimage was motivated by some report of Sutoku's vengeful spirit that is no longer extant, in the years following Saigyō's visit to Shikoku a *goryō* cult clearly began forming around the late emperor. As mentioned in chapter 5, the most visible sponsor of cultic activity devoted to Sutoku was his younger brother and sworn enemy, Emperor Go-Shirakawa. After a year in which Go-Shirakawa lost four close family members in rapid succession and immediately after finding himself placed under house arrest by his former ally Taira no Kiyomori, Go-Shirakawa began taking steps to pacify Sutoku's vengeful spirit in 1177. He first ordered that Sutoku no longer be referred to as the Sanuki-in (roughly, "the retired emperor in exile"), but as he is still known today: Sutoku ("reverent virtue"). He further ordered a series of eight lectures on the *Lotus Sutra* held at the Shingon temple established in the capital by Sutoku, Jōshōji. Finally, he ordered that Fujiwara Yorinaga—Sutoku's ally who had been mortally wounded in the Hōgen conflict—be restored posthumously to his former rank and office.[7] Such efforts were not limited to Go-Shirakawa, however: following a great fire in the capital in the fourth month of 1177, Minister of the Left Fujiwara Tsunemune linked the calamity to Sutoku's spirit, declaring that pacifying Sutoku was "a matter of unlimited importance."[8]

In 1183, the earliest rumors regarding a curse by Sutoku—supposedly written in his own blood, on the back of sutras he had personally copied—are attested in the capital.[9] It's unlikely a coincidence that in the same year Go-Shirakawa ordered the construction of a *goryō* shrine for both Sutoku and Sutoku's fallen ally, Fujiwara Yorinaga, built at the site of Sutoku's residence during the Hōgen. Consisting of two smaller shrines arranged side-by-side, one each for Sutoku and Yorinaga, roofed in *hinoki* bark and surrounded by a gated earthen wall, the site was completed and dedicated on 4/15/1184.[10] On that occasion it was noted that Fujiwara Norinaga—an ally of Sutoku who didn't return from exile following the Hōgen conflict until 1162—urged people to revere the evil spirit (*akuryō*) of the former emperor now as a divine spirit (*shinrei*), neatly articulating the structure of belief informing *goryō* cults.[11] In the period that followed, faced with ongoing personal crises, Go-Shirakawa kept up efforts to pacify Sutoku's spirit. In the eighth month of 1184, he contributed a shrine for Sutoku at Sutoku's temple, Jōshōji, and in 1191, stricken with illness a year before his own death, Go-Shirakawa ordered an image hall (*miedō*) built at the site of Sutoku's grave in exile.[12]

In the centuries following the construction of *goryō* shrines to Sutoku in the capital, the sites gradually transformed in function and eventually disappeared from the landscape.[13] Both the shrine built to pacify Sutoku and Yorinaga as well as Sutoku's own temple containing the shrine built by Go-Shirakawa were destroyed by fire during the Ōnin war that ravaged Kyoto beginning in 1467. Yet even as physical sites associated with Sutoku faded from the landscape, his presence in the cultural imagination continued to grow and take on new forms.

A major impetus for this was the *Hōgen monogatari,* the chronicle of the Hōgen conflict and its aftermath generally thought to have been written in the early to mid-thirteenth century.[14] Composed well after the events it described, the text incorporates as historical "truth" the rumors circulating at the time of its composition regarding a curse written by Sutoku in his own blood. The curse, supposedly written in exile while "submerged in evil meditation" by a long-haired and long-clawed Sutoku, isn't mentioned until nearly two decades after Sutoku's death, raising doubts about the veracity of its origins.[15] One truth can be extrapolated from the *Hōgen monogatari,* however: the further away from his actual death a text was written about Sutoku, the more his portrayal takes on the long-clawed and malcontented guise of a Tengu.[16]

Such depictions of a vengeful Sutoku were amplified in medieval and premodern texts and performances. In the Noh drama *Matsuyama Tengu,* the emperor is literally played as a Tengu; the play—classified as a "demon-type"—dramatizes the meeting between Saigyō and the deceased Sutoku at his gravesite. This popular theme reached a climax with Ueda Akinari's classic tale collection, *Ugetsu monogatari.* The opening story,

"Shiramine"—declared a "perfect masterpiece" by none other than Yukio Mishima[17]—explores the gravesite encounter between Saigyō and the malcontented spirit of Sutoku, now depicted as the "king of the Tengu," uttering curses against Go-Shirakawa and others who had opposed him, while vowing the demise of the Taira military clan. Written with the benefit of historical hindsight in 1776, the text correctly prophesies the annihilation of the Taira that occurred in 1185, decades after Sutoku's death. Depictions of Sutoku continued to spread with the circulation of woodblock prints: Utagawa Kuniyoshi (1797–1861) and Yoshitoshi (1839–1892) each produced well-known images of Sutoku, either showing his life in exile or his afterlife, rising from the grave.

The prominence of Sutoku within Akinari's *Ugetsu monogatari* is doubly significant because the author of that classic was also a noted *kokugakusha*—one of a number of scholars who looked back to an idealized Japanese past in order to probe questions regarding cultural identity in the present. The topic of Sutoku's vengeful spirit was popular in *kokugaku* circles, not for its entertainment value but for the clues it held regarding Japan's past, present, and possible future. Among disciples of the scholar Hirata Atsutane, for example, Sutoku's death in exile was given prominent historiographic weight. Noting that retired emperor Go-Shirakawa's reign ended in the drowning death of the child emperor Antoku, the apparent loss of one of the imperial regalia into the sea,[18] and the beginning of warrior rule in Japan, some among Hirata's disciples concluded that Sutoku's vengeful spirit was the cause of the fall of the imperial house from power.[19] Among these scholars by the mid-nineteenth century, Sutoku's vengeance was no longer evidenced by individual acts of spirit retribution but rather by what was felt to be a warped historical course Japan had fallen into, ruled by military leaders rather than the divinely appointed imperial house. As a consequence, the scholar Nakazui Unsai wrote a memorial to the throne suggesting that ending six hundred years of warrior rule and reestablishing imperial power would not be accomplished without first ensuring the complete pacification of Sutoku.[20]

This idea was persuasive enough that Emperor Kōmei—father of Emperor Meiji and the last emperor to live and die under military rule—made it his objective to achieve Sutoku's pacification once and for all. Though he did not live to see the project completed, in the last year of Kōmei's reign construction began in Kyoto once again on a shrine to welcome Sutoku's spirit back from exile.[21] Suspended due to Kōmei's death in the first month of 1867, construction was completed under Kōmei's son, Emperor Meiji. Then, in the eighth month of 1868—timed to coincide with the anniversary of Sutoku's death (and as imperial forces lay siege to a remnant of *bakufu* troops at Aizuwakamatsu Castle)—services were held at Sutoku's gravesite on Shikoku to initiate his return.[22] Following the logic of a "purified" Shinto advocated by the Hirata school, the service began with the recitation of *norito* to invoke and welcome Sutoku. Next, objects enshrining his spirit (*mitamashiro*)—in this case a wooden image along with a reed flute once owned by Sutoku—were ritually transferred to a sacred palanquin (*mikoshi*) in order to make the return journey to Kyoto. Arriving to a festive welcome on September 6, 1868, the *mitamashiro* were then transferred to the shrine built for Sutoku's spirit, mimetically named Shiramine-gū, after the mountain upon which Sutoku had been buried on Shikoku.[23]

As Yamada Yūji has pointed out, the act of transferring Sutoku's spirit from the site of his tomb in Shikoku to a shrine in Kyoto held not only religious but political significance. In the eyes of the Hirata line of *kokugakusha*—who were influential in the policies of the Jingikan (Department of Divinities) during this period[24]—the project to "recall" Sutoku's spirit from exile served to mark once and for all not only the final pacification of Sutoku, but with that, the final delegitimization of warrior rule in Japan.[25] For a country in the midst of the Boshin civil war, amid a fundamental transition in power and a transformation in governing ideology, such actions sought to convey to the populace—via the well-known figure of Sutoku—that the newly established imperial government was nothing new at all but merely the "restoration" of earlier, idealized structures of government, once again aligning Japan with the auspicious forces of creation represented by the "unbroken" line of imperial rule.[26] Two days after the enshrinement ceremony at Shiramine-gū in Kyoto, a new era name was proclaimed: the Meiji period had officially begun.[27]

What can we take away from all this? There are a number of things. At the most basic level, recalling the bricolage of practices used in the earliest attempts to soothe Sutoku's vengeful spirit helps to remind us of the seamless fusion of religious practice that was the norm, rather than the exception, prior to the "cultural revolution" of the Meiji period.[28] While perhaps a truism in some circles,[29] nevertheless the complex interweaving of Buddhist and *kami* cult idioms in premodern Japan is worth remembering amid a contemporary environment that in many ways continues the religious division announced in the early Meiji edicts "separating" Buddhas from *kami*.[30] This division lingers within the religious landscape of contemporary Japan, as at the Shiramine Shrine constructed for Sutoku in 1868, where Sutoku is worshipped to this day at annual festivals in Kyoto as a purely "Shinto" deity, all traces of Buddhist semiotics erased.

Such religious separation is also reflected at times in academic discussions of Japanese religion, where Saigyō has been lifted up as an emblem of the Buddhist "episteme" that is said to have dominated the premodern religious landscape,[31] while *kami* cults have been presented as part of a discrete religious tradition centered on the cultivation of the *makoto no kokoro,* or "mindful heart."[32] Even contemporary divisions of academic labor into Buddhist studies and Shinto studies—while helpful for specialization—can unwittingly reinforce the perception of Buddhism and Shinto as separate modes of discourse and practice in premodern Japan.[33] Such binary categories make it difficult to interpret the historical blending of practices seen in the case of Sutoku, where Buddhist sutras were recited to the enshrined soul force (*mitama*) of the deceased emperor, where a shrine was constructed to accompany the Buddhist temple founded by Sutoku, and where his imperial tomb (*misasagi*) in exile was joined by a Buddhist image hall (*miedō*). Indeed, the wooden image housed inside the *miedō* for the veneration of Sutoku as a Buddhist avatar (*daigongen*) was the same image used in 1868 to transfer Sutoku's spirit as a "purely Shinto" deity to the shrine in Kyoto.[34] We might conclude that the dimensions of religious practice in premodern Japan that blurred all boundaries (such as the *goryō* cults) were some of the most deeply influential in their time, while among the least understood and studied today.

A slightly more difficult point involves the study of exile, which in some ways presents the inverse challenge of the Shinto-Buddhist dichotomy mentioned above. With the advent of Meiji Japan and the adoption of new legal codes for the nascent state, for the first time in Japanese history exile disappeared from the codes of law.[35] In the new, national model of community, where sovereignty no longer "faded imperceptibly" at the margins but was meant to be "evenly operative over each square centimetre of legally demarcated territory,"[36] the penal sanction of exile was not merely irrelevant, but contradictory to the national imagination. Thus, unlike the separation of Shinto and Buddhism mentioned above—a division of labor upon which Japan's modernity was founded, reflected in the religious landscape of Japan today, and perpetuated in academic discussions of Japanese religion—we find that exile disappears with Japan's modernity, is contradictory to the lived experience of the modern nation, and is largely absent from academic discussions of Japanese culture, history, and religion. What should we make then of a trope such as exile that neither exists in modern Japan nor is echoed by any disciplinary configuration within the academy? What would it look like to consider fluidly the religious landscape of premodern Japan, outside of disciplinary boundaries? What were the "structuring structures" that governed the experiences and imaginations of those in the past, even in ways that may confound and contradict the present?

---

While we often hear about the importance of such concepts as *mujō* (impermanence), *mappō* (the end of the dharma), or *mono no aware* (poignant awareness) for understanding Heian Japan, I would suggest as a result of this study that exile should also be considered alongside such structuring categories of thought, as evidenced by the particular resonance held by exile in the life of the Japanese court. In studies drawn from myth, literature, cult, and legal practice in early and classical Japan, I've attempted to show how a storehouse of images, gestures, and quotations involving exile offered members of court society a wealth of signifying possibilities. Rather than a trope whose meaning was shared throughout court society, I've also argued that the meaning of exile was never static, but always subject to interpretation and appropriation. Such appropriation is recorded intact, for example, regarding the figure of the god Susano-o in the earliest myth-histories: "capricious" within Yamato-centered texts, yet benign within records collected from Izumo. Divergent and at times contested images can also be seen in the treatment of such fictional and historical figures of exile considered in this study as Kaguyahime, Genji, Michizane, and Emperor Sutoku.

Rather than ascribing agency to the signs themselves, I've tried to attend to the ways members of court society actively appropriated images, gestures, and quotations involving exile toward their own ends. In the *Taketori monogatari,* for example, the mytheme of a feather-robed maiden is woven into a narrative regarding the Japanese court, imagining the world of that court as the distant periphery of a more powerful, sacred center, the capital of the moon. In doing so, the *Taketori* renders the social order visible, enabling a critique of the sexual politics of the court as well as a piercing assessment of the "patriarchal desire" that motivated such politics in the first place.

It follows that the storehouse of images was not merely composed of abstract symbols, but was also embodied in specific practices, gestures, and meaningful actions. Thus when the historical statesman Michizane wrote about bowing to the lingering fragrance of the imperial robe he had carried with him into exile, he employed a particularly resonant trope with which to express his exclusion from power while also establishing affinity with those back in the capital. The fact that the fictional *Genji monogatari* directly quotes Michizane's poem when depicting Genji's own exile suggests that Michizane's signifying actions did not go unrecognized.

While the ethnologist Orikuchi Shinobu ascribed a single archetypal meaning to such stories of "exiled and wandering nobles," my readings have shown instead that narratives imagining exile were employed toward diverse ends. While at a common level every narrative of exile imagines a privileged sphere, as well as those who are excluded from it, this common structure or framework remained remarkably malleable. Among the possibilities, for those in positions of power the banishment of others provided a persuasive trope for asserting and maintaining their own "centrality"—as when it was woven into the ruling myths of the court or into the legal codes of the state, mapping various degrees of transgression onto various degrees of removal from the courtly center.

Yet narratives of exile from the Japanese court were employed not only to assert and inscribe various constellations of power, but also to render visible and at times reimagine the social order and the circulation of power within it. It was this ability to imagine and reimagine the world, we might say, that allowed the exiled emperor Sutoku to be reclassified first as a vengeful spirit and then to be enshrined back in the capital as a source of sacred power. Such reimagining itself constituted a form of social critique, enabling a posthumous redistribution of power that sent ripple effects throughout the entire court hierarchy.

To speak of the imagination of exile in this way raises questions about agency: about the degree to which members of the Japanese court were consciously involved in reshaping their world. While it is true that at the upper levels of court society, social criticism was raised to an art form—in ritually organized aesthetic competitions, for example—even such an articulate critic as Sei Shōnagon was likely unable to see beyond the contours of court society to imagine a radically different social order. It can't be denied, however, that through the outpourings of the social imagination, the constellation of power in society was continually reconfigured, as when three different oracles narrated the exiled Sugawara no Michizane's posthumous return to the capital as a vengeful deity, leading to the establishment of a shrine to Michizane later patronized by the state. While members of the court may not have been able to think outside of or beyond the categories provided by their society, they could and did make creative use of the categories and structures available to them. In this sense—at times with the sophistication of the *Tale of Genji* and at times with the enigmatic speech of an oracle—exile provided a deeply resonant trope through which members of the Japanese court imagined and reimagined their world and the circulation of power within it, whether sacred or otherwise.

# Notes

## Preface

*Epigraph.* Harold Arlen and E. Y. Harburg, "Munchkinland," in *The Wizard of Oz,* directed by Victor Fleming (Burbank: Metro-Goldwyn-Mayer, 1939).

1. Salman Rushdie, *The Wizard of Oz* (London: British Film Institute, 1993), 19. As Jane Gallop notes about Rushdie's case, following Gayatri Chakravorty Spivak, the post-structuralist rallying cry regarding the "death of the author" takes on an entirely different resonance when the death of actual living authors is considered. See Jane Gallop, *The Deaths of the Author: Reading and Writing in Time* (Durham, NC: Duke University Press, 2011), 1–2.

2. I discuss the definition and etymology of exile and banishment more fully in chapter 1, note 7.

## Chapter 1: Introduction

*Epigraph 1.* In the notes to his translation, Keene remarks that many commentators do not find it at all easy to imagine why Akimoto felt so. The goal of my study, put simply, is to recover the logic behind Akimoto and Kenkō's statements. Donald Keene, trans., *Essays in Idleness* (New York: Columbia University Press, 1967), 6; see also Nishio Minoru, ed., *Tsurezuregusa,* in Nihon koten bungaku taikei 30 (Tokyo: Iwanami Shoten, 1974), 93.

*Epigraph 2.* Julia Kristeva, from *Semiotike: Recherches pour une semanalyse* (Paris: Editions du Seuil, 1969), 146, translated in Jonathan Culler, *Structuralist Poetics* (Ithaca, NY: Cornell University Press, 1975), 139.

1. I adapt the term "myth-history" from Gary Ebersole to refer to the earliest chronicles of the Japanese court (the *Kojiki* and the later *Nihon shoki*), which are neither "purely" myth nor history but begin by recounting the "age of the gods" before moving on to narrate (with varying degrees of accuracy) the history of the Yamato court; a primary motive of both texts was to authenticate the court through a narrative of divine origins. See Gary Ebersole, *Ritual Poetry and the Politics of Death in Early Japan* (Princeton, NJ: Princeton University Press, 1989), 3 and passim.

2. While the Heian period lasted from 794 to 1185, execution was customarily commuted in favor of exile between 810 and 1056, as I discuss further in chapter 5.

3. See David Pollack, "The Informing Image: 'China' in *The Tale of Genji,*" in David Pollack, *The Fracture of Meaning: Japan's Synthesis of China from the Eighth through the Eighteenth Centuries* (Princeton, NJ: Princeton University Press, 1986), 55–76.

4. See Haruo Shirane, "The Poetics of Exile," in *The Bridge of Dreams: A Poetics of "The Tale of Genji"* (Stanford, CA: Stanford University Press, 1987), 17–23.

5. See Thomas LaMarre, *Uncovering Heian Japan: An Archaeology of Sensation and Inscription* (Durham, NC: Duke University Press, 2000), 7.

6. Michel de Certeau, *The Practice of Everyday Life,* trans. Steven Rendall (Berkeley: University of California Press, 1988), xviii.

7. A note about terminology. The English terms "exile" and "banishment" carry different connotations. *Exile* (rooted in the Latin *exilium*) has a broader semantic range, referring both to voluntary separation and forced removal of a person from their home or homeland. *Banishment* has a more specific connotation: derived from the Old German *bannan* ("to proclaim"), it connotes the state of being expelled by decree. While the majority of cases I examine in this project are instances of forced removal, or banishment (as in the myth of Susano-o), there are also cases where the agency is more ambiguous—as with Genji's exile to Suma—containing elements of both voluntary separation and forced removal. While recognizing the semantic distinction between the two terms, I will at times use the two interchangeably when appropriate. See Jonathan Tabori, *The Anatomy of Exile: A Semantic and Historical Study* (London: Harrap, 1972).

8. Inoue Mitsusada et al., eds., *Ritsuryō,* in Nihon shisō takei 3 (Tokyo: Iwanami Shoten, 1980), 15–16.

9. As Ross Bender notes, an even clearer example of the adaptive process within the legal codes is the establishment of the Council of Divinities (*Jingikan*) "charged with oversight of native (Shintō) institutions and clergy . . . [which] had no parallel in the Chinese bureaucratic structure." Ross Bender, "Emperor, Aristocracy, and the Ritsuryō State: Court Politics in Nara," in *Japan Emerging: Premodern History to 1850,* ed. Karl Friday (Boulder, CO: Westview Press, 2012), 113.

10. In the romanization of classical Japanese terms, I follow the guidelines provided in Haruo Shirane's *Classical Japanese: A Grammar* (New York: Columbia University Press, 2005), 4–5 and 18–23, aiming to approximate Heian sound values rather than to transliterate Heian orthography.

11. Kurano Kenji and Takeda Yūkichi, eds., *Kojiki/Norito,* in Nihon koten bungaku taikei 1 (Tokyo: Iwanami Shoten, 1966), 73 and 85. On the first occasion, Izanagi declares Susano-o's banishment; on the second occasion (quoted above), Susano-o is sentenced to banishment by the Council of Divinities.

12. Donald Philippi, trans., *Kojiki* (Tokyo: University of Tokyo, 1968), 73.

13. "Kamigami no sekai kara tsuihō suru," in Hayashi Ōki and Andō Chizuko, eds., *Kogorin* (Tokyo: Taishūkan, 1997), s.v. "*kamuyarau.*"

14. Helen McCullough, trans., *Okagami: The Great Mirror* (Princeton, NJ: Princeton University Press, 1980), p. 96, modified; Matsumura Hiroji, ed., *Ōkagami,* in Nihon koten bungaku taikei 21 (Tokyo: Iwanami Shoten, 1973), 72.

15. See Robert Borgen, *Sugawara no Michizane and the Early Heian Court* (Honolulu: University of Hawai'i Press, 1994), especially 289–305.

16. Benedict Anderson, *Imagined Communities: Reflections on the Origins and Spread of Nationalism* (New York: Verso, 1991), 19, cited in LaMarre, *Uncovering Heian Japan,* 1–2.

17. LaMarre, *Uncovering Heian Japan,* 5. LaMarre's work on the Heian period has generated diverse reactions. For two perspectives, see the reviews by Edward Kamens in *Journal of Japanese Studies,* vol. 27, no. 2 (summer 2001): 430–434, and by Richard Okada in *Harvard Journal of Asiatic Studies,* vol. 64, no. 1 (June 2004): 184–200. For the purpose of my study, I take LaMarre's comments regarding the national imagination as a helpful corrective when approaching the study of exile at the Japanese court.

18. Ryūichi Abe, *The Weaving of Mantra* (New York: Columbia University Press, 1999), 26. Ebersole also discusses how the center is defined by the location of the sovereign in his *Ritual Poetry and the Politics of Death,* 24.

19. Mikael Adolphson, Edward Kamens, and Stacie Matsumoto, eds., *Heian Japan: Centers and Peripheries* (Honolulu: University of Hawai'i Press, 2007), 2.

20. Ibid., p. 3.

21. Bruce Batten, "Cross-border Traffic on the Kyushu Coast, 794–1086," in Adolphson et al., *Heian Japan,* 357–383. Much of the attention now paid to the heterogeneity of space in premodern Japan has been stimulated by the influential work of Amino Yoshihiko; see, for example, his *Muen, kugai, raku: Nihon chūsei no jiyū to heiwa* (Tokyo: Heibonsha, 1987). In addition to Batten, other works in this vein include Thomas Keirstead, *The Geography of Power in Medieval Japan* (Princeton, NJ: Princeton University Press, 1992); Janet Goodwin, *Alms and Vagabonds: Buddhist Temples and Popular Patronage in Medieval Japan* (Honolulu: University of Hawai'i Press, 1994); D. Max Moerman, *Localizing Paradise: Kumano Pilgrimage and the Religious Landscape of Premodern Japan* (Cambridge, MA: Harvard University Press, 2005); and David Bialock, *Eccentric Spaces, Hidden Histories: Narrative, Ritual, and Royal Authority from The Chronicles of Japan to The Tale of the Heike* (Stanford, CA: Stanford University Press, 2007).

22. Kawashima's work is influenced by the writing of Catherine Bell and the emphasis Bell places on "ritualization" over ritual. See Catherine Bell, *Ritual Theory, Ritual Practice* (New York: Oxford University Press, 1992).

23. Terry Kawashima, *Writing Margins: The Textual Construction of Gender in Heian and Kamakura Japan* (Cambridge, MA: Harvard Asia Center, 2001), 1.

24. Ibid., 12.

25. Adolphson et al., *Heian Japan,* 10.

26. Jacques Le Goff, *The Medieval Imagination,* trans. Arthur Goldhammer (Chicago: University of Chicago Press, 1988), 6. Le Goff's work is one starting point for my reflections on the social imagination.

27. In addition to its use as popularized by Le Goff, the term *le imaginaire* has a diverse and long-standing history in France, from Jean-Paul Sartre's early work *Imaginaire: Psychologie phénoménologique de l'imagination* (Paris: Gallimard, 1940) to its role in the psychoanalytic theory of Jacques Lacan. As I discuss in the above section, however, my use of the term is not meant to imply an affiliation with any of these particular schools of thought.

28. I analyze these passages in detail in chapter 3.

29. Royall Tyler, trans., *The Tale of Genji* (New York: Viking, 2001), 325; see also Yamagishi Tokuhei, ed., *Genji monogatari,* in Nihon koten bungaku taikei 15 (Tokyo: Iwanami Shoten, 1975), 179.

30. Ibid.

31. Le Goff, *The Medieval Imagination*, 5. My understanding here contrasts with that of Le Goff, who refers to *le imaginaire* as "a collective, social, and historical phenomena,"

adding that the "images of interest . . . are collective images." In Le Goff's view, there is a correspondence between an image and the collective mind of society; indeed, the mark of an image is that it yields a shared meaning. Images whose meanings are *not* shared by society as a whole are, to Le Goff, suspect: falling under the category of "ideology," they indicate to him images whose meaning has been distorted by the interests of certain groups.

32. Umberto Eco's study, *The Open Work*, trans. Anna Cancogni (Cambridge, MA: Harvard University Press, 1989), remains pertinent to this discussion; see 1–23.

33. Sawara's exile and death are recorded in the *Nihon Kiryaku* entry for 785/9/28. For a detailed summary of Sawara's case, see Yamada Yūji, *Bakkosuru onryō: Tatari to chinkon no Nihon shi* (Tokyo: Yoshikawa Kōbunkan, 2007), 34–43. Other helpful sources include Herbert Plutschow, *Chaos and Cosmos: Ritual in Early and Medieval Japanese Literature* (Leiden: E. J. Brill, 1990), 207–209; Inoue Mitsuo, "Kodai no goryō shinkō," in *Tenman Tenjin: Goryō kara gakumongami e,* ed. Ueda Masaaki (Tokyo: Chikuma Shobo, 1988), 4; and Horimoto Masami, *Onryō no kodaishi* (Tokyo: Hokutosha, 1999), 139–228. I discuss Sawara's case in chapter 4, in the context of the emerging *goryō* cult.

34. Norbert Elias, *The Court Society,* trans. Edmund Jephcott (New York: Pantheon Books, 1983), 80. While *The Court Society* is based on Elias' study of the French aristocracy of the *ancien régime* (fifteenth to eighteenth centuries), many of his principles are suggestive for the case of Heian court society as well.

35. Note that Michizane also loses office when he goes into exile—a demotion—but he gains this back posthumously and is promoted further in rank as a means of appeasing his vengeful spirit.

36. Elias, *The Court Society,* 93.

37. Ibid., 94.

38. Ibid., 77.

39. Ibid., 84.

40. Ibid., 99, emphasis added.

41. Tyler, *The Tale of Genji,* 248, emphasis added; see also Yamagishi, *Genji monogatari,* 45.

42. Translated in Burton Watson, *Japanese Literature in Chinese,* vol. 1 (New York: Columbia University Press, 1975), 112; see also Kawaguchi Hisao, ed., *Kanke bunsō: Kanke goshū,* in Nihon koten bungaku taikei 72 (Tokyo: Iwanami Shoten, 1966), 484. Michizane's gesture is echoed in the Suma chapter of *The Tale of Genji* (Tyler, 246) as well as in Karen Brazell, trans., *The Confessions of Lady Nijō* (Stanford, CA: Stanford University Press, 1973), 208. The possession of the royal robes was also employed as a trope in poems and letters to argue for the incoherence and injustice of the courtier's estrangement from the capital.

43. See Inoue Mitsusada's commentary on exile in his annotated edition of the *ritsuryō* legal codes mentioned above: Inoue, *Ritsuryō,* 487.

44. Mikael Adolphson, *The Gates of Power* (Honolulu: University of Hawai'i Press, 2000), 153, emphasis added. The story of "the exile of the abbot" is also recounted in the *Heike monogatari;* see Royall Tyler, trans., *The Tale of the Heike* (New York: Viking Press, 2013), 65–74.

45. See Susan Matisoff, "Kintōsho: Zeami's Song of Exile," *Monumenta Nipponica* 32, no. 4 (winter 1977): 441. As I discuss in chapter 3, the valorization of exile relates to what has been called an "aesthetics of discontent"; on this topic, see Michele Marra, *The Aesthetics of Discontent: Politics and Reclusion in Medieval Japanese Literature* (Honolulu: University of Hawai'i Press, 1991).

46. Elias, *The Court Society*, 87.

47. An earlier version of chapter 2 was previously published as "Origin Myths: Susano-o, Orikuchi Shinobu, and the Imagination of Exile in Early Japan," *History of Religions* 52, no. 3 (February 2013): 236–266. I gratefully acknowledge the University of Chicago Press for permission to reprint this material.

48. "*Nihonshijō saidai no onryō,*" Yamada Yūji, *Bakkosuru onryō: Tatari to chinkon no Nihon shi* (Tokyo: Yoshikawa Kōbunkan, 2007), 86.

49. Catherine Gallagher and Stephen Greenblatt, *Practicing New Historicism* (Chicago: University of Chicago Press, 2000), 13.

50. Ibid., 7.

## Chapter 2: Origin Myths

*Epigraph 1.* Donald L. Philippi, trans., *Kojiki* (Tokyo: University of Tokyo, 1968), 73, modified; see also Kurano Kenji and Takeda Yūkichi, eds., *Kojiki/Norito,* in Nihon koten bungaku taikei 1 (Tokyo: Iwanami Shoten, 1966), 72–73.

*Epigraph 2.* Michel Foucault, *Discipline and Punish,* trans. Alan Sheridan (New York: Vintage Books, 1995), 29.

1. The ancient province of Izumo corresponds largely to present-day Shimane Prefecture.

2. Motoori Norinaga, *Kojikiden,* in *Motoori Norinaga zenshū,* vol. 1, ed. Motoori Toyokai (Tokyo: Yoshikawa Kōbunkan, 1926), 360. Along similar lines, see Takeshi Matsumae, "The Heavenly Rock-Grotto Myth and the Chinkon Ceremony," *Asian Folklore Studies* 39, no. 2 (1980): 9–22.

3. See C. Scott Littleton, "Susa-no-wo versus Ya-mata no woroti: An Indo-European Theme in Japanese Mythology," *History of Religions* 20, no. 3 (February 1981): 269–280; and Allan Grapard, "Visions of Excess and Excesses of Vision: Women and Transgression in Japanese Myth," *Japanese Journal of Religious Studies* 18, no. 1 (March 1991): 3–22.

4. See Cornelius Ouwehand, "Some Notes on the God Susa-no-o," *Monumenta Nipponica* 14, no. 3–4 (October 1958–January 1959): 384–407; and Robert Ellwood, "A Japanese Mythic Trickster Figure: Susa-no-o," in *Mythical Trickster Figures,* ed. William Hynes and William Doty (Tuscaloosa: University of Alabama Press, 1993), 141–158.

5. Alan Miller, "Ame No Miso-Ori Me (The Heavenly Weaving Maiden): The Cosmic Weaver in Early Shinto Myth and Ritual," *History of Religions* 24, no. 1 (August 1984): 27–48.

6. Nelly Naumann, "Sakahagi: The 'Reverse Flaying' of the Heavenly Piebald Horse," *Asian Folklore Studies* 41, no. 1 (January 1982): 7–38.

7. Wendy Doniger O'Flaherty, *Other Peoples' Myths: The Cave of Echoes* (New York: Macmillan Publishing Company, 1988), 31–32.

8. See particularly the epilogue "Scholarship as Myth" in Bruce Lincoln, *Theorizing Myth: Narrative, Ideology, and Scholarship* (Chicago: University of Chicago Press, 1999), 207–216.

9. Thomas LaMarre, *Uncovering Heian Japan: An Archaeology of Sensation and Inscription* (Durham, NC: Duke University Press, 2000), 5.

10. The work of probing Orikuchi's intellectual context has been carried out primarily among historians. On the political-historical context of the *minzokugaku* (native ethnology) discipline, including Orikuchi's involvement, see H. D. Harootunian, "Figuring the Folk:

History, Poetics, and Representation," in *Mirror of Modernity: Invented Traditions in Modern Japan,* ed. Stephen Vlastos (Berkeley: University of California Press, 1998), 155, as well as Kevin Doak, "Building National Identity through Ethnicity: Ethnology in Wartime Japan and After," *Journal of Japanese Studies* 27, no. 1 (winter 2001): 1–39.

11. Scholars in the West who have examined exile narratives from Heian Japan have largely focused on uncovering the models on which fictional characters were based. See the helpful discussions in "The Informing Image" chapter of David Pollack's *The Fracture of Meaning* (Princeton, NJ: Princeton University Press, 1986) and "The Poetics of Exile" chapter of Haruo Shirane's *The Bridge of Dreams: A Poetics of "The Tale of Genji"* (Stanford, CA: Stanford University Press, 1987).

12. Western scholars of Japanese literature frequently cite Orikuchi's concept in their own discussions of works that fall under his category (such as the *Taketori monogatari* or the *Tale of Genji*), though generally without examining Orikuchi's larger theoretical framework or contextualizing his position as an influential scholar working at Kokugakuin University during the inter- and postwar periods. See Norma Field, *The Splendor of Longing in the* Tale of Genji (Princeton, NJ: Princeton University Press, 1987), 33–34; Shirane, *The Bridge of Dreams,* 3–4 and passim; and more recently, Monika Dix, "Hachikazuki: Revealing Kannon's Crowning Compassion in Muromachi Fiction," *Japanese Journal of Religious Studies* 36, no. 2 (January 2009): 286–287.

13. Orikuchi Shinobu, *Orikuchi Shinobu zenshū,* ed. Orikuchi Hakushi Kinenkai (Tokyo: Chūōkōronsha, 1955), 7:344. While *ryūri* is frequently translated as "wandering," important figures within Orikuchi's genre (such as Kaguyahime) remain in a single, fixed location throughout their period on the margins. I translate the term accordingly as "exile and wandering."

14. Helpful discussions of Orikuchi's *kishu ryūritan* theory can be found in Takahashi Tōru, "Kishu ryūritan no kōzō," *Kokubungaku kaishaku to kanshō* 56, no. 10 (October 1991): 123–128; and Yamaoka Yoshikazu, "Kishu ryūritan to wa nanika," *Kokubungaku: Kaishaku to kyōzai no kenkyu* 54, no. 4 (March 2009): 6–14.

15. The portion of *Nihon bungaku no hassei* introducing Orikuchi's term *kishu ryūritan* was published in 1924. Takahashi Tōru points out that Orikuchi's mentor in the field of Japanese ethnology, Yanagita Kunio, had earlier touched on the theme of the royal exile in his 1920 essay "Nagasare-ō" ("The Exiled King"), which can be found in Yanagita Kunio, *Hitotsume kozō: Sono hoka* (Tokyo: Oyama Shoten, 1934), 274–291. Yanagita, in turn, had been influenced by his reading of *Die Götter im Exil* (*Gods in Exile*), an 1854 work by the German poet and literary critic Heinrich Heine. See Takahashi Tōru, "Kishu ryūritan no kōzō," 127–128.

16. Orikuchi, *Orikuchi Shinobu zenshū,* 7:351.

17. Ibid., 7:344, 351. Tokue Motomasa argues that the spirit of the *kishu ryūritan* tradition continued on within the performing arts of the medieval period; see his article, "Kishu ryūritan igo—Orikuchigaku no tenkai," *Kokubungaku: kaishaku to kyōzai no kenkyū* 20, no. 1 (January 1975): 111–116.

18. Orikuchi, *Orikuchi Shinobu zenshū,* 7:244.

19. Ariyama Daigo and Ishiuchi Toru, eds., *Chōkū/Orikuchi Shinobu jiten* (Tokyo: Bensei Shuppan, 2000), s.v. "*Kishu ryūritan,*" by Nomura Jun'ichi. See also the discussion of transgression within the *kishu ryūritan* genre in Yamaoka, "Kishu ryūritan to wa nanika," 6–7.

20. Orikuchi, *Orikuchi Shinobu zenshū,* 7:351. For a discussion of Orikuchi's attraction to narratives of suffering and sorrow, see Takahashi Tōru, "Kishu ryūritan no kōzō," 123 and 128.

21. Orikuchi, *Orikuchi Shinobu zenshū,* 7:352.

22. Ibid., 7:344, emphasis added.

23. Philippi, *Kojiki,* 71–73, modified; see Kurano and Takeda, *Kojiki/Norito,* 73. Note that in the *Kojiki* text, Susano-o himself identifies his "mother's land" as Ne-no-katasu-kuni, the "Land of Firm Roots," a subterranean region usually associated by scholars of Japanese myth with Yomi no kuni, the realm of the dead where Izanagi encountered Izanami's corpse.

24. Orikuchi, *Orikuchi Shinobu zenshū,* 2:6, emphasis added.

25. Ibid., 2:4–5, emphasis added; see also the translation in Tōji Kamata, "The Disfiguring of Nativism: Hirata Atsutane and Orikuchi Shinobu," in *Shinto in History,* ed. John Breen and Mark Teeuwen (Honolulu: University of Hawai'i Press, 2000), 310.

26. Orikuchi was a noted poet whose work garnered literary prizes under the pen name Shaku Chōkū; in the postwar period, he participated in the annual imperial poetry gatherings. Like earlier Kokugaku scholars, he too felt that classical poetic forms provided a means for developing an empathetic relation to authors of the ancient literary tradition.

27. Orikuchi, *Orikuchi Shinobu zenshū,* 2:5, emphasis in the original; see also Kamata, "The Disfiguring of Nativism," 310.

28. For Orikuchi, the journey from center to periphery continued to trace itself over and over again in the Japanese imagination, producing recurring stories of estranged heroes who were at the same time rare or divine visitors. Thus in addition to his ideas regarding *tokoyo,* a further concept helpful for understanding the *kishu ryūritan* theme is his theory of *marebito,* or divine visitors. In Orikuchi's view, when a hero "as of an offspring of divinity" was exiled and forced to wander in a peripheral or lowly place, while he or she may be regarded as a pariah to those who occupy the center from which they were expelled, those who encounter the person on the periphery receive them as a rare or sacred visitor: a *marebito.* In this regard, Nomura Jun'ichi writes, the *kishu ryūritan* theme and the *marebito* category should be understood as two aspects of a similar principle, with the *marebito* functioning as a kind of reverse image of the *kishu ryūritan* theme (the hero's journey to the periphery as seen from two different perspectives). See Nomura Jun'ichi, "*Kishu ryūritan,*" in *Chōkū/Orikuchi Shinobu Jiten,* as well as Takahashi Tōru, "Kishu ryūritan no kōzō," 124–125.

29. For further critical reflections on Orikuchi's work, see Kamata, "The Disfiguring of Nativism," 295–317, as well as Osamu Murai, *Han Orikuchi Shinobu ron* (Tokyo: Sakuhinsha, 2004), 24–46 and passim.

30. As Thomas LaMarre describes this kind of move, "scholars must posit the existence of an already-unified Japan before the advent of Chinese practices; the scholarly emphasis therefore falls on whatever seems to come before, or lie outside, continental customs, scripts, institutions, and so on. This involves a tendentious search for anything that does not seem marked as 'foreign'; these (by default) 'native' elements are then drawn into the imagination of a Japan before and beyond China." LaMarre, *Uncovering Heian Japan,* 2–3.

31. Orikuchi, *Orikuchi Shinobu zenshū,* 7:348.

32. His full sentence reads, "What a dreadful thing, being confined within the expressions of Chinese verse, and Japanese forms don't arise." Orikuchi, *Orikuchi Shinobu zenshū,* 7:347. Compare Motoori Norinaga's comment from *Naobi no mitama:* "[People

are] going astray, fenced in within the confines of the Chinese classics." Motoori Norinaga, *Motoori Norinaga,* in Nihon no meicho 21, ed. Ishikawa Jun (Tokyo: Chūōkōronsha, 1970), 179.

33. For discussions of the Kokugaku project focusing on various early modern Japanese scholars, see Peter Nosco, *Remembering Paradise: Nativism and Nostalgia in Eighteenth-Century Japan* (Cambridge, MA: Council on East Asian Studies, 1990); H. D. Harootunian, *Things Seen and Unseen: Discourse and Ideology in Tokugawa Nativism* (Chicago: University of Chicago Press, 1988); Mark McNally, *Proving the Way: Conflict and Practice in the History of Japanese Nativism* (Cambridge, MA: Harvard University Asia Center, 2005); and Wilburn Hansen, *When Tengu Talk: Hirata Atsutane's Ethnography of the Other World* (Honolulu: University of Hawai'i Press, 2008).

34. See LaMarre, *Uncovering Heian Japan,* 5.

35. See Burton Watson, trans., *Po Chu-I: Selected Poems* (New York: Columbia University Press, 2000), vii–xvi. Bai Juyi is the poet's name in the pinyin system of romanization; in Japan he is also known as Haku Rakuten.

36. While I draw attention here to influences on Orikuchi from the older Kokugaku movement, Orikuchi believed himself to be at the vanguard of a "New Kokugaku" (Shin Kokugaku), a movement that would combine the classical training of the older nativist scholars with the emerging discipline of native ethnology (*minzokugaku*) in order to trace links between archaic Japan and the contemporary Japanese "folk." See Orikuchi, *Orikuchi Shinobu zenshū,* 3:496–497, as well as H. D. Harootunian, "Figuring the Folk," 144–145.

37. Jun'ichi Isomae, *Japanese Mythology: Hermeneutics on Scripture* (Oakville, CT: Equinox Publishing, 2010), 27.

38. Ibid., 28–29. As Isomae mentions, "this close linkage of the Kojiki and Nihonshoki myths to the non-ruling strata does not appear before the advent of Nativism: it was an epochal development."

39. Harootunian, "Figuring the Folk," 155.

40. On this process, see Joan Piggott, *The Emergence of Japanese Kingship* (Stanford, CA: Stanford University Press, 1997); Gary Ebersole, *Ritual Poetry and the Politics of Death in Early Japan* (Princeton, NJ: Princeton University Press, 1989); Herman Ooms, *Imperial Politics and Symbolics in Ancient Japan: The Tenmu Dynasty, 650–800* (Honolulu: University of Hawai'i Press, 2009); and Michael Como, *Weaving and Binding: Immigrant Gods and Female Immortals in Ancient Japan* (Honolulu: University of Hawai'i Press, 2009), among others.

41. "Whereupon the Emperor said, 'This is the framework of the state, the great foundation of the imperial influence. Therefore . . . discarding the mistaken and establishing the true, I desire to hand them on to later generations." Philippi, *Kojiki,* 41; see also Kurano and Takeda, *Kojiki/Norito,* 45–47.

42. Kōnoshi Takamitsu, "Constructing Imperial Mythology: *Kojiki* and *Nihon shoki,*" trans. Iori Joko, in *Inventing the Classics: Modernity, National Identity, and Japanese Literature,* ed. Haruo Shirane and Tomi Suzuki (Stanford, CA: Stanford University Press, 2001), 52. The term *ritsuryō* here refers to the *ritsu* (penal) and *ryō* (administrative) law codes, which established the legal charter for the Yamato state. As I discuss in chapter 5, the Taihō legal code (Taihō ritsuryō), the earliest complete law code of the Yamato state, was promulgated in 702, a decade before the completion of the *Kojiki.*

43. Ibid.

44. Isomae, *Japanese Mythology,* 30.

45. Ibid., 25.

46. Kōnoshi indicates that this mythology became homogenized only in retrospect, after the compilation of the *Kojiki* and *Nihon shoki* narratives, through the retroactive labor of exegetical commentary. Kōnoshi, "Constructing Imperial Mythology," 56–59.

47. Ooms, *Imperial Politics and Symbolics,* 32.

48. Ibid.

49. From Julia Kristeva's *Semiotike:* "Every text takes shape as a mosaic of citations, every text is the absorption and transformation of other texts." Translated in Jonathan Culler, *Structuralist Poetics* (Ithaca, NY: Cornell University Press, 1979), 139. See also Julia Kristeva, *Desire in Language: A Semiotic Approach to Literature and Art,* ed. Leon Roudiez (New York: Columbia University Press, 1980), 66.

50. One explanation for the numerous variants found within the *Nihon shoki* may be related to the court's project to collect *fudoki,* an effort begun during the interval between the compilation of the two myth-histories. See Michiko Aoki, *Records of Wind and Earth: A Translation of* Fudoki *with Introduction and Commentaries* (Ann Arbor, MI: Association of Asian Studies, 1997), 2.

51. Isomae, *Japanese Mythology,* 51.

52. Ibid., 42–49. Three variants within the *Nihon shoki* name Susano-o (rather than Amaterasu) as the parent of Ame no Oshihomimi, who in turn fathered the "heavenly offspring" Ninigi. See W. G. Aston, trans., *Nihongi: Chronicles of Japan from the Earliest Times to A.D. 697* (Tokyo: Charles E. Tuttle Co., 1972), 33–40.

53. Isomae, *Japanese Mythology,* 47–49 and passim. For a more detailed comparison of the *Kojiki* and *Nihon Shoki* texts, see David Lurie, *Realms of Literacy: Early Japan and the History of Writing* (Cambridge, MA: Harvard University Press, 2011), 213–253.

54. Joan Piggott, "Sacral Kingship and Confederacy in Early Izumo," *Monumenta Nipponica* 44, no. 1 (spring 1989), 54.

55. Ibid., 60.

56. Ibid.; see also Piggott's *Emergence of Japanese Kingship,* 1–14, 150–151, and passim.

57. As Michael Como demonstrates, the process of integrating deities and cults between center and periphery was not merely a "top-down" process initiated by the state, but also flowed upward, as immigrant lineages from the Asian mainland brought with them newly popular deities, cults, and innovative technologies that spread widely through grassroots channels. See Michael Como, *Weaving and Binding,* xiv, 162, and passim.

58. Piggott, "Sacral Kingship and Confederacy in Early Izumo," 62.

59. Aoki, *Records of Wind and Earth,* 141 n. 165. This is suggestive, though not conclusive, of his status as a deity centered in Izumo, as no other *fudoki* is extant in its entirety.

60. This sword is more widely known as Kusanagi, the name retroactively given the weapon after Yamato Takeru used it on missions narrated later in the *Kojiki* and *Nihon shoki.* A variant in the *Nihon shoki* records the sword's original name as the Ama no murakumo, or "Heavenly Cloud-Gathering" sword. See Aston, *Nihongi,* 53.

61. Miyazawa Akihisa, "Izumo no saishi iseki," in *Izumo no kamigami: Shinwa to shizoku,* ed. Ueda Masaaki (Chikuma Shobō, 1987), 47.

62. Akimoto Kichiro, ed., *Fudoki,* in Nihon koten bungaku taikei 2 (Tokyo: Iwanami Shoten, 1970), 217; see also Aoki, *Records of Wind and Earth,* 140–141.

63. Inoue Mitsusada, *Nihon no rekishi: Shinwa kara rekishi e* (Tokyo: Chūō Kōronsha, 1965), 62.

64. It should be noted that the *ritsuryō* system of shrine offerings was breaking down even while the *Engishiki* was being compiled, as the state gradually lost its ability to patronize such an extensive system of shrines and as newly consecrated sites competed for state support. By the end of the Heian period, the extensive list recorded in the *Engishiki* had been replaced by a much more truncated system of twenty-two shrines. See Allan Grapard, "Institution, Ritual, and Ideology: The Twenty-Two Shrine-Temple Multiplexes of Heian Japan," *History of Religions* 27, no. 3 (fall 1988): 246–269.

65. Matsumoto Hisashi, "Susano-o shinkō no rekishi," in *Susano-o shinkō jiten,* ed. Ōbayashi Taryō (Tokyo: Ebisu Kōshō, 2004), 51. Bingo, adjacent to Izumo, would be equivalent to Hiroshima Prefecture today; Kii Province would now be equivalent to Wakayama Prefecture.

66. Once again this is suggestive, though not conclusive, evidence for the worship of Susano-o across the archipelago, because not all existing shrines were listed in the *jinmyōchō.* According to the *Izumo Fudoki,* for example, out of a total of 399 shrines in Izumo, only 184 were listed as "officially recognized shrines" (*kansha*) by the centralized Jingikan, or Department of Divinities. See Ueda Masaaki, "Kamigami no genzō," in *Izumo no kamigami: Shinwa to shizoku,* ed. Ueda Masaaki (Chikuma Shobō, 1987), 3–4. In the Heian period, Susano-o came to be worshipped as a manifestation of the Buddhist Heavenly King Gozu (Gozu Tennō) at the Gion shrine-temple complex in Kyoto, but the Gion complex did not exist prior to the ninth century.

67. See Matsumae Takeshi, "Izumo no shinwa," in Ueda, ed., *Izumo no kamigami,* 90; and Mizuno Yū, *Kodai no Izumo to Yamato* (Tokyo: Daiwashobō, 1994), 17.

68. The tumult surrounding this period is illustrated clearly in the era name chosen by the female ruler Kōtoku in 645: Taika, or "Great Change." See also the discussion by Como, who characterizes the period as one of "tremendous ferment in both the nature of the royal cult and in the cast of deities that formed its core." Como, *Weaving and Binding,* 2.

69. Matsumae Takeshi, *Nihon no kamigami* (Tokyo: Chūō Kōronsha, 1974), 47.

70. Mizuno, *Kodai no Izumo to Yamato,* 19.

71. Kōnoshi, "Constructing Imperial Mythology," 67. A full historical accounting of Susano-o worship would also need to take into consideration influences from the Korean peninsula on the development of the cult.

72. See the discussion in Ebersole, *Ritual Poetry,* 101–122. On the Niiname-sai, see the study by Robert Ellwood, *The Feast of Kingship: Accession Ceremonies in Ancient Japan* (Tokyo: Sophia University Press, 1973).

73. We should bear in mind that at no time do Izumo texts such as the *Izum*[illegible] name Ōnamuchi/Ōkuninushi as the offspring of Susano-o.

74. According to the *Nihon shoki* main text, three deities were sent down initially but failed to perform their mission: Ame no hohi, Take mikuma no ushi, and Ame wakahiko. Aston, *Nihongi,* 64–65.

75. Philippi, *Kojiki,* 134–135, modified. See Kurano and Takeda, *Kojiki/Norito,* 123.

76. Some premodern sources considered the shrine a seat of worship for Susano-o as well. See Matsumoto, "Susano-o shinkō no rekishi," 57.

77. Sakamoto Tarō et al., eds., *Nihon shoki,* in Nihon koten bungaku taikei 67 (Tokyo: Iwanami, 1967), 150–151.

78. See the discussion of theories regarding early Izumo in Matsumae, *Nihon no kamigami,* 49.

79. Anders Carlqvist, "The Land-Pulling Myth and Some Aspects of Historic Reality," *Japanese Journal of Religious Studies* 37, no. 2 (January 2010): 196–201; Shiraishi Taichirō, "Wakoku tanjō," in Nihon no jidaishi 1 (Tokyo: Yoshikawa Kōbunkan, 2002), 43–44.

80. See Carlqvist, "The Land-Pulling Myth," 196–204; Shiraishi, "Wakoku tanjō," 45; Mizuno, *Kodai no Izumo to Yamato,* 20; and Matsumae, *Nihon no kamigami,* 49.

81. Mizuno, *Kodai no Izumo to Yamato,* 24.

82. Watanabe Sadayuki, "Chi-iki ōken no jidai," in *Shimane-ken no rekishi,* ed. Matsuo Hisashi (Yamakawa Shuppansha, 2005), 57; See also Shiraishi, "Wakoku tanjō," 48, 90–94; Carlqvist, "The Land-Pulling Myth," 201; and Piggott, *Emergence of Japanese Kingship,* 32–33.

83. Piggott, "Sacral Kingship and Confederacy in Early Izumo," 60, and Carlqvist, "The Land-Pulling Myth," 203.

84. Piggott, "Sacral Kingship and Confederacy in Early Izumo," 60.

85. The position of Izumo no kuni no miyatsuko was appointed by the state and filled by the head of the leading family among the Izumo elite, the Izumo no Omi. While the office of *kuni no miyatsuko* was officially discontinued throughout the archipelago following the Taika reform of 645 and amid the Yamato state's attempt to exercise greater centralized control over the provinces, the Izumo no miyatsuko continued to hold office through the Nara period and beyond.

86. Matsumae, "Izumo no shinwa," 110–111.

87. The ritual grew still more elaborate over time: in its complete form, the year-long period of purification followed by recitation at court was repeated again upon completing the first praise ritual—a process aptly illustrating Mary Douglas' notion that "ideas concerning pollution and purification are used to mark the gravity of the event and the power of ritual." See Aoki Kazuo et al., eds., *Shoku Nihongi II,* in Shin nihon koten bungaku taikei 13 (Tokyo: Iwanami Shoten, 1997), 456–457, and the entry in Kokugakuin Daigaku Nihon Bunka Kenkyūjo, ed., *Shintō Jiten* (Tokyo: Kobundo, 1999), s.v. "Izumo Shinko," as well as Maeda Haruto, *Kodai Izumo* (Tokyo: Yoshikawa Kōbunkan, 2006), 108, and Mary Douglas, *Purity and Danger: An Analysis of the Concepts of Pollution and Taboo* (New York: Routledge, 1991), 96.

88. Donald Philippi, *Norito* (Princeton, NJ: Princeton University Press, 1990), 72–75, modified; see also Kurano and Takeda, *Kojiki/Norito,* 452–457.

89. See Felicia Bock, trans., *Engi-shiki: Procedures of the Engi Era, Books I-V* (Tokyo: Sophia University, 1972), 114–115.

90. The praise liturgy names the "blessed offspring of Izanagi" as Kushimikeno no mikoto, the great deity of the Kumano Shrine in Izumo, a principle shrine worshipped by the Izumo Omi family. Kushimikeno is frequently presented in scholarship as an alternate name for Susano-o (see Kurano and Takeda, *Kojiki/Norito,* 452–453), although this connection isn't clearly made in either the Izumo Kamuyogoto liturgy or in the *Izumo Fudoki.* On this point, see Matsumoto, "Susano-o shinkō no rekishi," 53.

91. As I discuss later, this represents a deviation from the official narrative of the Yamato court chronicles.

92. Philippi, *Norito,* 72–73; see also Kurano and Takeda, *Kojiki/Norito,* 454–457.

93. Matsumae, "Izumo no shinwa," 95.

94. See Matsumae, "Izumo no shinwa," 112, and Carlqvist, "The Land-Pulling Myth," 221–215.

95. Matsumae, "Izumo no shinwa," 111–112. See also Isomae, *Japanese Mythology,* 41–42.

96. According to the Kamuyogoto liturgy, Ōnamuchi presented three of his divine offspring to serve as "close protector deities" (近守神) for the sovereign. See Philippi, *Norito,* 74, and Kurano and Takeda, *Kojiki Norito,* 454–455.

97. See the discussion of the Kamuyogoto in Inoue Mitsusada, *Nihon no rekishi,* 84.

98. Aoki et al., *Shoku Nihongi,* entry for 716/2/10. The Yamato sovereign was not present for the first recorded performance of the liturgy in 716 but was represented on that occasion by an official from the Jingikan; see also Matsumae, "Izumo no shinwa," 111.

99. Aoki et al., *Shoku Nihongi,* 457; see also Maeda, *Kodai Izumo,* 118–119.

100. Obinata Katsumi, "Kodai kokka no tenkai to Izumo, Iwami, Oki sangoku," in *Shimane-ken no rekishi,* ed. Matsuo Hisashi et al. (Yamakawa Shuppensha, 2005), 103.

101. Philippi, *Norito,* 75; Kurano and Takeda, *Kojiki Norito,* 454–457.

102. See the discussion in Ebersole, *Ritual Poetry,* 89–91.

103. Here I mean to draw attention to mythic parallels between Susano-o's gift to Amaterasu (of the divine sword from Izumo) and the Izumo miyatsuko's ritual offerings to the Yamato sovereign (of jeweled beads, a sword, etc.). It is striking, however, that there are two instances recorded in the *Nihon shoki* regarding rulers who are keen to examine the sacred treasures of Izumo, with at times lethal consequences for some of those involved. See the *Nihon shoki* entries for Sūjin 60.7.14 and Suinin 26.8.3.

104. See Paul Veyne, *Did the Greeks Believe in Their Myths?* trans. Paula Wissing (Chicago: University of Chicago Press, 1988).

105. The two works alluded to here regarding double burial and silkworm cults—Ebersole's *Ritual Poetry* and Como's *Weaving and Binding,* respectively—remain among the leading works in English for examining the interplay between symbolic structure and editorial agency within the earliest myth-histories.

106. Frits Vos, *A Study of the Ise Monogatari,* vol. 2 (The Hague: Mouton & Co., 1957), 2.

107. Though my discussion moves in a somewhat different direction, there exists a growing body of scholarship critiquing the notion of "belief" as an operative category for the study of contemporary Japanese religions. Among others, see Karen Smyers, *The Fox and the Jewel* (Honolulu: University of Hawai'i Press, 1999), 1–13; Thomas Kasulis, *Shinto: The Way Home* (Honolulu: University of Hawai'i Press, 2004), 27–37; and Ian Reader, *Religion in Contemporary Japan* (Honolulu: University of Hawai'i Press, 1991), 1–22.

108. James Scott, *Domination and the Arts of Resistance: Hidden Transcripts* (New Haven, CT: Yale University Press, 1990), 18.

109. Ibid., 4.

110. Ibid., 20.

111. If this sounds too egalitarian for the elite world of the Japanese court, we might recall that the oracles narrating the exiled Sugawara no Michizane's posthumous return to the capital as a vengeful deity were revealed by a child, an ascetic, and a female shaman, leading to the establishment of a shrine to Michizane eventually patronized by the state.

## Chapter 3: The Radiance of Exile

*Epigraph.* Ivan Morris, trans., *The Pillow Book of Sei Shōnagon* (New York: Penguin Books, 1971), 125, modified. The passage refers to "a clear, moonlit night a little after the tenth day of the eighth month"—hence, shortly before the great autumn moon of the fifteenth day (according to the traditional Japanese lunar calendar) referenced in both the *Taketori* and the Suma chapter of the *Genji monogatari.* See also Ikeda Kikan et al., eds., *Makura no Sōshi,* in Nihon koten bungaku taikei 19 (Tokyo: Iwanami Shoten, 1971), 155–156.

1. Both have been the subject of much speculation. Because of details in the story such as the smoke rising from Mt. Fuji and because the tale is mentioned in various Heian era sources, the outermost dates possible for authorship have been established as between 810 and 949. Most scholars believe the tale to have been in circulation by 900. Regarding authorship, the tale is obviously a recasting of popular material, but several scholars believe it to have been put into the form of this tale by a single male author whose knowledge of Chinese comes through in the *kanbun*-like endings of sentences and other grammatical traces. See Sakakura Atsuyoshi et al., eds., *Taketori monogatari, Ise monogatari, Yamato monogatari,* in Nihon koten bungaku taikei 9 (Tokyo: Iwanami Shoten, 1974), 5–18, and Mitani Eichi, *Monogatari bungaku no sekai* (Tokyo: Yuseido, 1975), 30–32.

2. "*Monogatari no idekihajime no oya naru Taketori no okina,*" Royall Tyler, trans., *The Tale of Genji* (New York: Viking, 2001), 325; Yamagishi Tokuhei, ed., *Genji monogatari,* in Nihon koten bungaku taikei 15 (Tokyo: Iwanami Shoten, 1959), 179. Later in this chapter I touch on the relationship between the *Genji* and *Taketori* tales.

3. A simplistic identification of kana writing with women falls short of the complex ways in which gender was constructed through literature during the Heian period. The example most often cited for this is the *Tosa Nikki,* written by Ki no Tsurayuki, a male author passing as a female author writing in a male genre—a genre later popular among female authors. On the topic of gender and Heian literature, see especially Edith Sarra, *Fictions of Femininity: Literary Inventions of Gender in Japanese Court Women's Memoirs* (Stanford, CA: Stanford University Press, 1999); Tomiko Yoda, *Gender and National Literature: Heian Texts in the Constructions of Japanese Modernity* (Durham, NC: Duke University Press, 2004); Richard Okada, *Figures of Resistance: Language, Poetry, and Narrating in* The Tale of Genji *and Other Mid-Heian Texts* (Durham, NC: Duke University Press, 1991), especially 160–163; and Joshua Mostow, *At the House of Gathered Leaves: Shorter Biographical and Autobiographical Narratives from Japanese Court Literature* (Honolulu: University of Hawai'i Press, 2004), 1–44.

4. Among Japanese scholars, see particularly Mitani, *Monogatari bungaku no sekai,* and Kojima Naoko, *Kaguyahime gensō: Kōken to kinki* (Tokyo: Shinwa, 1995). Western scholars who have addressed the *Taketori* include Haruo Shirane, *The Bridge of Dreams: A Poetics of "The Tale of Genji"* (Stanford, CA: Stanford University Press, 1987); Okada, *Figures of Resistance;* Michele Marra, *The Aesthetics of Discontent: Politics and Reclusion in Medieval Japanese Literature* (Honolulu: University of Hawai'i Press, 1991); and Alan Miller, "The Swan-Maiden Revisited," *Asian Folklore Studies* 46, no. 1 (1987): 55–86.

5. Orikuchi Shinobu (1887–1953) considered the *Taketori* a pure example of his *kishu ryūritan* genre, or "tales of exiled and wandering nobles." As I discuss in chapter 2 and briefly in this chapter, however, Orikuchi's analysis of exile in the *Taketori* as the repetition of a timeless archetype failed to address the gendered and historical contexts from which the *Taketori* and other narratives of exile arose. Orikuchi's discussion of the *kishu ryūritan* genre can be found in *Orikuchi Shinobu zenshū,* ed. Orikuchi Hakushi Kinenkai (Tokyo: Chūōkōronsha, 1955), 7:344–353. For a more contemporary discussion connecting the *Taketori* to the *kishu ryūritan* genre, see Takahashi Tōru, *Monogatari bungei no hyōgenshi* (Nagoya: Nagoya Daigaku Shuppankai, 1987), 124–125.

6. I adopt this term from Shirane (*Bridge of Dreams*), used originally in reference to the *Tale of Genji.*

7. *Tsuki no miyako* refers to the "capital" (*miyako*) of the moon. In classical Japanese, *miyako* is defined as the site where the sovereign's palace is located. By extension, as in Donald Keene's translation of the *Taketori monogatari*, "*tsuki no miyako*" may also be translated as "palace of the moon." See note 12, below.

8. "*Monoguruoshiki yo.*" This quote comes from the Suma chapter of the *Tale of Genji*, a section that narrates Genji's exile from the Heian court. Yamagishi, *Genji monogatari*, 20; Tyler, *The Tale of Genji,* 233.

9. The *fudoki* are valuable sources of comparison with the court-centered royal works of myth-history. *Fudoki* usually list a place name along with a fragment of mythic narrative providing the genealogy for that name. From these sources it is evident that the royal deities—Amaterasu in particular—were not necessarily worshipped in every province and that other regions retained their own local narratives about the descent of gods and the creation of the land. See Michiko Aoki, *Records of Wind and Earth* (Ann Arbor, MI: Association for Asian Studies, 1987).

10. Akimoto Kichiro, ed., *Fudoki,* in Nihon koten bungaku taikei 2 (Tokyo: Iwanami Shoten, 1970), 468.

11. See the discussion of the *fudoki* fragment in Okada, *Figures of Resistance*, 44–47.

12. Sakakura, *Taketori monogatari*, 29. Translations from the *Taketori* are my own; for a full translation of the text, see Donald Keene, trans., "The Tale of the Bamboo Cutter," in *Modern Japanese Fiction and Its Traditions,* ed. J. Thomas Rimer (Princeton, NJ: Princeton University Press, 1978), 275–305.

13. Sakakura, *Taketori monogatari,* 29–30.

14. Ibid., 30.

15. Ibid., 31; see Keene, "Tale of the Bamboo Cutter," 277. See Nakamura Hajime et al., eds., *Iwanami bukkyō jiten* (Tokyo: Iwanami Shoten, 1989), s.v. "*henge.*"

16. Sakakura, *Taketori monogatari*, 32; see Keene, "Tale of the Bamboo Cutter," 278.

17. For a succinct discussion of the rise of the Fujiwara regent's line, see Mikael Adolphson, "Oligarchy, Shared Rulership, and Power Blocs," in *Japan Emerging: Premodern History to 1850,* ed. Karl Friday (Boulder, CO: Westview Press, 2012), 122–134.

18. See Robert Borgen, *Sugawara no Michizane and the Early Heian Court* (Honolulu: University of Hawai'i Press, 1994), 63–64.

19. Mitani, *Monogatari bungaku no sekai*, 46–51. In contrast to texts that adopt a critical stance toward the Fujiwara regent's line, Joshua Mostow has explored how Fujiwara regents were also the patrons of texts presenting themselves in more favorable light. See Mostow, *At the House of Gathered Leaves*, 1–44.

20. As further evidence of a textual critique of Fujiwara ascendance within the *Taketori,* scholars have identified names among Kaguyahime's suitors and other figures in the tale that appear to make punning reference to key members of the Fujiwara line. Prince Kuramochi, given the task of obtaining the branch from a tree on a mountain of immortality, has been linked to Fujiwara no Fubito, the adopted son of Fujiwara no Kamatari and ancestor of the powerful Heian regent Fujiwara no Yoshifusa. While Fujiwara no Fubito was a leading member of the Fujiwara line some two centuries before the *Taketori* was written, his descendent Yoshifusa was the powerful regent living around the time of its composition responsible for the Ōtenmon incident mentioned above. Others have suggested that the character Nakatomi

no Fusako, the messenger in the story sent by the emperor to determine whether Kaguyahime is indeed as beautiful as rumored (but whom Kaguyahime refuses to see), is a composite referring most directly to Fujiwara no Fusasaki, who began the Fujiwara's Northern Branch. See the discussion of names in Marra, *The Aesthetics of Discontent*, 28–33, which in turn references Kano Morohira, "Taketori monogatari Ko," in *Taketori no okina no monogatari kai,* ed. Tanaka Ohide and Kano Morohira (Tokyo: Kokubun Meicho Kankōkai, 1934); see also Kojima Naoko, *Kaguyahime gensō*, 74–75, and Okada, *Figures of Resistance*, 57–61.

21. Sakakura, *Taketori monogatari,* 53; see also Keene, "Tale of the Bamboo Cutter," 294.

22. Or "shadow," as in Keene's translation. The word *kage* at the time could suggest either light or shadow; in keeping with Kaguyahime's renowned radiance, I consider the former meaning more appropriate.

23. "*Tama o todometaru kokochi shite*," Sakakura, *Taketori monogatari,* 57.

24. Keene translates as an "obligation incurred in a former life," though the phrase *mukashi no chigiri* literally means simply an obligation from the past. Sakakura, *Taketori monogatari,* 59; see Keene, "Tale of the Bamboo Cutter," 299.

25. Sakakura, *Taketori monogatari*, 63; see also Keene, "Tale of the Bamboo Cutter," 302.

26. Orikuchi, *Orikuchi Shinobu zenshū* 7:344–353.

27. Marra, *Aesthetics of Discontent,* 14–34.

28. Okada, *Figures of Resistance*, 13.

29. Shirane, *Bridge of Dreams*, 194.

30. Marra, *Aesthetics of Discontent,* 34.

31. Ibid., 26.

32. Ibid., emphasis added. The phrase *onri edo gongu jōdo* is introduced by Marra; it does not appear in the story itself.

33. See especially William LaFleur, *The Karma of Words* (Berkeley: University of California Press, 1983), xii.

34. See Kojima Naoko, *Kaguyahime gensō,* 77, as well as the general discussion of Pure Land belief and *monogatari* in Takahashi Tōru, *Monogatari bungei no hyōgenshi,* 120–125.

35. Marra, *Aesthetics of Discontent,* 26.

36. The extant text of the *ritsuryō* codes can be found in Inoue Mitsusada, ed., *Ritsuryō,* in Nihon shisō taikei 3 (Tokyo: Iwanami Shoten, 1980). See my discussion of the *ritsuryō* codes in chapter 5.

37. Sakakura, *Taketori monogatari*, 65.

38. I am grateful to Michele Marra for suggesting this line of inquiry.

39. On the intertextual poetics of exile in the *Genji,* see especially the chapter by Haruo Shirane, "The Poetics of Exile," in his *Bridge of Dreams*, 17–23.

40. See Kojima Naoko's essay, "Araburu hikari: Kaguyahime kara Hikaru Genji e," in *Ōken no kiso e,* ed. Akasaka Norio (Tokyo: Shin'yosha, 1992), 186 and passim.

41. This term is taken from Richard Okada, "Displacements of Conquest, or Exile: *The Tale of Genji*, and Post-Cold War Learning," in *Reading the Tale of Genji: Its Picture-Scrolls, Texts and Romance,* ed. Richard Stanley-Baker et al. (Folkestone, UK: Global Oriental, 2009), 71.

42. Ibid., 69.

43. Ibid.

44. Details of this popular account are taken from Okada, *Figures of Resistance,* 159.

45. Yamagishi, *Genji monogatari,* 41.

46. Tyler, *The Tale of Genji*, 319.

47. Ibid., xii.

48. Thomas LaMarre, *Uncovering Heian Japan: An Archeology of Sensation and Inscription* (Durham, NC: Duke University Press, 2000), 70–71, emphasis added.

49. In LaMarre's discussion of poetics and the Heian imagination, he passes over the subtext of exile structuring the narrative of the Picture Contest scroll in the *Genji.* Thus he locates Genji's eventual victory primarily in the quality of his artwork, while failing to note the significance of the previous rounds leading up to Genji's victory that I discuss later in the chapter.

50. Tyler, *The Tale of Genji,* 325, modified; Yamagishi, *Genji monogatari,* 179; see also my discussion in chapter 1.

51. "*Miyako ni ariwabite,*" Sakakura, *Taketori monogatari,* 115. The *Ise monogatari* is not today considered the work of a single author.

52. Tyler, *The Tale of Genji,* 326; also Yamagishi, *Genji monogatari,* 180.

53. Tyler, *The Tale of Genji,* 326; also Yamagishi, *Genji monogatari,* 181, emphasis added.

54. Tyler, *The Tale of Genji,* 329; Yamagishi, *Genji monogatari,* 184–185. Later in the chapter, in the afterglow of the contest, as the moon begins to rise and sake cups are passed around, conversation turns to the "His Late Eminence": the departed emperor who had been father both to Genji and the current retired emperor, and Genji is praised as the one among the departed emperor's princes and princesses who most fully developed his aesthetic capabilities—who "put to shame the finest artists of the past." Genji's connection to his late father serves as a contrast to the regime that sent Genji into exile, the court of the now retired emperor. The way is thus paved for Genji to set new standards for the court: at the close of the picture contest chapter, the narrator states that due to Genji's "touches," "this was an extraordinarily brilliant reign." Tyler, *The Tale of Genji,* 329–330; Yamagishi, *Genji monogatari,* 185–188.

55. Tyler, *The Tale of Genji,* 358, emphasis added; Yamagishi, *Genji monogatari,* 239.

56. See the discussion in Okada, *Figures of Resistance,* 166–167.

57. Shirane, *Bridge of Dreams,* 23, emphasis added.

58. Tyler, *The Tale of Genji,* 325; Yamagishi, *Genji monogatari,* 179.

## Chapter 4: Spirits in Exile

*Epigraph 1.* Ikeda Kikan, ed., *Makura no Sōshi,* in Nihon koten bungaku taikei 19 (Tokyo: Iwanami Shoten, 1971), 114, "*Kokochi yogenaru mono.*" At the annual Gion spirit-pacification festival, the master of horses—adorned with flowers—led the procession of horses from the imperial palace.

*Epigraph 2.* Michel de Certeau, *The Practice of Everyday Life,* trans. Steven Rendall (Berkeley: University of California Press, 1988), 21.

1. Kuroita Katsumi, ed., *Nihon kiryaku,* in Kokushi taikei 11 (Tokyo: Yoshikawa Kōbunkan, 1979), 25. The *Nihon kiryaku* is a chronicle of the Japanese court from the "age of the gods" to 1036, written in Chinese, which provides helpful information regarding the court especially for the period after the Six National Histories end (post-887).

2. Helen McCullough, trans., *Okagami: The Great Mirror* (Princeton, NJ: Princeton University Press, 1980), 217; see also Matsumura Hiroji, ed., *Ōkagami,* in Nihon koten bungaku taikei 21 (Tokyo: Iwanami Shoten, 1973), 253. By the time the *Okagami* was written, around 1100, Michizane had been deified and was known as the Kitano god (among other names). He would not yet have been known as the Kitano god in 930, the time that this passage refers back to. It's possible that the story is apocryphal—though no less valuable a clue into the imagination of Michizane in the later Heian period.

3. Robert Borgen, *Sugawara no Michizane and the Early Heian Court* (Honolulu: University of Hawai'i Press, 1994), 336.

4. Following common academic use, I employ the term cult here (rooted in the Latin *cultus*) to refer simply to the worship of a particular deity within a larger pantheon of divinities.

5. On a similar point, see Allan Grapard, "Japan's Ignored Cultural Revolution," *History of Religions* 23, no. 3 (February 1984): 253.

6. On the *goryō* cults, see especially the collection edited by Shibata Minoru: *Goryō shinkō* (Tokyo: Yūzankaku Shuppan, 1984), and more recently Yamada Yūji, *Bakkosuru onryō: Tatari to chinkon no Nihon shi,* (Tokyo: Yoshikawa Kōbunkan, 2007). Also helpful are Ueda Masaaki, ed., *Tenman Tenjin: Goryō kara gakumongami e* (Tokyo: Chikuma Shobō, 1988); Murayama Shūichi, *Tenjin goryō shinkō* (Tokyo: Hanawa Shobō, 1996); and the more popular work by Horimoto Masami, *Onryō no kodaishi* (Tokyo: Hokutosha, 1999). In English, see Hori Ichiro, *Folk Religion in Japan* (Chicago: University of Chicago Press, 1968); H. E. Plutschow, *Chaos and Cosmos: Ritual in Early and Medieval Japanese Literature* (Leiden: E. J. Brill, 1990); Doris Bargen, *A Woman's Weapon: Spirit Possession in* The Tale of Genji (Honolulu: University of Hawai'i Press, 1997); Neil McMullen, "On Placating the Gods and Pacifying the Populace: The Case of the Gion Goryō Cult," *History of Religions* 27, no. 3 (February 1988): 270–293; Kuroda Toshio, "The World of Spirit Pacification: Issues of State and Religion," *Japanese Journal of Religious Studies* 23, no. 3–4 (fall 1996): 321–351; Herman Ooms, *Imperial Politics and Symbolics in Ancient Japan: The Tenmu Dynasty, 650–800* (Honolulu: University of Hawai'i Press, 2009), 224–252; and Michael Como, *Weaving and Binding: Immigrant Gods and Female Immortals in Ancient Japan* (Honolulu: University of Hawai'i Press, 2009), 193–196.

7. On deification in general, see the discussion of *hitogami* in Hori, *Folk Religion,* 31–38.

8. This is not to say that malevolent spirits had not existed previously. *Tatarigami,* or curse-bearing deities, were commonly held responsible for pestilence and plague, yet they were not classified into a group of vengeful spirits of aristocratic or royal dead known specifically as *goryō,* nor were they necessarily identified as the deceased spirits of specific individuals. Spirits of the living were also believed capable of possessing others and even causing death; see Bargen, *A Woman's Weapon,* for a discussion of this type of spirit possession.

9. Sakurai Tokutarō, drawing upon the discovery of *mokkan* and wooden effigies used for making curses from the Nara and Heian periods, makes an important connection between the cult of vengeful spirits and the widespread culture of magical curses in Yamato Japan: Sakurai, "Onryō kara Goryō e," in *Goryō shinkō,* ed. Shibata Minoru (Tokyo: Yūzankaku Shuppan, 1984), 3–12.

10. Fujiwara no Hirotsugu, executed in 740 for starting a rebellion after having been exiled to Kyushu, is also considered an early *goryō* prototype. However, the *Shoku Nihongi* does not use the term *goryō* to refer to his vengeful spirit, but simply *ryō,* and his name is not

included among those listed in the first official record of *goryō* mentioned in the *Nihon sandai jitsuroku.* See Aoki Kazuo et al., eds., *Shoku Nihongi,* in Shin nihon koten bungaku taikei 13 (Tokyo: Iwanami Shoten, 1997), entry for 746/6/18, as well as Yamada, *Bakkosuru onryō,* 18–19.

11. Sawara's exile and death are recorded in the *Nihon kiryaku* 785/9/28. For a detailed discussion of Sawara's case, see Yamada, *Bakkosuru onryō,* 34–43, as well as Plutschow, *Chaos and Cosmos,* 207–209; Inoue Mitsuo, "Kodai no goryō shinkō," in *Tenman Tenjin: Goryō kara gakumongami e,* ed. Ueda Masaaki (Tokyo: Chikuma Shobō, 1988), 34; and Horimoto, *Onryō no kodaishi,* 139–228.

12. The official number of *goryō* fluctuated over time. The *Nihon sandai jitsuroku,* the official court history that records the first *goryō-e,* specifically records that six spirits were worshipped at that time and lists them by name or title. Later, as I mention below, this list expanded to eight (although not always the same eight, depending on the place of worship).

13. Neil McMullen, following Shibata Minoru, writes that the Fujiwara male mentioned in the 863 *goryō-e* was Fujiwara no Hirotsugu, rather than Nakanari, which contradicts current scholarly opinion. The confusion arises because the Fujiwara in question is mentioned in the text only by his title the *kansatsushi.* See McMullen, "On Placating the Gods," 286 and 288.

14. Inoue Mitsuo, "Kodai no goryō shinkō," 33–36.

15. See the *Nihon sandai jitsuroku* entry for 863/5/20: 事に座し誅せられ、冤魂癘をなす. The character for *en* (冤) conveys the meaning "false charge." Kuroita Katsumi, ed., *Nihon sandai jitsuroku,* in Kokushi taikei 4 (Tokyo: Yoshikawa Kōbunkan, 2000); see also Takeda Yūkichi and Satō Kenzō, eds., *Kundoku Nihon sandai jitsuroku* (Tokyo: Rinsen Shoten, 1986).

16. Nihon Daijiten Kankōkai, eds., *Nihon kokugo daijiten* (Tokyo: Shogakkan, 1972–1976), s.v. "*enkon.*" Originally a Chinese term (*yuanhun*), the phrase appears in Chinese texts as early as the third century BCE, referring to grieved spirits who carried out their vengeance as an act of justice. See Alvin Cohen, "Avenging Ghosts and Moral Judgment in Ancient Chinese Historiography: Three Examples from Shih-chi," in *Legend, Lore, and Religion in China,* ed. Sarah Allan and Alvin Cohen (San Francisco: Chinese Materials Center, 1979), 99.

17. See *Nihon sandai jitsuroku* 863/5/20. See also the discussion of the passage by Inoue Mitsuo, "Kodai no goryō shinkō," 32.

18. Kuroda, "World of Spirit Pacification," 326.

19. *Nihon sandai jitsuroku* 863/5/20.

20. Ibid., 863/5/20.

21. The Gion shrine-temple complex was purged of its Buddhist elements as part of the "separation of Buddhas and *kami*" policy of the Meiji period, and it has been known since that time simply as Yasaka Shrine. During the Heian period, for example, the deity Susano-o came to be worshipped at Gion as a manifestation of the Buddhist Heavenly King Gozu (Gozu Tennō).

22. Fujiwara Munetada, *Chūyūki,* 1127/6/14, quoted in Kuroda, "World of Spirit Pacification," 340, modified.

23. Kuroda, "World of Spirit Pacification," 338–339.

24. Ibid., 333.

25. Ibid., 337.

26. For the two different lists of the eight goryō worshipped at the Upper and Lower Goryō Shrines, see Shibata Minoru, "Goryō shinkō to Tenjin," in *Sugawara Michizane to*

*Dazaifu Tenmangū,* vol. 1, ed. Dazaifu Tenmangū Bunka Kenkyūjo (Tokyo: Yoshikawa Kōbunkan, 1975), 351.

27. Yamada, *Bakkosuru onryō,* 48–49.

28. See the discussion in Yamada, *Bakkosuru onryō,* 53–54.

29. See Borgen, *Sugawara no Michizane,* 63–64.

30. For some of the ramifications of the Ōtenmon Incident within the world of Heian culture and politics, see Michele Marra, *The Aesthetics of Discontent: Politics and Reclusion in Medieval Japanese Literature* (Honolulu: University of Hawai'i Press, 1991), 30.

31. H. Paul Varley, for example, in a table of "major periods and cultural epochs of Japanese history" within his widely used text *Japanese Culture*, refers to a "Fujiwara epoch" lasting from "the tenth century to the late eleventh century." Varley, *Japanese Culture* (Honolulu: University of Hawai'i Press, 1984), x.

32. See, for example, Mimi Hall Yiengpruksawan, in "What's in a Name? Fujiwara Fixation in Japanese Cultural History," *Monumenta Nipponica* 49, no. 4 (winter 1994): 423–453, where she questions whether the Fujiwara were as powerful as many historians assume and has pointed out the degree to which the Fujiwara were losing cultural and financial capital—unable even to repair their own villas—during the very years that others place them at the height and center of Heian cultural politics. In effect, she argues, scholars have at times accepted the self-representation of the Fujiwara found in such works as the *Eiga monogatari*—works that are dedicated to glorifying the Fujiwara line—without looking more closely into the actual context of Heian cultural and political practices.

33. For accounts emphasizing the importance of the Fujiwara in this period, see Helen McCullough, "The Fujiwara Role in Japanese Court History from Kamatari to Michinaga," Appendix D in Helen Craig McCullough, trans., *Okagami: The Great Mirror* (Princeton, NJ: Princeton University Press, 1980), 335–355, as well as George Sansom, *A History of Japan to 1334* (Stanford, CA: Stanford University Press, 1958) especially chapter 8, "The Fujiwara Regents."

34. Only one other scholar had attained the rank of minister of the right: Kibi no Makibi, from 766 to 771. See McCullough, *Okagami*, 343 note 8.

35. Retired emperor Uda, known during his retirement as the Teiji no In, attempted to prevent the edict banishing Michizane from being carried out but was refused entrance to the palace.

36. See McCullough, *Okagami*, Appendix D, 343.

37. Because the immediate political maneuvering that led to Michizane's banishment has received extensive treatment by scholars elsewhere, I have omitted further details here. See especially Borgen, *Sugawara no Michizane*, 270–289; for a detailed analysis in Japanese of Michizane's exile, see Tokoro Isao, "Michizane no hairu," in *Sugawara Michizane to Dazaifu Tenmangū,* vol. 1, ed. Dazaifu Tenmangū Bunka Kenkyūjo (Tokyo: Yoshikawa Kōbunkan, 1975), 54–100.

38. *Nihon kiryaku* 901/1/25 (Engi 1/1/25).

39. *Nihon kiryaku* 901/2/4. See also the entry for 901/1/25 in Kuroita Katsumi, ed., *Seiji yōryaku*, in Kokushi taikei 28 (Tokyo: Yoshikawa Kōbunkan, 1972), 2. The *Seiji yōryaku* is another unofficial court history, which also uses the term *sasen* in reference to Michizane's appointment to the Dazaifu and states that offerings were to be made to appease the imperial ancestors. (A new era name, Engi, was adopted after Michizane's banishment. Therefore, the year 901 can be referred to both as the first year of the Engi period (as in the *Nihon kiryaku*) or the fourth year of Shōtai (as in the *Seiji yōryaku*).

40. Jeffrey Mass, *Antiquity and Anachronism in Japanese History* (Stanford, CA: Stanford University Press, 1992), 45

41. Kawaguchi Hisao, ed., *Kanke bunsō: Kanke goshū*, in Nihon koten bungaku taikei 72 (Tokyo: Iwanami Shoten, 1966), 483 (item 479): 哀哉放逐者.

42. Kobayashi Shinmei, ed., *Shinsen kanwa jiten* (Tokyo: Shōgakukan, 2000), s.v. "*hōchiku*."

43. Burton Watson, trans., *Japanese Literature in Chinese,* vol. 1 (New York: Columbia University Press, 1975), 111. See *Kanke Kōshū*, 481 (item 478 不出門): 一從謫落在柴荊/万死兢々跼蹐情.

44. Kobayashi, *Shinsen kanwa jiten*, s.v. "*takuraku*." The characters for *takuraku* are not commonly used in modern Japanese. A classical cognate of *taku* that illustrates the twin meanings of exile and demotion is *takusennin*, "immortals banished from heaven to the world of humans."

45. See the *Kodansha Encyclopedia of Japan* (New York: Kodansha, 1983), s.v. "Dazaifu."

46. Borgen, *Sugawara no Michizane,* 289.

47. Ibid., 378, emphasis added; see Kuroita Katsumi, ed., *Seiji yōryaku*, 3.

48. On Michizane's journey to the Dazaifu, see Borgen, *Sugawara no Michizane,* 279 and 289. The instructions to Michizane's guards en route to the Dazaifu are recorded in Kuroita Katsumi, ed., *Seiji yōryaku*, 3: "食馬給无."

49. McCullough, *Okagami*, 96. See Tachibana Kenji et al., ed., *Okagami*, in Nihon koten bungaku zenshū 34 (Tokyo: Shogakkan, 1974), 74.

50. Delmer Brown and Ichiro Ishida, trans. and eds., *The Future and the Past: A Translation and Study of the Gukanshō* (Berkeley: University of California Press, 1979), 42; see also Okami Masao et al., ed., *Gukanshō*, in Nihon koten bungaku taikei 86 (Tokyo: Iwanami Shoten, 1968), 154–155.

51. For details on those sent into exile beside Michizane, see Borgen, *Sugawara no Michizane,* 279, as well as Kuroita Katsumi, ed., *Seiji yōryaku,* 3.

52. The Dazaifu, an administrative outpost of the Japanese court in Tsukushi (Kyushu), was originally built in the seventh century as a fortification and defensive base with an eye toward invaders from the mainland. Under the *ritsuryō* legal system, the Dazaifu took on greater importance, and by the eighth century the outpost was responsible for the administration of Tsukushi and its districts. Due to its proximity to the Korean peninsula, the Dazaifu played an important role in diplomacy, receiving foreign officials and Japanese returning from the Asian mainland. While ordinarily under the *ritsuryō* system, the central government bureau (Daijōkan) had responsibility for the governance of all provinces, the Dazaifu was exceptional in that it had direct responsibility for the governance of Tsukushi. See especially Bruce Batten, *To the Ends of Japan: Premodern Frontiers, Boundaries, and Interactions* (Honolulu: University of Hawai'i Press, 2003), as well as Furuhashi Nobuyoshi, ed., *Nihon bungeishi* (Tokyo: Kawade, 1986), 77 and 110, and the *Kodansha Encyclopedia of Japan*, s.v. "Dazaifu."

53. In charge of the Dazaifu, nominally, was a governor-general. In the Heian period, this office was customarily given to a prince, but the holder of the office nearly always remained in the capital, sending a provisional governor-general to occupy the office on their behalf. Furuhashi Nobuyoshi, ed., *Nihon bungeishi*, 110.

54. During the Heian period it became common to reduce some princes to the status of commoners, partly to lessen the drain on the imperial treasury and partly to reduce the field of potential competitors for the throne. This change of status resulted in their receiving a sur-

name, the most common of which was Minamoto, or Genji. These figures frequently emerge as powerful emblems of discontent—the most familiar example being the hero of the *Tale of Genji,* a prince-turned-commoner who himself is exiled for two chapters.

55. Ariwara no Narihira is popularly attributed authorship of the *Ise monogatari,* although scholars assume the work to be the result of redactions and contributions from several anonymous hands. On the production of a literature of disaffection in general and the *Ise monogatari* in particular, see Marra, *The Aesthetics of Discontent,* especially 35–53.

56. Regarding the Anna Incident (Anna no Hen), see Richard Okada, *Figures of Resistance: Language, Poetry, and Narrating in* The Tale of Genji *and Other Mid-Heian Texts* (Durham, NC: Duke University Press, 1991), 166–170.

57. *Nihon kiryaku*, 110, cited in Okada, *Figures of Resistance,* 168.

58. William and Helen Craig McCullough, trans., *A Tale of Flowering Fortunes: Annals of Japanese Aristocratic Life in the Heian Period,* vol. 1 (Stanford, CA: Stanford University Press, 1980), 100; see also Matsumura Hiroji et al., eds., *Eiga monogatari*, in Nihon koten bungaku takei 75 (Tokyo: Iwanami Shoten, 1974), 58, as well as the discussion in Okada, *Figures of Resistance,* 168.

59. Edward Seidensticker, trans., *The Gossamer Years* (Charles E. Tuttle, 1964), 72–73; see also Suzuki Tomotarō et al., eds., *Kagerō nikki*, in Nihon koten bungaku takei 20 (Tokyo: Iwanami Shoten, 1974), 175.

60. Yamada, *Bakkosuru onryō,* 65.

61. This was the *Kanke Kōshū*, cited above. Ki no Haseo's name has been proposed as one of the possible authors of the *Taketori monogatari*.

62. See Yamada, *Bakkosuru onryō,* 67.

63. For contemporary chronicles that record the lightning strike, see the *Fusō Ryakki* and *Nihon kiryaku* entries for Enchō 8 (930)/6/26. The incident is discussed by Borgen, *Sugawara no Michizane,* among others, and is vividly portrayed in the *Kitano Tenjin Engi* picture scroll, Komatsu, ed., Kuroita Katsumi, ed., *Fusō ryakki*, in Kokushi taikei 12 (Tokyo: Yoshikawa Kōbunkan, 1999).

64. Dōken's revelation is recorded in Makabe Toshinobu, ed., *Kitano,* in Shinto Taikei (Jinja-hen) 11 (Tokyo: Shinto Taikei Hensankai, 1979), 77–80.

65. Makabe, *Kitano,* 80.

66. Shinbo Tōru, ed., *Kitano Tenjin engi emaki* (Tokyo: Shibundō, 1991), 114–115.

67. Makabe, *Kitano,* 30–31: "彼の輸得処に我が禿倉を構結."

68. Hokora—sometimes written 宝倉, or "jewel storehouse"—refers to a small shrine.

69. Yamada, *Bakkosuru onryō,* 77.

70. Yoshitane's son's oracle is recorded in Makabe, *Kitano,* 42–44.

71. Yamada, *Bakkosuru onryō,* 77–78.

72. Kokugakuin Daigaku Nihon Bunka Kenkyūjo, eds., *Shintō jiten* (Tokyo: Kōbundō, 1999), s.v. "*raijin*."

73. Ibid.

74. Morosuke's prayer is recorded in Makabe, *Kitano,* 11, 29–30.

75. The temple Anrakuji was eventually known historically as the Anrakuji Tenmangū, then was renamed the Dazaifu Jinja during the Meiji period, and from the postwar period it has been known as the Dazaifu Tenmangū. The site today is second in importance among Tenjin shrines only to the Kitano Tenmangū in Kyoto. See Yamada, *Bakkosuru onryō,* 65.

76. See Makabe, *Kitano,* p. 12, as well as Borgen, *Sugawara no Michizane,* 324, and Yamada, *Bakkosuru onryō,* 82.

77. Ikeda, *Makura no Sōshi*, 161. Some versions of the Pillow Book refer to this lord as the *Kitano no saishō*, referencing the lord's position as a consultant (*saishō*, or *sangi*) on the Council of State (Daijōkan). For a discussion of titles and ranks within the Japanese court, see William and Helen Craig McCullough, *Tale of Flowering Fortunes,* vol. 2, Appendix A, 789–831.

78. For information linking Michizane's final promotions to an epidemic, see Plutschow, *Chaos and Cosmos,* 211. For the edicts promoting Michizane, see Makabe, *Kitano,* 53.

79. As Kuroda Toshio pointed out, "the social control of belief systems has always been an object of struggle." Kuroda, "World of Spirit Pacification," 330.

80. Ibid., 334.

81. Borgen, *Sugawara no Michizane,* 324; the list of nineteen shrines was a precursor to the set of twenty-two shrines finalized by 1039.

82. From Kokan Shiren's *Genkō Shakusho*, cited in Bernard Faure, *Visions of Power: Imagining Medieval Japanese Buddhism* (Princeton, NJ: Princeton University Press, 1996), 104.

83. For a sense of the considerable transformations the Michizane cult has undergone over time, see Borgen, *Sugawara no Michizane,* 325–336.

84. Yamada, *Bakkosuru onryō,* 53. See also Allan Grapard, "Religious Practices," in *The Cambridge History of Japan,* Vol. 2: *Heian Japan,* ed. Donald Shively and William McCullough (New York: Cambridge University Press, 1999), 558–564.

85. See the conclusion of Yonei Teruyoshi's "Kodai Nihon no 'tatari *shisutemu*'," *Tokyo Daigaku Shūkyō Nenpyō* 10 (1992): unpaginated.

86. An entry in the *Nihon sandai jitsuroku* from 865, for example, indicates that in the relatively early years of the *goryō* cult, the court actually prohibited a *goryō-e* from being held. See *Nihon sandai jitsuroku* 865/6/14. Discussed and quoted in Kitayama Shigeo, *Heian-kyō*, in Nihon no rekishi 4 (Tokyo: Chūō Kōronsha, 1965), 228, and Kikuchi Kyōko, "Goryō shinkō no seiritsu to hatten," in *Goryō shinkō,* ed. Shibata Minoru (Tokyo: Yūzankaku Shuppan, 1984), 37–61. As Kikuchi points out, the enormously popular Gion *goryō-e* later came to be held on the same date as the banned *goryō-e* (44). See also the discussion by McMullen, "On Placating the Gods," 290 and note 43.

87. Both Kitayama and McMullen point out that because the prohibition refers to crowds gathering and engaging in horseback riding and archery contests during the *goryō-e,* the court may have been anxious about the potential for uprising on such occasions.

88. Yamada, *Bakkosuru onryō,* 71–72, and Kuroda, "World of Spirit Pacification," 329–330.

89. See Matsuo Kenji, "Explaining the 'Mystery' of the *Ban Dainagon ekotoba,*" *Japanese Journal of Religious Studies* 28, no. 1–2 (spring 2001): 103–132.

90. See the *Fusō Ryakki*, 292: "今年始入末法." For a discussion of the "last age of the law" in Japanese history, see Marra, *The Aesthetics of Discontent,* especially 71–75.

91. Yiengpruksawan, in "What's in a Name?" has suggested that the grand work patronized by the Fujiwara, such as the Amida Hall of the Byōdō-in, "was a strategy, a form of rhetoric, by which order momentarily reigned" (450). She also notes, "This is the society of a frightened cultural elite, for whom anarchy is not an abstraction" (449).

## Chapter 5: Cosmologies of Law

*Epigraph 1.* One year after the oracle cited in this passage, retired emperor Toba died, the Hōgen rebellion broke out (a succession dispute among Toba's sons), and the practice of execution returned to the Heian capital. William R. Wilson, trans., *Tale of the Disorder in Hōgen* (Ithaca, NY: Cornell University East Asia Program, 2001), 5, as well as Nagazumi Yasuaki and Shimada Isao, eds., *Hōgen monogatari, Heiji monogatari,* in Nihon koten bungaku taikei 31 (Tokyo: Iwanami Shoten, 1961), 58. Regarding the historical accuracy of the *Hōgen monogatari,* see note 79 below.

*Epigraph 2.* Jacques Le Goff, *The Medieval Imagination,* Arthur Goldhammer, trans. (Chicago: University of Chicago Press, 1988), 12.

1. The *Nihon Ryōiki* was compiled around 822 and is attributed to the priest Kyōkai. The collection contains one chapter for each of the 116 regnal periods of the fifty-three sovereigns traditionally said to have ruled up to that point. Emperor Saga's reign was known by the era name Kōnin (弘仁), lasting from 810 through 823.

2. Nakada Norio, ed., *Nihon ryōiki,* in Shinpen Nihon koten bungaku zenshū 6 (Tokyo: Shogakukan, 1995), 376.

3. "*Fukō no daigyaku, fugi no shigoku.*" Wilson, *Tale of the Disorder in Hōgen,* 69, emphasis added, and Nagazumi and Shimada, *Hōgen monogatari,* 380.

4. The work of a committee of drafters, the Taihō ritsuryō was completed in 701 and enacted in 702. Details about the text of the *ritsuryō* codes will be discussed later in this chapter; at this point it is important to note that not long after the Taihō ritsuryō was completed, the court began work on a revised set of codes. These, known as the Yōrō ritsuryō, were drafted at some point around 718 but not enacted into law until 757.

Earlier attempts to construct a legal code appear to have begun in the court of Emperor Tenji at Otsu in Ōmi, perhaps around 668, although nothing survives of the code other than the mention of its name, and it was possibly never enacted. The next effort at codifying law was made by Emperor Tenmu's court at Kiyomihara in Asuka, perhaps around 681. Again, this code does not survive, except for a few provisions quoted in later works. In 689, Empress Jito ordered copies of the *ryō* distributed to local officials; it is not known whether these administrative codes (*ryō*) were accompanied by penal codes (*ritsu*). See the article by Cornelius Kiley in the *Kodansha Encyclopedia of Japan* (New York: Kodansha, 1983), s.v. "*ritsuryō.*"

5. Ryūichi Abe, *The Weaving of Mantra: Kūkai and the Construction of Esoteric Buddhist Discourse* (New York: Columbia University Press, 1999), 26.

6. Ibid.

7. William Wayne Farris, *Sacred Texts and Buried Treasures* (Honolulu: University of Hawai'i Press, 1998), 209.

8. Inoue Mitsusada et al., eds., *Ritsuryō,* in Nihon shisō takei 3 (Tokyo: Iwanami Shoten, 1980), 16.

9. Ibid.

10. Ibid.

11. See the annotations for "plotting rebellion" in Inoue, *Ritsuryō,* 16. I later discuss the punishments, as well as the distinction between death by beheading and by strangulation.

12. Geoffrey MacCormack points out that while in the original Chinese codes these offenses didn't necessarily entail the most severe punishments—not all of them are punishable by execution, for example—the abominations were not to be commuted during general amnesties nor mitigated for any reason; the same was also true in Japan. It should also be noted

that in the Chinese codes there were a total of ten abominations; the compilers of the Japanese codes removed those (such as incest) that were not considered transgressions of the Japanese social order. See Geoffrey MacCormack, *Traditional Chinese Penal Law* (Edinburgh, UK: Edinburgh University Press, 1990), 100–133.

13. This is not to say that the codes were implemented exactly as written; later I discuss important changes to the practice of punishment following the promulgation of the codes in Japan.

14. Some scholars believe the increased perception of beheading as severe was related to a Confucian aversion to dismembering the body. As stated in the *Classic of Filial Piety* (*Xiao Jing,* ca. 400 BCE), "One's body, hair, and skin are received from one's parents. Not daring to harm them is the beginning of filiality." Translated in Stephen Bokenkamp, *Ancestors and Anxiety: Daoism and the Birth of Rebirth in China* (Berkeley: University of California Press, 2007), 22. See also Wallace Johnson, *The T'ang Codes,* vol. 1: *General Principles* (Princeton, NJ: Princeton University Press, 1979), 59 note 74.

15. While it's beyond the scope of this chapter to detail the complex system by which punishments were increased or decreased in severity, it's worth noting that one of the initial considerations was a person's social status. A taxonomy of six levels of consideration for persons of high status, known as the *rokugi* (六議), was employed. One effect of the *rokugi* was that court officials customarily had their sentence reduced, although as noted above, for the most serious transgressions (the *hachigyaku*) no ameliorations were to be considered. See the text of the law codes in Inoue, *Ritsuryō,* 19–20. For a discussion of these procedures, see also Rikō Mitsuo, *Nihon kodai hōseishi* (Tokyo: Keiō Tsūshin, 1986), especially 106–107.

16. Aoki Kazuo et al., eds., *Shoku Nihongi,* in Shin Nihon koten bungaku taikei 13 (Tokyo: Iwanami Shoten, 1997), entry for 724/3/1. Mention of the "three classes of banishment" also appears in the *Nihon Shoki* during Tenmu's reign in the year 676, indicating that the practice of exile in three degrees was already known prior to the promulgation of the Taihō penal code. See W. G. Aston, trans., *Nihongi: Chronicles of Japan from the Earliest Times to A.D. 697,* vol. 2 (Tokyo: Charles Tuttle, 1972), 333.

17. In every instance of the first three of the eight outrages, the death penalty is mandated. For the fourth outrage, which consists of a variety of types of transgressions of violence or murder against members of one's own family, execution is prescribed in some but not all cases.

18. A particularly striking display of the penal system in action is recorded in the *Shoku Nihongi* following the suppression of a rebellion led by Fujiwara no Hirotsugu in 740. After Hirotsugu's death in Kyushu, the official history lists the following punishments given to his supporters: "twenty-six executions, forty-seven banishments, five confiscations of property, thirty-two beatings, and one hundred and seventy-seven whippings, sentenced according to the law (*hō ni yorite sadameshimu*)." Aoki et al., eds., *Shoku Nihongi,* entry for 741/1/22. Hirotsugu's case is doubly significant to our discussion, as he is the first person mentioned in the court chronicles whose deceased spirit was believed responsible for the death of another member of court. See the *Shoku Nihongi* entry for 746/6/18 regarding the death of the Buddhist priest Genbō attributed to Hirotsugu; see also Herman Ooms, *Imperial Politics and Symbolics in Ancient Japan: The Tenmu Dynasty, 650–800* (Honolulu: University of Hawai'i Press, 2009), 231.

19. Rebecca Redwood French's phrase "legal cosmology" underscores the point that law codes are inseparably bound to the religious worldviews of the societies that produce them,

a theme she explores in her study of Tibetan law, culture, and legal commentary, *The Golden Yoke: The Legal Cosmology of Buddhist Tibet* (Ithaca, NY: Cornell University Press, 1995). Here I use the term to suggest similarly that early Japanese law codes imagined a particular vision of the social order centered around the figure of a divine sovereign and further that the codes attempted to represent that social order as a manifestation of the divine/natural order.

20. French, *The Golden Yoke,* 16.

21. Rebecca Redwood French, "The Legal Cosmology of Buddhist Tibet," *Criterion* 33 (winter 1994): 24, emphasis added.

22. French, *The Golden Yoke,* 59.

23. For ways in which the Japanese ecclesiastic code both connected to and departed from the *Vinaya* attributed to Shakyamuni, as well as the complex interaction in Nara and Heian Japan between *ritsuryō* law and Buddhist law, see Abe, *The Weaving of Mantra,* 32–33 and passim, as well as, more generally, William Bodiford, ed., *Going Forth: Visions of Buddhist Vinaya* (Honolulu: University of Hawai'i Press, 2005).

24. On the legal cosmology of the Chinese codes, see especially Johnson, *The T'ang Codes,* 3–38, as well as Geoffrey MacCormack, *The Spirit of Traditional Chinese Law* (Athens: University of Georgia Press, 1996), 52–68.

25. This line appears in the seventeen-article constitution customarily attributed to Prince Shōtoku, from a *Nihon shoki* entry for 604/4/3, in Theodore de Bary et al., eds., *Sources of Japanese Tradition,* vol. 1: *From Earliest Times to 1600* (New York: Columbia University Press, 2001), 51.

26. MacCormack, *Traditional Chinese Penal Law,* 25.

27. Abe, *The Weaving of Mantra,* 21.

28. MacCormack, *Traditional Chinese Penal Law,* 27.

29. As Livia Kohn further explains regarding the influence of five phases theory on Chinese law, "No sharp cutting or executions, associated with metal, took place in the spring, the season of growth and of wood." Livia Kohn, *Daoism and Chinese Culture* (Cambridge, MA: Three Pines Press, 2001), 45.

30. From the *Xiao jing yuan shen ji,* a Han-period text on the *Classic of Filial Piety* (*Xiao jing*), quoted in Johnson, *The T'ang Codes,* 56.

31. "A corpus of knowledge, techniques, 'scientific' discourses is formed and becomes entangled with the practice of the power to punish." Michel Foucault, *Discipline and Punish,* trans. Alan Sheridan (New York: Vintage Books, 1995), 23.

32. Ibid., 24, emphasis added.

33. Ibid., 23, emphasis added.

34. As an example of this larger project, in an imperial edict as early as 646, land throughout the archipelago was recast as belonging to the Yamato state; the privilege of occupying that land was to be compensated by subjects through taxes and compulsory labor.

35. Foucault, *Discipline and Punish,* 23, emphasis added.

36. Ibid., 24, emphasis added.

37. Ibid., 25.

38. See William H. and Helen Craig McCullough, trans., *A Tale of Flowering Fortunes: Annals of Japanese Aristocratic Life in the Heian Period,* vol. 2 (Stanford, CA: Stanford University Press, 1980), 790–791. A more literal term for these members of court was simply *tenjōbito,* with a still higher group of senior nobles (*kugyō*) ranking above them.

39. Foucault, *Discipline and Punish,* 29, emphasis added.

40. In the introductory chapter, I quoted Sugawara no Michizane's poetry on the subject of an emperor's robes clung to at the margins of society. See also the Suma chapter in Royall Tyler, trans., *The Tale of Genji* (New York: Viking, 2001), 246, as well as Karen Brazell, trans., *The Confessions of Lady Nijō* (Stanford, CA: Stanford University Press, 1973), 208. This also helps to explain why the possession of the imperial robes is employed as a rhetorical device in poems and letters implying the incoherence and injustice of the courtier's estrangement from the capital.

41. George Sansom, *A History of Japan to 1334* (Stanford, CA: Stanford University Press, 1958), 107–108.

42. For an introduction to *mokkan* within the context of the development of writing in Japan, see David Lurie, *Realms of Literacy: Early Japan and the History of Writing* (Cambridge, MA: Harvard University Press, 2011), especially 121–125; see also Farris, *Sacred Texts,* 201–232.

43. Joan Piggott, *The Emergence of Japanese Kingship* (Stanford, CA: Stanford University Press, 1997), 13.

44. Ibid., 168.

45. Ibid., xx.

46. Ibid., 232.

47. Ibid., 169.

48. Ibid., 234.

49. Ibid., 234.

50. It's also questionable to what extent the early Japanese state gained its knowledge of the Chinese codes through direct contact with the Middle Kingdom. It is reasonable to assume, as some have argued, that Japan's knowledge of Chinese law came in the same way as many of its importations from the mainland—through families of Korean immigrants. The Korean kingdom of Silla, for example, circulated its own copy of the T'ang law as early as 520—evidence that the Korean peninsula was far in advance of Japan in adopting this particular feature of Chinese bureaucratic statecraft (Farris, *Sacred Texts,* 220, note 161). In addition, it is known that among the members of the committee that drafted the Taihō code, 8 of 19 were members of Korean immigrant families (ibid., 105, note 163). It seems probable that as the early Japanese state was engaged in compiling its own version of the Chinese codes, much of the information regarding those codes and their implementation came from sources originating in the Korean peninsula.

51. Ross Bender, "Emperor, Aristocracy, and the Ritsuryō State: Court Politics in Nara," in *Japan Emerging: Premodern History to 1850,* ed. Karl Friday (Boulder, CO: Westview Press, 2012), 113.

52. *Kodansha Encyclopedia of Japan,* s.v. "*ritsuryō.*" Another area where the drafters of the Japanese codes revised the T'ang model concerns the issue of rank—specifically rank automatically conferred on the descendents of officials within the court bureaucracy. In both cases, male children of court officials were granted rank automatically, at a level several ranks below that of their parent. In this way, the bureaucracy worked to ensure that the aristocracy replicated itself, as children of ranked officials automatically started off within the court hierarchy as ranked officials rather than commoners. Where the two codes differed, however, was on how much rank they automatically conferred upon descendents. In the Japanese instance, the compilers of the codes systematically granted a higher rank than their T'ang counterparts to the children of court officials. To cite one example, if an official in Japan

achieved the first rank in the court bureaucracy, that official's heir automatically assumed the Junior Lower Fifth rank upon entering the court hierarchy. In China, the children of the same official at the first rank were automatically ceded only the Senior Upper Seventh rank.

53. See, for example, Farris, *Sacred Texts,* 231–232.

54. Piggott, *The Emergence of Japanese Kingship,* 318.

55. *Kodansha Encyclopedia of Japan,* s.v. "*ritsuryō.*"

56. In 834 the court also sponsored the compilation of the Ryō no Gige, which was intended to be the authoritative interpretation of the administrative and civil portions of the Yōrō ryō; it contained the original text of the *ryō* along with commentaries, and itself was enacted as law.

57. The Engi Shiki were compiled in 927 but not enacted until 967.

58. See Mikael Adolphson, *The Gates of Power: Monks, Courtiers, and Warriors in Premodern Japan* (Honolulu: University of Hawai'i Press, 2000), 1–20, for his discussion of Kuroda Toshio's *kenmon taisei* theory.

59. William Wayne Farris, *Japan to 1600: A Social and Economic History* (Honolulu: University of Hawai'i Press, 2009), 68.

60. Farris, *Sacred Texts,* 199.

61. Kuroda Toshio, "The World of Spirit Pacification: Issues of State and Religion," *Japanese Journal of Religious Studies* 23, no. 3–4 (fall 1996): 338–339.

62. It was during this time that Saga created the *kurōdodokoro,* an office not chartered within the legal codes, which allowed Saga to issue edicts without going through the usual bureaucratic channels. Later in the Heian period, the same office would be used by the Fujiwara to wrest control of governmental administration from the emperor.

63. Okada, for example, states that Kusuko was "forced to drink poison." Richard Okada, *Figures of Resistance* (Durham, NC: Duke University Press, 1991), 140. Borgen mentions that blame for the incident also fell on Heizei's advisers, who were members of the same ceremonial branch of the Fujiwara clan as Kusuko. Several advisers were sent into exile, after which the ceremonial branch of the Fujiwara never regained its power. See Robert Borgen, *Sugawara no Michizane and the Early Heian Court* (Honolulu: University of Hawai'i Press, 1994), 38.

64. Retired emperor Heizei's son, Prince Abo, was also punished in the affair and exiled to the Dazaifu in Tsukushi. When he returned to the capital fourteen years later, his sons were reduced to commoner status and given the surname Ariwara; later, Ariwara Narihira and Yukihira would produce some of the most important literature of exile of the Heian period.

65. Inoue, *Ritsuryō,* 687. See also the supplemental notes on page 487. Inoue, by using such phrases as "they say" and "it is said that" (*to iwarete iru*), appears to hedge slightly his statement that executions did not take place at all.

66. See the entry for *shikei* written by Takashio Hiroshi in Tsunoda Bun'ei, ed., *Heian jidaishi jiten* (Tokyo: Kadokawa Shoten, 1994). Nearly identical phrasing and reasoning can be found in Ishii Ryōsuke's *Keibatsu no rekishi* (Tokyo: Akashi Shoten, 1992), 71–72.

67. Tsunoda et al., *Heian jidaishi jiten,* s.v. "*shikei.*"

68. The basis for this religious model of expiation through offerings and sanction is found by many scholars initially in myth, specifically when the god Susano-o was forced to offer one thousand offering tables and cut his hair, beard, and nails—*and* was sentenced to divine banishment from the High Heavenly Plain. On this episode as a model both for ar-

chaic religious law and for the practice of exile in general, see Miura Hiroyuki, "Tsuihōkeiron," in *Hōseishi no kenkyū* (Tokyo: Iwanami Shoten, 1919), 988–989.

69. Ishio Yoshihisa, *Nihon kodaihō no kenkyū* (Tokyo: Hōritsu Bunkasha, 1991), 172.

70. See Ishio, *Nihon kodaihō no kenkyū,* 172–173; Inoue, *Ritsuryō,* 678; Tsunoda, *Heian jidaishi jiten,* s.v. "*shikei.*"

71. Ishii, *Keibatsu no rekishi,* 73 note 8.

72. Ibid.: "*Waga kokuminsei no onwa naru ni yoru mono de arō.*"

73. Rikō, *Nihon kodai hōseishi,* 138. Also see the chapter "Sagacho ni okeru shikei teishi ni tsuite" in his work, *Ritsu no kenkyū* (Tokyo: Meiji Shoin, 1961), 304–334.

74. Prince Iyo, also a son of Emperor Kammu, was arrested in 807 for plotting treason and confined in a temple where, along with his mother Fujiwara Yoshiko, he is said to have committed suicide by taking poison. Iyo was Saga's half brother.

75. See Rikō, *Nihon kodai hōseishi,* especially 166, note 49.

76. Kuroita Katsumi et al., eds., *Nihon kiryaku,* in Kokushi taikei 11 (Tokyo: Yoshikawa Kōbunkan, 1929), 174.

77. See Rikō, *Nihon kodai hōseishi,* 138–139, and 166 note 47.

78. For a discussion of Japan's "worldwide first abolition of capital punishment," see Petra Schmidt, *Capital Punishment in Japan* (Leiden: E. J. Brill, 2002), 11 note 10.

79. Wilson, *Tale of the Disorder in Hōgen,* 5. See also Nagazumi and Shimada, *Hōgen monogatari,* 58. While the *Hōgen monogatari* is the most complete account of the Hōgen conflict available, the text itself was written well after the events it describes, and its account is filtered through a partisan historiographic lens. Nor does there exist a single *Hōgen monogatari* text: as with other medieval narratives that were initially popularized by *biwa hōshi* (traveling reciters), multiple versions of the text were eventually set down in writing over time. The earliest reference to the existence of the *Hōgen monogatari* dates to 1297, but the version referred to is not itself extant. The earliest extant text dates to 1318, but only a portion of that text is preserved. For a fuller discussion of the existing variants, see Paul Varley, *Warriors of Japan as Portrayed in the War Tales* (Honolulu: University of Hawai'i Press, 1994), 50–53, and Elizabeth Oyler, *Swords, Oaths, and Prophetic Visions: Authoring Warrior Rule in Medieval Japan* (Honolulu: University of Hawai'i Press, 2006), 18–19. Oyler suggests a probable composition date for the *Hōgen monogatar*i around the early to mid-thirteenth century. I discuss further historiographical issues related to the Hōgen text later in this chapter.

80. The Hōgen disturbance thus exemplifies the kind of power struggle characteristic of the *insei* system of the late Heian period, when several retired emperors might exist in addition to the emperor at any given moment, all vying to wield power (Wilson, *Tale of the Disorder in Hōgen,* 110). See G. Cameron Hurst, "*Insei,*" in *The Cambridge History of Japan,* vol. 2, ed. Donald Shively and William McCullough (Cambridge: Cambridge University Press, 1999), 576–643.

81. Wilson, *Tale of the Disorder in Hōgen,* 84; Nagazumi and Shimada, *Hōgen monogatari,* 163.

82. Yamada Yūji, *Bakkosuru onryō: Tatari to chinkon no Nihon shi* (Tokyo: Yoshikawa Kōbunkan, 207), 89–91.

83. Wilson, *Tale of the Disorder in Hōgen,* 69; see also Nagazumi and Shimada, *Hōgen monogatari,* 380. This passage appears to be the primary text on which many scholars of Japanese law base their claim for a 347-year period in which capital punishment was never practiced.

84. Wilson, *Tale of the Disorder in Hōgen,* 69–70; see also Nagazumi and Shimada, *Hōgen monogatari,* 380.

85. Wilson, *Tale of the Disorder in Hōgen,* 109, quoting from the *Nakaraibon* version of the *Hōgen* in Takahashi Sadaichi, *Heike monogatari shohon no kenkyū* (Tokyo: Fuzanbō, 1943), 519–520.

86. Wilson, *Tale of the Disorder in Hōgen,* 99; Nagazumi and Shimada, *Hōgen monogatari,* 395: "*Sutokuin no go-tatari to zo moshikeru.*"

87. Yamada Yūji, *Bakkosuru onryō,* 91–95.

88. Ibid., 95–97.

89. Benedict Anderson, *Imagined Communities: Reflections on the Origins and Spread of Nationalism* (New York: Verso, 1991), 19.

90. Ibid.

## Chapter 6: Conclusion

*Epigraph 1.* Michel Foucault, *Discipline and Punish,* trans. Alan Sheridan (New York: Vintage Books, 1995, 30–31.

*Epigraph 2.* Caroline Walker Bynum, *Fragmentation and Redemption: Essays on Gender and the Human Body in Medieval Religion* (New York: Zone Books, 1991), 14.

1. Yamada Yūji, *Bakkosuru onryō: Tatari to chinkon no Nihon shi* (Tokyo: Yoshikawa Kōbunkan, 2007), 86.

2. See William LaFleur, *Awesome Nightfall: The Life, Times, and Poetry of Saigyō* (Boston: Wisdom Publications, 2003), 32–41.

3. Ibid., 6.

4. Donald Keene, *Seeds in the Heart: Japanese Literature from Earliest Times to the Late Sixteenth Century* (New York: Henry Holt, 1993), 678. Kūkai's birthplace was on Shikoku.

5. Burton Watson, trans., *Saigyō: Poems of a Mountain Home* (New York: Columbia University Press, 1992), 181, modified; see also Kazamaki Keijirō et al., *Sankashū: Kinkai wakashū,* in Nihon koten bungaku taikei 29 (Tokyo: Iwanami Shoten, 1974), 232.

6. Anthony Chambers, trans., *Tales of Moonlight and Rain* (New York: Columbia University Press, 2007), 68, modified; see also LaFleur, *Awesome Nightfall,* 34, and Kazamaki et al., *Sankashū,* 233.

7. On these pacification attempts, see Yamada, *Bakkosuru onryō,* 91–95.

8. Ibid., 93: "*Mukyoku no daiji nari.*"

9. Regarding the curse attributed to Sutoku, see Yamada, *Bakkosuru onryō,* 88–93.

10. Ibid., 96.

11. Ibid., 94.

12. Ibid., 96–97.

13. The shrine ordered built by Go-Shirakawa at the site of Sutoku's former residence later came to be known as the Awata no miya, and was visited among other reasons to pray for safe childbirth. Ibid., 99.

14. Elizabeth Oyler, *Swords, Oaths, and Prophetic Visions: Authoring Warrior Rule in Medieval Japan* (Honolulu: University of Hawai'i Press, 2006), 18–19.

15. In addition, the sutras upon which the curse was written were said to have disappeared into the sea shortly before Sutoku's death.

16. Tengu—a kind of Japanese goblin characterized by birdlike features and martial prowess—are associated with mountains (such as the mountain temple where Sutoku was buried). Chambers, *Tales of Moonlight and Rain,* 17. On the conjoining of Tengu belief, mountain asceticism, political activism, and Sutoku's spirit, see Sarah Thal, *Rearranging the Landscape of the Gods: The Politics of a Pilgrimage Site in Japan, 1573–1912* (Chicago: University of Chicago, 2005), 118–126.

17. Chambers, *Tales of Moonlight and Rain,* 56–57.

18. The regalia believed lost was the sword originally said to have been discovered in Izumo by the god Susano-o and offered to the sun goddess Amaterasu, who bequeathed it to her earthly descendants, the rulers of Japan.

19. Yamada Yūji, "Sutoku tennō shinrei no kikan," in Ōhama Tetsuya, ed., *Kindai Nihon no rekishiteki isō: Kokka, minzoku, bunka* (Tokyo: Tōsui Shobō, 1999), 4–8.

20. Ibid., 6–7.

21. Ibid., 13.

22. Ibid., 21–22.

23. Ibid., 23. The shrine is now called Shiramine Jingū.

24. The Jingikan had been "reestablished" in the third month of 1868.

25. Yamada, "Sutoku tennō shinrei no kikan," 21.

26. Ibid., 25–26.

27. Yamada, *Bakkosuru onryō,* 87.

28. See Allan Grapard, "Japan's Ignored Cultural Revolution: The Separation of Shinto and Buddhist Divinities in Meiji and a Case Study: Tōnomine," *History of Religions* 23, no. 3 (February 1984), 240–265.

29. For a leading collection of essays on this topic, see Mark Teeuwen and Fabio Rambelli, eds., *Buddhas and Kami in Japan: Honji Suijaku as a Combinatory Paradigm* (New York: Routledge, 2003).

30. The "*shinbutsu bunri*" edicts, issued beginning in the first year of the Meiji period, aimed officially to disentangle Buddhism from Shinto. The edicts specified that Buddhist priests could no longer serve at Shinto shrines, Buddhist iconography could no longer be used in the worship of Shinto deities, and Buddhist names could no longer be used in reference to Shinto *kami.* In actuality, the edicts resulted in an enormous destruction of Buddhist material and social culture. See Grapard, "Japan's Ignored Cultural Revolution," as well as James Ketelaar, *Of Heretics and Martyrs in Meiji Japan: Buddhism and Its Persecution* (Princeton, NJ: Princeton University Press, 1990).

31. See, for example, William LaFleur, *The Karma of Words: Buddhism and the Literary Arts in Medieval Japan* (Berkeley: University of California Press, 1983). In contrast, as Donald Keene notes, Saigyō spent more than five years at Ise—*after* joining the Buddhist priesthood and living on Mt. Koya—composing poems inspired by the Great Shrine of Ise, drawing correspondences between Buddhas and *kami,* and lamenting the court's failure to keep up the shrine or fill the post of high priestess. See Keene, *Seeds in the Heart,* 678–679. LaFleur's later work on Saigyō (*Awesome Nightfall*) takes better account of this synthesis of Buddhas and *kami.*

32. Thomas Kasulis, *Shinto: The Way Home* (Honolulu: University of Hawai'i Press, 2004). Kasulis' account is a theoretically rich treatment of Shinto; my point here is simply that any account of Shinto as an autonomous religious tradition is made possible only following the Meiji "invention" of a purified Shinto, as Kasulis himself notes. On the Meiji con-

struction of a "pure" Shinto, see Sarah Thal, "A Religion That Was Not a Religion: The Creation of Modern Shinto in Nineteenth-Century Japan," in *The Invention of Religion: Rethinking Belief in Politics and History,* ed. Derek Peterson and Darren Walhof (New Brunswick, NJ: Rutgers University Press 2002), 100–114. On the problematic term "Shinto" in Japanese history more generally, see Mark Teeuwen, "What Used to Be Called Shinto: The Question of Japan's Indigenous Religion," in *Japan Emerging: Premodern History to 1850,* ed. Karl Friday (Boulder, CO: Westview Press, 2012), 66–76. On the creation of religion itself as a sui generis category of thought in Meiji Japan, see Jason Josephson, *The Invention of Religion in Japan* (Chicago: University of Chicago Press, 2012).

33. Grapard, "Japan's Ignored Cultural Revolution," 242.

34. Sonoda Minoru and Hashimoto Masanobu, eds., *Shinto-shi daijiten* (Tokyo: Yoshikawa Kōbunkan, 2004), s.v. "Shiramine Jingū."

35. In the penal code promulgated by the Meiji Ministry of Justice in 1873, banishment was replaced with the punishment of "imprisonment with hard labor (*chōeki*)." See Daniel Botsman, *Punishment and Power in the Making of Modern Japan* (Princeton, NJ: Princeton University Press, 2005), 160, 175–176.

36. Benedict Anderson, *Imagined Communities: Reflections on the Origins and Spread of Nationalism* (New York: Verso, 1991), 19.

# Character Glossary

*akuryō* 悪霊
Anrakuji 安楽寺
Bai Juyi 白居易
*chizai* 笞罪
*chōeki* 懲役
*daibutsu* 大仏
*daigongen* 大権現
Daijōkan 太政官
*emaki* 絵巻
Enchō 延長
Engishiki 延喜式
*enkon* 冤魂
*enkonrei* 冤魂癘
Fujiwara Hirotsugu 藤原広嗣
Fusō Ryakki 扶桑略記
Genbō 玄昉
Gokei 五刑
*goryō* 御霊
*goryō-e* 御霊会
Gozu Tennō 牛頭天王
Hachigyaku 八逆
*hagoromo* 羽衣
*henge* 変化
*hōchiku* 放逐
*hōgyo* 崩御
Hoke Sanmaidō 法花三昧堂
*hokora* 禿倉; 宝倉
Hokumen no bushi 北面の武士
*jigoku* 地獄
Jingikan 神祇官
Jinmyōchō 神名帳
Jōshōji 成勝寺
*jōzai* 杖罪
*kamiyo* 神代
*kanpaku* 関白
*kansha* 官社
*karai tenjin* 火雷天神
*kebiishi* 検非違使
*kishu ryūritan* 貴種流離譚
Kitano Tenjin Engi 北野天神縁起
Kofun 古墳
*Kojiki* 古事記
Kokugaku 国学
Kōnin 弘仁
kugyō 公卿
Kūkai 空海
kumo no uebito 雲の上人
Kusanagi 草薙
Kushimikeno no mikoto 櫛御気野命
Kusuko no hen 薬子の変
*kyaku* 客
*kyō* 梟
Manyōshū 万葉集
*mappō* 末法
Matsuyama 松山
*miedō* 御影堂
*miko* 巫
*misasagi* 陵

*mitamashiro* 御霊代
*mono no aware* 物の哀れ
*mujō* 無情
*myōjin* 名神
Nakazui Unsai 中瑞雲斎
Ne-no-katasu-kuni 根之堅州国
Nihon Daijō Itokuten 日本太政威徳天
*Nihon Kiryaku* 日本紀略
*Nihon Sandai Jitsuroku* 日本三代実録
*Nihon Shoki* 日本書紀
*nin* 任
*ōharae* 大祓
oidasu 追い出す
*onryō* 怨霊
*raijin* 雷神
*rei* 癘
*reiza* 霊座
Rokugi 六議
*ruzai* 流罪
*ryō* 霊
*Ryō no Gige* 令義解
*saishō* 宰相
*sakō* 左降
Sanuki-in 讃岐院
*sasen* 左遷
Seiji Yōryaku 政事要略
Seiryōden 清涼殿
*seisai* 制裁
*sekkanke* 摂関家
*sekkan seido* 摂関制度
*sesshō* 摂政
*shiki* 式
*shima-nagashi* 島流し
*shinbutsu bunri* 神仏分離
*shinrei* 神霊
Shinsen'en 神泉苑
Shiramine-gū 白峰宮
*shizai* 死罪
Sutoku 崇徳
Taihō Ritsuryō 大宝律令
Taika 大化
*taisha* 大社
*Taketori monogatari* 竹取物語
*takuraku* 謫落
*tengu* 天狗
*tenjin* 天神
*tenjōbito* 殿上人
Tenjō no ma 殿上の間
Tenman Daijizai Tenjin 天満大自在天神
*tokoyo* 常世
*tsuihō* 追放
*tsuki no miyako* 月の都
*tsumi* 罪
Yayoi 弥生
Yomi no kuni 黄泉国
Yōrō Ritsuryō 養老律令
*zuzai* 徒罪

# Bibliography


Abe, Ryūichi. *The Weaving of Mantra: Kūkai and the Construction of Esoteric Buddhist Discourse.* New York: Columbia University Press, 1999.

Adolphson, Mikael. *The Gates of Power: Monks, Courtiers, and Warriors in Premodern Japan.* Honolulu: University of Hawai'i Press, 2000.

———. "Oligarchy, Shared Rulership, and Power Blocs." In *Japan Emerging: Premodern History to 1850,* edited by Karl Friday (Boulder, CO: Westview Press, 2012), 122–134.

Adolphson, Mikael, Edward Kamens, and Stacie Matsumoto, eds. *Heian Japan: Centers and Peripheries.* Honolulu: University of Hawai'i Press, 2007.

Akimoto Kichiro, ed. *Fudoki.* In Nihon koten bungaku taikei 2. Tokyo: Iwanami Shoten, 1970.

Amino Yoshihiko. *Muen, kugai, raku: Nihon chūsei no jiyū to heiwa.* Tokyo: Heibonsha, 1987.

———. *Nihon no rekishi o yominaosu.* Tokyo: Chikuma Shobo, 1991.

———. *Zoku Nihon no rekishi o yominaosu.* Tokyo: Chikuma Shobo, 1998.

Anderson, Benedict. *Imagined Communities: Reflections on the Origins and Spread of Nationalism,* revised edition. New York: Verso, 1991.

Aoki Kazuo et al., eds. *Shoku Nihongi II.* In Shin Nihon koten bungaku taikei 13. Tokyo: Iwanami Shoten, 1997.

Aoki, Michiko. *Records of Wind and Earth: A Translation of* Fudoki, *with Introduction and Commentaries.* Ann Arbor, MI: Association for Asian Studies, 1987.

Ariyama Daigo and Ishiuchi Toru, eds. *Chōkū/Orikuchi Shinobu jiten.* Tokyo: Bensei Shuppan, 2000.

Arlen, Harold, and E. Y. Harburg. "Munchkinland." In *The Wizard of Oz,* directed by Victor Fleming. Burbank: Metro-Goldwyn-Mayer, 1939.

Aston, W. G., trans. *Nihongi: Chronicles of Japan from the Earliest Times to A.D. 697.* Tokyo: Charles E. Tuttle, 1972.

Bargen, Doris. *A Woman's Weapon: Spirit Possession in* The Tale of Genji. Honolulu: University of Hawai'i Press, 1997.

Batten, Bruce. "Cross-border Traffic on the Kyushu Coast, 794–1086." In *Heian Japan: Centers and Peripheries,* edited by Mikael Adolphson et al. (Honolulu: University of Hawai'i Press, 2007), 357–383.

———. *To the Ends of Japan: Premodern Frontiers, Boundaries, and Interactions.* Honolulu: University of Hawai'i Press, 2003.

Bell, Catherine. *Ritual Theory, Ritual Practice.* New York: Oxford University Press, 1992.

Bender, Ross. "Emperor, Aristocracy, and the Ritsuryō State: Court Politics in Nara." In *Japan Emerging: Premodern History to 1850,* edited by Karl Friday (Boulder, CO: Westview Press, 2012), 111–121.

Bialock, David. *Eccentric Spaces, Hidden Histories: Narrative, Ritual, and Royal Authority from The Chronicles of Japan to The Tale of the Heike.* Stanford, CA: Stanford University Press, 2007.

Bock, Felicia Gressitt, trans. *Engi-Shiki: Procedures of the Engi Era, Books I–V.* Tokyo: Sophia University, 1970.

Bodiford, William, ed. *Going Forth: Visions of Buddhist Vinaya.* Honolulu: University of Hawai'i Press, 2005.

Bokenkamp, Stephen. *Ancestors and Anxiety: Daoism and the Birth of Rebirth in China.* Berkeley: University of California Press, 2007.

Borgen, Robert. *Sugawara no Michizane and the Early Heian Court.* Honolulu: University of Hawai'i Press, 1994.

Botsman, Daniel. *Punishment and Power in the Making of Modern Japan.* Princeton, NJ: Princeton University Press, 2005.

Bourdieu, Pierre. *Outline of a Theory of Practice.* Trans. Richard Nice. New York: Cambridge University Press, 1977.

Brazell, Karen, trans. *The Confessions of Lady Nijō.* Stanford, CA: Stanford University Press, 1973.

Brown, Delmer, and Ichiro Ishida, trans. and eds. *The Future and the Past: A Translation and Study of the Gukanshō.* Berkeley: University of California Press, 1979.

Bynum, Caroline Walker. *Fragmentation and Redemption: Essays on Gender and the Human Body in Medieval Religion.* New York: Zone Books, 1991.

Carlqvist, Anders. "The Land-Pulling Myth and Some Aspects of Historic Reality." *Japanese Journal of Religious Studies* 37, no. 2 (January 2010): 185–222.

Chambers, Anthony, trans. *Tales of Moonlight and Rain.* New York: Columbia University Press, 2007.

Cohen, Alvin. "Avenging Ghosts and Moral Judgment in Ancient Chinese Historiography: Three Examples from Shih-chi." In *Legend, Lore, and Religion in China,* edited by Sarah Allan and Alvin Cohen (San Francisco: Chinese Materials Center, 1979), 97–108.

Como, Michael. *Weaving and Binding: Immigrant Gods and Female Immortals in Ancient Japan.* Honolulu: University of Hawai'i Press, 2009.

Culler, Jonathan. *Structuralist Poetics.* Ithaca, NY: Cornell University Press, 1975.

Dazaifu Tenmangū Bunka Kenkyūjo, ed. *Sugawara Michizane to Dazaifu Tenmangū.* Tokyo: Yoshikawa Kōbunkan, 1975.

de Bary, Theodore, Donald Keene, George Tanabe, and Paul Varley, eds. *Sources of Japanese Tradition.* Vol. 1: *From Earliest Times to 1600.* New York: Columbia University Press, 2001.

de Certeau, Michel. *The Practice of Everyday Life.* Trans. Steven Rendall. Berkeley: University of California Press, 1988.

Dix, Monika. "Hachikazuki: Revealing Kannon's Crowning Compassion in Muromachi Fiction." *Japanese Journal of Religious Studies* 36, no. 2 (January 2009): 279–294.

Doak, Kevin. "Building National Identity through Ethnicity: Ethnology in Wartime Japan and After." *Journal of Japanese Studies* 27, no. 1 (winter 2001): 1–39.

Douglas, Mary. *Purity and Danger: An Analysis of the Concepts of Pollution and Taboo.* New York: Routledge, 1991.

Ebersole, Gary. *Ritual Poetry and the Politics of Death in Early Japan.* Princeton, NJ: Princeton University Press, 1989.

Eco, Umberto. *The Open Work.* Trans. Anna Cancogni. Cambridge, MA: Harvard University Press, 1989.

Elias, Norbert. *The Court Society.* Trans. Edmund Jephcott. New York: Pantheon Books, 1983.

Ellwood, Robert. *The Feast of Kingship: Accession Ceremonies in Ancient Japan.* Tokyo: Sophia University Press, 1973.

———. "A Japanese Mythic Trickster Figure: Susa-no-o." In *Mythical Trickster Figures,* edited by William Hynes and William Doty (Tuscaloosa: University of Alabama Press, 1993), 141–158.

Farris, William Wayne. *Japan to 1600: A Social and Economic History.* Honolulu: University of Hawai'i Press, 2009.

———. *Sacred Texts and Buried Treasures: Issues in the Historical Archeology of Ancient Japan.* Honolulu: University of Hawai'i Press, 1998.

Faure, Bernard. *Visions of Power: Imagining Medieval Japanese Buddhism.* Princeton, NJ: Princeton University Press, 1996.

Field, Norma. *The Splendor of Longing in the* Tale of Genji. Princeton, NJ: Princeton University Press, 1987.

Foucault, Michel. *Discipline and Punish.* Trans. Alan Sheridan. New York: Vintage Books, 1995.

French, Rebecca Redwood. *The Golden Yoke: The Legal Cosmology of Buddhist Tibet.* Ithaca, NY: Cornell University Press, 1995.

———. "The Legal Cosmology of Buddhist Tibet." *Criterion* 33 (winter 1994): 24.

Furuhashi Nobuyoshi, ed. *Nihon bungeishi.* Tokyo: Kawade, 1986.

Gallagher, Catherine, and Stephen Greenblatt. *Practicing New Historicism.* Chicago: University of Chicago Press, 2000.

Gallop, Jane. *The Deaths of the Author: Reading and Writing in Time.* Durham, NC: Duke University Press, 2011.

Goodwin, Janet. *Alms and Vagabonds: Buddhist Temples and Popular Patronage in Medieval* Japan. Honolulu: University of Hawai'i Press, 1994.

Grapard, Allan. "Institution, Ritual, and Ideology: The Twenty-Two Shrine-Temple Multiplexes of Heian Japan." *History of Religions* 27, no. 3 (fall 1988): 246–269.

———. "Japan's Ignored Cultural Revolution: The Separation of Shinto and Buddhist Divinities in Meiji and a Case Study: Tōnomine." *History of Religions* 23, no. 3 (February 1984): 240–265.

———. "Religious Practices." In *The Cambridge History of Japan,* vol. 2: *Heian Japan,* edited by Donald Shively and William McCullough (New York: Cambridge University Press, 1999), 558–564.

———. "Visions of Excess and Excesses of Vision: Women and Transgression in Japanese Myth." *Japanese Journal of Religious Studies* 18, no. 1 (March 1991): 3–22.

Hansen, Wilburn. *When Tengu Talk: Hirata Atsutane's Ethnography of the Other World.* Honolulu: University of Hawai'i Press, 2008.

Harootunian, H. D. "Disciplining Native Knowledge and Producing Place: Yanagita Kunio, Origuchi Shinobu, Takata Yasuma." In *Culture and Identity: Japanese Intellectuals During the Interwar Years,* edited by J. Thomas Rimer (Princeton, NJ: Princeton University Press, 1990), 99–127.

———. "Figuring the Folk: History, Poetics, and Representation." In *Mirror of Modernity: Invented Traditions in Modern Japan,* edited by Stephen Vlastos (Berkeley: University of California Press, 1998), 144–159.

———. *Things Seen and Unseen: Discourse and Ideology in Tokugawa Nativism.* Chicago: University of Chicago Press, 1988.

Hayashi Ōki and Andō Chizuko, eds. *Kogorin.* Tokyo: Taishūkan, 1997.

Hori, Ichiro. *Folk Religion in Japan.* Chicago: University of Chicago Press, 1968.

Horimoto Masami. *Onryō no kodaishi.* Tokyo: Hokutosha, 1999.

Hurst, G. Cameron. "*Insei.*" In *The Cambridge History of Japan,* vol. 2. Edited by Donald Shively and William McCullough (Cambridge: Cambridge University Press, 1999), 576–643.

Ikeda Kikan et al., eds. *Makura no Sōshi.* In Nihon koten bungaku taikei 19. Tokyo: Iwanami Shoten, 1971.

Imai Tadayoshi, ed. *Kundoku Shoku Nihongi.* Kyoto: Rinkawa Shoten, 1986.

Inoue Mitsuo. "Kodai no goryō shinkō." In *Tenman tenjin: Goryō kara gakumongami e,* edited by Ueda Masaaki (Tokyo: Chikuma Shobo, 1988), 25–48.

Inoue Mitsusada, *Nihon no rekishi: Shinwa kara rekishi e.* Tokyo: Chūō Kōronsha, 1965.

Inoue Mitsusada et al., eds. *Ritsuryō.* In Nihon shisō taikei 3. Tokyo: Iwanami Shoten, 1980.

Inoue Nobutaka et al., eds. *Shinto jiten.* Tokyo: Kōbundō, 1994.

Ishii Ryōsuke. *Keibatsu no rekishi.* Tokyo: Akashi Shoten, 1992.

Ishikawa Jun, ed. *Motoori Norinaga.* In Nihon no meicho 21. Tokyo: Chūōkōronsha, 1970.

Ishio Yoshihisa. *Nihon kodaihō no kenkyū.* Tokyo: Hōritsu Bunkasha, 1991.

Isomae, Jun'ichi. *Japanese Mythology: Hermeneutics on Scripture.* Oakville, CT: Equinox Publishing, 2010.

———. "Reappropriating the Japanese Myths: Motoori Norinaga and the Creation Myths of the *Kojiki* and *Nihonshoki.*" *Japanese Journal of Religious Studies* 27, no. 1–2 (spring 2000): 15–39.

Iwasa Masashi et al., eds. *Jinnō shōtōki.* In Nihon koten bungaku taikei 87. Tokyo: Iwanami Shoten, 1969.

Johnson, Wallace. *The T'ang Codes.* Vol. 1: *General Principles.* Princeton, NJ: Princeton University Press, 1979.

Josephson, Jason. *The Invention of Religion in Japan.* Chicago: University of Chicago Press, 2012.

Kamata, Tōji. "The Disfiguring of Nativism: Hirata Atsutane and Orikuchi Shinobu." In *Shinto in History,* edited by John Breen and Mark Teeuwen (Honolulu: University of Hawai'i Press, 2000): 295–317.

Kamens, Edward. "Review—Uncovering Heian Japan: An Archeology of Sensation and Inscription." *Journal of Japanese Studies* 27, no. 2 (summer 2001): 430–434.

Karaki Junzō. *Muyōsha no keifu.* Tokyo: Chikuma Shobō, 1960.

Kasulis, Thomas. *Shinto: The Way Home.* Honolulu: University of Hawai'i Press, 2004.

Kawaguchi Hisao, ed. *Kanke bunsō: Kanke goshū.* In Nihon koten bungaku taikei 72. Tokyo: Iwanami Shoten, 1966.

Kawashima, Terry. *Writing Margins: The Textual Construction of Gender in Heian and Kamakura Japan.* Cambridge, MA: Harvard Asia Center, 2001.

Kazamaki Keijirō et al., eds. *Sankashū: Kinkai wakashū.* In Nihon koten bungaku taikei 29. Tokyo: Iwanami Shoten, 1974.

Keene, Donald, trans. *Essays in Idleness: The Tsurezuregusa of Kenkō.* New York: Columbia University Press, 1967.

———. *Seeds in the Heart: Japanese Literature from Earliest Times to the Late Sixteenth Century.* New York: Henry Holt, 1993.

———. "The Tale of the Bamboo Cutter." In *Modern Japanese Fiction and Its Traditions,* edited by J. Thomas Rimer (Princeton, NJ: Princeton University Press, 1978), 275–305.

Keirstead, Thomas. *The Geography of Power in Medieval Japan.* Princeton, NJ: Princeton University Press, 1992.

Ketelaar, James. *Of Heretics and Martyrs in Meiji Japan: Buddhism and Its Persecution.* Princeton, NJ: Princeton University Press, 1990.

Kikuchi Kyōko. "Goryo shinkō no seiritsu to hatten." In *Goryō shinkō,* edited by Shibata Minoru (Tokyo: Yūzankaku Shuppan, 1984), 37–61.

Kishi Toshio. *Tojō no seitai.* In Nihon no kodai 9. Tokyo: Chūōkōronsha, 1987.

Kitayama Shigeo. *Heian-kyo.* In Nihon no rekishi 4. Tokyo: Chūōkōronsha, 1965.

Kobayashi Shinmei, ed. *Shinsen kanwa jiten.* Tokyo: Shōgakukan, 2000.

*The Kodansha Encyclopedia of Japan.* New York: Kodansha, 1983.

Kohn, Livia. *Daoism and Chinese Culture.* Cambridge, MA: Three Pines Press, 2001.

Kojima Naoko. "Araburu hikari: Kaguyahime kara Hikaru Genji e." In *Ōken no kisō e,* edited by Akasaka Norio (Tokyo: Shin'yosha, 1992), 154–186.

———. *Kaguyahime gensō: Kōken to kinki.* Tokyo: Shinwa, 1995.

Kojima Noriyuki, ed. *Nihon shoki: Jō.* In Nihon koten bungaku zenshū 2. Tokyo: Shōgakkan, 1994.

Kokugakuin Daigaku Nihon Bunka Kenkyūjo, ed. *Shintō jiten.* Tokyo: Kōbundō, 1999.

Komatsu Shigemi, ed. *Kitano Tenjin engi.* In Zoku Nihon no Emaki 15. Tokyo: Chūōkōronsha, 1991.

Kōnoshi Takamitsu. "Constructing Imperial Mythology: *Kojiki* and *Nihon shoki.*" Trans. Iori Joko. In *Inventing the Classics: Modernity, National Identity, and Japanese Literature,* edited by Haruo Shirane and Tomi Suzuki (Stanford, CA: Stanford University Press, 2001), 51–67.

Kristeva, Julia. *Desire in Language: A Semiotic Approach to Literature and Art.* Ed. Leon Roudiez. New York: Columbia University Press, 1980.

Kurano Kenji and Takeda Yūkichi, eds. *Kojiki/Norito.* In Nihon koten bungaku taikei 1. Tokyo: Iwanami Shoten, 1966.

Kuroda, Toshio. "The World of Spirit Pacification: Issues of State and Religion." *Japanese Journal of Religious Studies* 23, no. 3–4 (fall 1996): 321–351.

Kuroita Katsumi, ed. *Fusō ryakki.* In Kokushi taikei 12. Tokyo: Yoshikawa Kōbunkan, 1999.

———. *Nihon kiryaku.* In Kokushi taikei 11. Tokyo: Yoshikawa Kōbunkan, 1979.

———. *Nihon sandai jitsuroku.* In Kokushi taikei 4. Tokyo: Yoshikawa Kōbunkan, 2000.

———. *Seiji yōryaku.* In Kokushi taikei 28. Tokyo: Yoshikawa Kōbunkan, 1972.

LaFleur, William. *Awesome Nightfall: The Life, Times, and Poetry of Saigyō.* Boston: Wisdom Publications, 2003.

———. "The Death and 'Lives' of the Poet-Monk Saigyō." In *The Biographical Process,* edited by Frank Reynolds and Donald Capps (The Hague: Mouton, 1976), 343–361.

———. *The Karma of Words: Buddhism and the Literary Arts in Medieval Japan.* Berkeley: University of California Press, 1983.

LaMarre, Thomas. *Uncovering Heian Japan: An Archeology of Sensation and Inscription.* Durham, NC: Duke University Press, 2000.

Le Goff, Jacques. *The Medieval Imagination.* Trans. Arthur Goldhammer. Chicago: University of Chicago Press, 1988.

Lincoln, Bruce. *Theorizing Myth: Narrative, Ideology, and Scholarship.* Chicago: University of Chicago Press, 1999.

Littleton, C. Scott. "Susa-no-wo versus Ya-mata no woroti: An Indo-European Theme in Japanese Mythology." *History of Religions* 20, no. 3 (February 1981): 269–280.

Lurie, David. *Realms of Literacy: Early Japan and the History of Writing.* Cambridge, MA: Harvard University Press, 2011.

MacCormack, Geoffrey. *The Spirit of Traditional Chinese Law.* Athens: University of Georgia Press, 1996.

———. *Traditional Chinese Penal Law.* Edinburgh, UK: Edinburgh University Press, 1990.

Maeda Haruto. *Kodai Izumo.* Tokyo: Yoshikawa Kōbunkan, 2006.

Makabe Toshinobu, ed. *Kitano.* In Shinto taikei (Jinja-hen) 11. Tokyo: Shinto Taikei Hensankai, 1979.

Marra, Michele. *The Aesthetics of Discontent: Politics and Reclusion in Medieval Japanese Literature.* Honolulu: University of Hawai'i Press, 1991.

———. *Representations of Power: The Literary Politics of Medieval Japan.* Honolulu: University of Hawai'i Press, 1993.

Mass, Jeffrey. *Antiquity and Anachronism in Japanese History.* Stanford, CA: Stanford University Press, 1992.

Matisoff, Susan. "Kintōsho: Zeami's Song of Exile." *Monumenta Nipponica* 32, no. 4 (winter 1977): 441–465.

Matsumae, Takeshi. "The Heavenly Rock-Grotto Myth and the Chinkon Ceremony." *Asian Folklore Studies* 39, no. 2 (1980): 9–22.

———. "Izumo no shinwa." In *Izumo no kamigami: Shinwa to shizoku,* edited by Ueda Masaaki (Tokyo: Chikuma Shobō, 1987), 81–114.

———. *Nihon no kamigami.* Chūō Kōronsha, 1974.

Matsumoto Hisashi. "Susano-o shinkō no rekishi." In *Susano-o shinkō jiten,* ed. Ōbayashi Taryō (Tokyo: Ebisu Kōshō, 2004), 48–75.

Matsumura Hiroji et al., eds. *Eiga monogatari.* In Nihon koten bungaku taikei 75. Tokyo: Iwanami Shoten, 1974.

———. *Ōkagami.* In Nihon koten bungaku taikei 21. Tokyo: Iwanami Shoten, 1973.

Matsuo Kenji. "Explaining the 'Mystery' of the *Ban Dainagon ekotoba.*" *Japanese Journal of Religious Studies* 28, no. 1–2 (spring 2001): 103–132.

McCullough, Helen Craig, trans. *Okagami: The Great Mirror.* Princeton, NJ: Princeton University Press, 1980.

McCullough, William, and Helen Craig McCullough, trans. *A Tale of Flowering Fortunes: Annals of Japanese Aristocratic Life in the Heian Period.* Stanford, CA: Stanford University Press, 1980.

McMullen, Neil. "On Placating the Gods and Pacifying the Populace: The Case of the Gion Goryō Cult." *History of Religions* 27, no. 3 (February 1988): 270–293.

McNally, Mark. *Proving the Way: Conflict and Practice in the History of Japanese Nativism.* Cambridge, MA: Harvard University Press, 2005.

Miller, Alan. "*Ame No Miso-Ori Me* (The Heavenly Weaving Maiden): The Cosmic Weaver in Early Shinto Myth and Ritual." *History of Religions* 24, no. 1 (August 1984): 27–48.

———. "The Swan-Maiden Revisited." *Asian Folklore Studies* 46, no. 1 (January 1987): 55–86.

Miner, Earl, Hiroko Odagiri, and Robert Morrell, eds. *The Princeton Companion to Classical Japanese Literature.* Princeton, NJ: Princeton University Press, 1985.

Mitani Eichi. *Monogatari bungaku no sekai.* Tokyo: Yuseido, 1975.

Miura Hiroyuki. *Hōseishi no kenkyu.* Tokyo: Iwanami Shoten, 1919.

Miyazawa Akihisa. "Izumo no saishi iseki." In *Izumo no kamigami: Shinwa to shizoku,* edited by Ueda Masaaki (Tokyo: Chikuma Shobō, 1987), 25–52.

Mizubayashi Takeshi. *Kiki shinwa to ōken no matsuri.* Tokyo: Iwanami Shoten, 1991.

Mizuno Yū. *Kodai no Izumo to Yamato.* Tokyo: Daiwashobō, 1994.

Moerman, D. Max. *Localizing Paradise: Kumano Pilgrimage and the Religious Landscape of Premodern Japan.* Cambridge, MA: Harvard University Press, 2005.

Morris, Ivan, trans. *The Pillow Book of Sei Shōnagon*. New York: Penguin Books, 1971.
Mostow, Joshua. *At the House of Gathered Leaves: Shorter Biographical and Autobiographical Narratives from Japanese Court Literature*. Honolulu: University of Hawai'i Press, 2004.
Motoori Norinaga. *Kojikiden*. In *Motoori Norinaga zenshū* (*Complete Works of Motoori Norinaga*), vol. 1, edited by Motoori Toyokai. Tokyo: Yoshikawa Kōbunkan, 1926.
———. *Motoori Norinaga*. In Nihon no meicho 21, edited by Ishikawa Jun. Tokyo: Chūōkōronsha, 1970.
Murayama, Shūichi. *Tenjin goryō shinkō*. Tokyo: Hanawa Shobō, 1996.
Nagazumi Yasuaki and Shimada Isao, eds. *Hōgen monogatari, Heiji monogatari*. In Nihon koten bungaku taikei 31. Tokyo: Iwanami Shoten, 1961.
Nakada Norio, ed. *Nihon ryōiki*. In Shinpen Nihon koten bungaku zenshū 6. Tokyo: Shogakukan, 1995.
Nakamura Hajime et al., eds. *Iwanami bukkyō jiten*. Tokyo: Iwanami Shoten, 1989.
Naumann, Nelly. "Sakahagi: The 'Reverse Flaying' of the Heavenly Piebald Horse." *Asian Folklore Studies* 41, no. 1 (January 1982): 7–38.
Nickerson, Peter. "The Meaning of Matrilocality: Kinship, Property, and Politics in Mid-Heian." *Monumenta Nipponica* 48, no. 4 (winter 1993): 429–467.
Nihon Daijiten Kankōkai, eds. *Nihon kokugo daijiten*. Tokyo: Shōgakkan, 1972–1976.
Nishimura Toru. *Orikuchi shinobu jiten*. Tokyo: Taishukan Shoten, 1998.
Nishio Minoru, ed. *Tsurezuregusa*. In Nihon koten bungaku taikei 30. Tokyo: Iwanami Shoten, 1974.
Nosco, Peter. *Remembering Paradise: Nativism and Nostalgia in Eighteenth-Century Japan*. Cambridge, MA: Council on East Asian Studies, 1990.
Obinata Katsumi. "Kodai kokka no tenkai to Izumo, Iwami, Oki sangoku." In *Shimane-ken no rekishi,* edited by Matsuo Hisashi et al. (Yamakawa Shuppensha, 2005), 81–116.
O'Flaherty, Wendy Doniger. *Other Peoples' Myths: The Cave of Echoes*. New York: Macmillan Publishing Company, 1988.
Okada, Richard. "Displacements of Conquest, or Exile, *The Tale of Genji,* and Post-Cold War Learning." In *Reading the Tale of Genji: Its Picture-Scrolls, Texts and Romance,* edited by Richard Stanley-Baker et al. (Folkestone, UK: Global Oriental, 2009), 63–79.
———. *Figures of Resistance: Language, Poetry, and Narrating in* The Tale of Genji *and Other Mid-Heian Texts*. Durham, NC: Duke University Press, 1991.
———. "Review—Uncovering Heian Japan: an Archeology of Sensation and Inscription." *Harvard Journal of Asiatic Studies* 64, no. 1 (June 2004): 184–200.
Okami Masao et al., eds. *Gukanshō*. In Nihon koten bungaku taikei 86. Tokyo: Iwanami Shoten, 1968.
Ooms, Herman. *Imperial Politics and Symbolics in Ancient Japan: The Tenmu Dynasty, 650–800*. Honolulu: University of Hawai'i Press, 2009.

Orikuchi Hakushi Kinenkai, ed. *Orikuchi Shinobu zenshū.* Tokyo: Chūōkōronsha, 1955.
Osamu Murai. *Han Orikuchi Shinobu ron.* Tokyo: Sakuhinsha, 2004.
Ouwehand, Cornelius. "Some Notes on the God Susa-no-o." *Monumenta Nipponica* 14, no. 3–4 (October 1958–January 1959): 384–407.
Oyler, Elizabeth. *Swords, Oaths, and Prophetic Visions: Authoring Warrior Rule in Medieval Japan.* Honolulu: University of Hawai'i Press, 2006.
Philippi, Donald L., trans. *Kojiki.* Tokyo: University of Tokyo, 1968.
———. *Norito.* Princeton, NJ: Princeton University Press, 1990.
Piggott, Joan. *The Emergence of Japanese Kingship.* Stanford, CA: Stanford University Press, 1997.
———. "Sacral Kingship and Confederacy in Early Izumo." *Monumenta Nipponica* 44, no. 1 (spring 1989): 45–74.
Plutschow, H. E. *Chaos and Cosmos: Ritual in Early and Medieval Japanese Literature.* Leiden: E. J. Brill, 1990.
Pollack, David. *The Fracture of Meaning: Japan's Synthesis of China from the Eighth through the Eighteenth Centuries.* Princeton, NJ: Princeton University Press, 1986.
Reader, Ian. *Religion in Contemporary Japan.* Honolulu: University of Hawai'i Press, 1991.
Rekishigaku Kenkyūkai, ed. *Nihon rekishi kōza 2: Kodai.* Tokyo: Tokyo Daigaku Shuppankai, 1984.
Rikō Mitsuo. *Nihon kodai hōseishi.* Tokyo: Keiō Tsūshin, 1986.
———. *Ritsu no kenkyū.* Tokyo: Meiji Shoin, 1961.
———. *Ritsuryōsei no kenkyū.* Tokyo: Keiō Tsūshin, 1981.
Rushdie, Salman. *The Wizard of Oz.* London: British Film Institute, 1993.
Sakakura Atsuyoshi et al., eds. *Taketori monogatari, Ise monogatari, Yamato monogatari.* In Nihon koten bungaku taikei 9. Tokyo: Iwanami Shoten, 1974.
Sakamoto Tarō et al., eds. *Nihon shoki.* In Nihon koten bungaku taikei 67. Tokyo: Iwanami Shoten, 1967.
Sakurai Tokutarō. "Onryō kara Goryō e." In *Goryō shinkō,* edited by Shibata Minoru (Tokyo: Yūzankaku Shuppan, 1984), 3–12.
Sansom, George. *A History of Japan to 1334.* Stanford: Stanford University Press, 1958.
Sarra, Edith. *Fictions of Femininity: Literary Inventions of Gender in Japanese Court Women's Memoirs.* Stanford, CA: Stanford University Press, 1999.
Schmidt, Petra. *Capital Punishment in Japan.* Leiden: E. J. Brill, 2002.
Scott, James. *Domination and the Arts of Resistance: Hidden Transcripts.* New Haven, CT: Yale University Press, 1990.
Seidensticker, Edward, trans. *The Gossamer Years.* Tokyo: Charles E. Tuttle, 1964.
Shibata Minoru, ed. *Goryō shinkō.* Tokyo: Yūzankaku Shuppan, 1984.
———. "Goryō shinkō to Tenjin." In *Sugawara Michizane to Dazaifu Tenmangū,* vol. 1, edited by Dazaifu Tenmangū Bunka Kenkyūjo (Tokyo: Yoshikawa Kōbunkan, 1975), 333–351.
Shinbo Tōru, ed. *Kitano Tenjin engi emaki.* Tokyo: Shibundō, 1991.
Shintani Nakanori. *Nihonjin no sōshiki.* Tokyo: Kinokuniya Shoten, 1992.

Shinto Taikei Hensankai, ed. *Kitano.* In Shinto Taikei 11: Jinja-hen. Tokyo: Shinto Taikei Hensankai, 1979.

Shiraishi Taichirō. "Wakoku tanjō." In Nihon no jidaishi 1. Tokyo: Yoshikawa Kōbunkan, 2002.

Shirane, Haruo. *The Bridge of Dreams: A Poetics of "The Tale of Genji."* Stanford, CA: Stanford University Press, 1987.

———. *Classical Japanese: A Grammar.* New York: Columbia University Press, 2005.

Smyers, Karen. *The Fox and the Jewel.* Honolulu: University of Hawai'i Press, 1999.

Sonoda Minoru and Hashimoto Masanobu, eds. *Shinto-shi daijiten.* Tokyo: Yoshikawa Kōbunkan, 2004.

Stockdale, Jonathan J. "Origin Myths: Susano-o, Orikuchi Shinobu, and the Imagination of Exile in Early Japan," *History of Religions* 52, no. 3 (February 2013): 236–266.

Suzuki Tomotarō et al., eds. *Kagerō nikki.* In Nihon koten bungaku taikei 20. Tokyo: Iwanami Shoten, 1974.

Tabori, Jonathan. *The Anatomy of Exile: A Semantic and Historical Study.* London: Harrap, 1972.

Tachibana Kenji et al., eds. *Okagami.* In Nihon koten bungaku zenshū 34. Tokyo: Shogakkan, 1974.

Takahashi Sadaichi. *Heike monogatari shohon no kenkyū.* Tokyo: Fuzanbō, 1943.

Takahashi Tōru. "Kishu ryūritan no kōzō." *Kokubungaku kaishaku to kanshō* 56, no. 10 (October 1991): 123–128.

———. *Monogatari bungei no hyōgenshi.* Nagoya: Nagoya Daigaku Shuppankai, 1987.

Takeda Yūkichi and Satō Kenzō, eds. *Kundoku Nihon sandai jitsuroku.* Tokyo: Rinsen Shoten, 1986.

Tanaka Ōhide and Kanō Morohira, eds. *Taketori no okina no monogatari kai.* Tokyo: Kokubun Meicho Kankōkai, 1934.

Teeuwen, Mark. "What Used to Be Called Shinto: The Question of Japan's Indigenous Religion." In *Japan Emerging: Premodern History to 1850*, edited by Karl Friday (Boulder, CO: Westview Press, 2012), 66–76.

Teeuwen, Mark, and Fabio Rambelli, eds. *Buddhas and Kami in Japan: Honji Suijaku as a Combinatory Paradigm.* New York: Routledge, 2003.

Thal, Sarah. *Rearranging the Landscape of the Gods: The Politics of a Pilgrimage Site in Japan, 1573–1912.* Chicago: University of Chicago, 2005.

———. "A Religion That Was Not a Religion: The Creation of Modern Shinto in Nineteenth-Century Japan." In *The Invention of Religion: Rethinking Belief in Politics and History,* edited by Derek Peterson and Darren Walhof (New Brunswick, NJ: Rutgers University Press 2002), 100–114.

Tokoro Isao. "Michizane no hairu." In *Sugawara Michizane to Dazaifu Tenmangū,* vol. 1, edited by Dazaifu Tenmangū Bunka Kenkyūjo (Tokyo: Yoshikawa Kōbunkan, 1975), 54–100.

Tokue Motomasa. "Kishu ryūritan igo—Orikuchigaku no tenkai." *Kokubungaku: Kaishaku to kyōzai no kenkyū* 20, no. 1 (January 1975): 111–116.

Tsuda Sōkichi. *Nihon koten no kenkyu: Jō.* Tokyo: Iwanami Shoten, 1953.
Tsunoda Bun'ei, ed. *Heian jidaishi jiten.* Tokyo: Kadokawa Shoten, 1994.
Tyler, Royall, trans. *The Tale of Genji,* vol. 1–2. New York: Viking, 2001.
———. *The Tale of the Heike* (New York: Viking Press, 2013) 65–74.
Ueda Masaaki. "Kamigami no genzō." In *Izumo no kamigami: Shinwa to shizoku,* edited by Ueda Masaaki (Tokyo: Chikuma Shobō, 1987), 3–24.
———, ed. *Tenman Tenjin: Goryō kara gakumongami e.* Tokyo: Chikuma Shobō, 1988.
Varley, H. Paul, trans. *A Chronicle of Gods and Sovereigns: Jinnō Shōtōki of Kitabatake Chikafusa.* New York: Columbia University Press, 1980.
———. *Japanese Culture.* Honolulu: University of Hawai'i Press, 1984.
———. *Warriors of Japan as Portrayed in the War Tales.* Honolulu: University of Hawai'i Press, 1994.
Veyne, Paul. *Did the Greeks Believe in Their Myths?* Trans. Paula Wissing. Chicago: University of Chicago Press, 1988.
Vos, Frits. *A Study of the Ise-monogatari,* vol. 2. The Hague: Mouton & Co., 1957.
Watanabe Sadayuki. "Chi-iki ōken no jidai." In *Shimane-ken no rekishi,* edited by Matsuo Hisashi et al. (Yamakawa Shuppansha, 2005), 49–80.
Watson, Burton, trans. *Japanese Literature in Chinese,* vol. 1. New York: Columbia University Press, 1975.
———, trans. *Po Chu-I: Selected Poems.* New York: Columbia University Press, 2000.
———, trans. *Saigyō: Poems of a Mountain Home.* New York: Columbia University Press, 1992.
Williams, Yoko. *Tsumi: Offence and Retribution in Early Japan.* New York: RoutledgeCurzon, 2003.
Wilson, William R., trans. *Tale of the Disorder in Hōgen.* Ithaca, NY: Cornell University East Asia Program, 2001.
Yamada Yūji. *Bakkosuru onryō: Tatari to chinkon no Nihon shi.* Tokyo: Yoshikawa Kōbunkan, 2007.
———. *Sutoku-in onryō no kenkyū.* Kyoto: Shibunkaku Shuppan, 2001.
———. "Sutoku tennō shinrei no kikan." In *Kindai Nihon no rekishiteki isō: Kokka, minzoku, bunka,* edited by Ōhama Tetsuya (Tokyo: Tōsui Shobō, 1999), 4–29.
Yamagishi Tokuhei, ed. *Genji monogatari.* In Nihon koten bungaku taikei 14–18. Tokyo: Iwanami Shoten, 1959.
Yamaguchi Masao. *Chi no enkinhō.* Tokyo: Iwanami Shoten, 1984.
Yamaoka Yoshikazu. "Kishu ryūritan to wa nanika." *Kokubungaku: Kaishaku to kyōzai no kenkyū* 54, no. 4 (March 2009): 6–14.
Yanagita Kunio. *Hitotsume kozō: Sono hoka.* Tokyo: Oyama Shoten, 1934.
Yiengpruksawan, Mimi Hall. "What's in a Name? Fujiwara Fixation in Japanese Cultural History." *Monumenta Nipponica* 49, no. 4 (winter 1994): 423–453.
Yoda, Tomiko. *Gender and National Literature: Heian Texts in the Constructions of Japanese Modernity.* Durham, NC: Duke University Press, 2004.
Yonei Teruyoshi. "Kodai Nihon no 'tatari *shisutemu.*'" *Tokyo Daigaku Shūkyō Nenpyō* 10 (1992): unpaginated.

# Index

*Page numbers in **bold** refer to figures and tables.*

## ABOUT THE AUTHOR

JONATHAN STOCKDALE is an associate professor of religion at the University of Puget Sound in Tacoma, Washington.

Production Notes for Stockdale | *Imagining Exile in Heian Japan: Banishment in Law, Literature, and Cult*

Jacket Design by Julie Matsuo-Chun

Display type in Bembo Std and text type in Times New Roman

Composition by Westchester Publishing Services

Printing and binding by Sheridan Books, Inc.

Printed on 55 lb. House White Hi-Bulk D37, 360 ppi.